Asset Analytics

Performance and Safety Management

Series Editors

The main aim of this book series is to provide a floor for researchers, industries, asset managers, government policy makers and infrastructure operators to cooperate and collaborate among themselves to improve the performance and safety of the assets with maximum return on assets and improved utilization for the benefit of society and the environment.

Assets can be defined as any resource that will create value to the business. Assets include physical (railway, road, buildings, industrial etc.), human, and intangible assets (software, data etc.). The scope of the book series will be but not limited to:

- Optimization, modelling and analysis of assets
- Application of RAMS to the system of systems
- Interdisciplinary and multidisciplinary research to deal with sustainability issues
- Application of advanced analytics for improvement of systems
- Application of computational intelligence, IT and software systems for decisions
- Interdisciplinary approach to performance management
- Integrated approach to system efficiency and effectiveness
- Life cycle management of the assets
- Integrated risk, hazard, vulnerability analysis and assurance management
- Adaptability of the systems to the usage and environment
- Integration of data-information-knowledge for decision support
- Production rate enhancement with best practices
- Optimization of renewable and non-renewable energy resources

Review Process

The proposal for each volume follows multi-pronged review process. The first level of review (single blind) is conducted by the series editors who may or may not decide to enlist the help of editorial board members for a second level of review. Proposals may also undergo a third level of peer review (double blind) if recommended by the Series Editors.

The series follows Ethics Statement found in the Springer standard guidelines here. https://www.springer.com/us/authors-editors/journal-author/journal-author-helpdesk/before-you-start/before-you-start/1330#c14214.

Reggie Davidrajuh

Petri Nets for Modeling Complex Discrete-Event Systems

An Approach Based on GPenSIM

Springer

Reggie Davidrajuh
School of Computer Science
and Engineering
Chongqing Three Gorges University
Chongqing, China

University of Stavanger
Stavanger, Norway

ISSN 2522-5162 ISSN 2522-5170 (electronic)
Asset Analytics
ISBN 978-981-96-6395-8 ISBN 978-981-96-6396-5 (eBook)
https://doi.org/10.1007/978-981-96-6396-5

This Springer imprint is published by the registered company Springer Nature Singapore Pte Ltd.
The registered company address is: 152 Beach Road, #21-01/04 Gateway East, Singapore 189721, Singapore

This book is dedicated to the faculty members of the ***School of Computer Science and Engineering*** *(SCSE), the* ***Chongqing Three Gorges University*** *(CTGU),*

Especially to ***Prof. Wei Zhang*** *(The President of CTGU) and* ***Prof. Yuming Feng*** *(The Dean of SCSE).*

Photo of the author's family at CTGU in June 2024

From left to right:
Prof. Hongbing Li (Vice Dean), Prof. Chunzhe Zhao (Vice Dean), Ada (the author's daughter), Ruglin (the author's wife), the author, Prof. Wei Zhang (The President of CTGU), Prof. Yuming Feng (The Dean), Mr. Hongfu Liao, Dr. Xiangguang Dai, and Dr. Longzhou Cao.

Foreword

I am privileged to write this Foreword for Prof. Reggie Davidrajuh's latest book on GPenSIM. From Prof. Reggie's previous books, we have witnessed various practical scenarios and application techniques of GPenSIM. Sometimes, we are curious about how GPenSIM is designed and to what extent we can reach it, so this book comes. The current book is a reference manual on GPenSIM, which will help GPenSIM users quickly understand the different ways of interacting with GPenSIM so that users can tap the full potential of GPenSIM.

The beauty of GPenSIM is the tight integration with MATLAB. This feature not only means that it is easy to deploy and run but also indicates that we can employ the comprehensive toolboxes in MATLAB to realize practical applications in various fields. Even more, it is very effective for all practitioners.

Through Prof. Reggie's visit to my laboratory, I realized he is an energic tech-geek, humble but prolific. Professor Reggie also promised me that he would develop a dedicated library for "Queuing Petri Nets" during his sabbatical stay in China during Spring 2025; I am looking forward to this library and a book on it! I wish Prof. Reggie all the best!

Liang Zhang
Professor of Computer Science
Fudan University
Shanghai, China

Preface

This book is an advanced book that shows how complex discrete-event systems can be modeled, simulated, and implemented with Petri nets and GPenSIM. Its focus and scope are to show how GPenSIM's interface can be used to model and implement complex discrete-event systems. Part I of this book explains the internals of GPenSIM (how to interface with GPenSIM) so that a user can develop his functions to circumvent existing functions or extend them. Part II describes how Petri net models can interact with the external environment. Supervisory Control is used as an example to show how GPenSIM's processor files can be used as the interface between the Petri nets and the external world. In Part II, we will see that supervisory control techniques expand the Petri net model of the controlled system with the addition of the controller (control places and arcs). In contrast, GPenSIM maps the controller into processors, thus keeping the original Petri net intact.

GPenSIM

General-Purpose Petri net Simulator (GPenSIM) is a toolbox (set of functions) that runs on MATLAB for modeling, simulation, and performance analysis of discrete-event systems. Academics in some universities chose GPenSIM as it is easy to learn, use, and extend. Also, the fact that GPenSIM runs on MATLAB allows Petri net models implemented with GPenSIM to use hundreds of functions that are available in the other MATLAB toolboxes.

For modeling real-world discrete-event systems, though Ordinary Petri nets (P/T Petri nets) are an obvious choice (due to their advantages such as self-documentation and graphical representation), they lack modeling power as they speak regular (type 3) or context-free (type 2). Ordinary Petri nets do not possess modeling power type 1 or 0 languages. Hence, there are many extensions to make extended Petri net languages possess modeling power type 1 or 0 languages.

GPenSIM provides extensions through processors (pre-processors and post-processors). In the processor files, a user can add colors and logical conditions in

MATLAB language and use GPenSIM's built-in functions. Also, GPenSIM allows a Petri net model to be either untimed (all transitions in the model are "primitive" and take zero time to fire) or timed (all transitions in the model are "non-primitive" as they take finite time to fire). Note that GPenSIM is fine-tuned for timed Petri nets.

The Structure of This Book

This book consists of two parts:

- Part I, *Interfacing with GPenSIM*, consisting of five chapters, explains the internals of GPenSIM (how to interface with GPenSIM) so that a user can develop his functions to circumvent existing functions or extend them.
- Part II, *Interfacing with the External Environment*, describes how to allow Petri net models to interact with the external environment. Supervisory Control is used as a tool to show how processor files can be used as the interface between the Petri nets and the external world.

Part I: Interfacing with GPenSIM

Chapter 1, "File Structure in GPenSIM", introduces the file structure in GPenSIM and describes how different files (such as the main simulation file (MSF), Petri net Definition Files (PDFs), and processor files) communicate with each other to make up a Petri net model. This chapter discusses files both in monolithic (non-modular) and modular Petri nets.

Chapter 2, "Data Structures in GPenSIM", explains the data structures of different elements in GPenSIM. Some of the data structures are simple as they represent the basic elements such as a place, transition, token, token colors, and resource. The other data structures, such as the Petri net structure with initial dynamics, are large (and sometimes complex).

Chapter 3, "Virtual Tokens and Virtual State", explains the new concepts in GPenSIM. GPenSIM realizes the "atomicity" property differently, as the tokens consumed by a transition are kept inside the transition during the firing time, causing virtual tokens and virtual states.

Chapter 4, "Log Files", describes the log files (simulation results) that are output from functions such as "gpensim" and "cotree".

Chapter 5, "Retention of Tokens in Input Places", is on holding (retention of) tokens in places. In GPenSIM, by default, whenever a transition becomes enabled and the conditions in the pre-processor files are satisfied, the transition is allowed to consume the input tokens and start firing immediately. This chapter introduces two approaches for holding (retaining) the tokens in the input places for a while: (1) "Time Windows", a function that can be used in the pre-processor. (2) "Delayed Enabled

Transitions" is an approach in which delays are declared in the main simulation file; Delayed Enabled Transitions is a new functionality that was introduced in version 11.

Part II: Interfacing with External Environment

Chapter 6, "Processor Files as Interfaces", is a continuation of Chap. 1; In this chapter, we focus on how we can use the processor files as the entry points (the interface) to allow a Petri net model to access and control external hardware and software.

Chapter 7, "Introduction to Supervisory Control with GPenSIM", proposes a unique approach in which the controller of a Petri net (the plant) is mapped into processor files for implementation. Since Petri net models of a real-life plant are usually huge, adding a controller with many control places and their arcs to the transitions of the plant will make the resulting controlled system huge and complicated. The GPenSIM approach, while keeping the plant as it is and mapping the controller into processor files, not only reduces the overall size of the controlled system but also allows coding the processors into embedded processors for real-life hardware control.

Chapter 8, "Supervisory Control with GPenSIM", presents two simple examples to introduce the GPenSIM way of synthesizing controllers for Petri nets and then implementing the controllers via the processor files.

Chapter 9, "GPenSIM Built-in Functions for Supervisory Control", presents the details of the most important GPenSIM built-in functions for supervisory Control.

Chapter 10, "Case Study on Supervisory Control with GPenSIM", puts the stages of implementing supervisory control-based controllers into action. This chapter presents a case study in which we will develop controllers and then map them into processors.

What is not Given in This Book: Basics of GPenSIM and Petri Nets

This book takes a deeper look into the internals of GPenSIM and about interfacing with GPenSIM. The basics of GPenSIM and the basics of Petri nets and Supervisory Control are not covered in this book. Appendix B lists some basic books on GPenSIM.

GPenSIM Website: http://www.davidrajuh.net/gpensim/

Users can download source code for the examples in this book and GPenSIM source files from the GPenSIM website.

Chongqing, China Reggie Davidrajuh

Acknowledgments I thank many colleagues and friends for helping me complete this book; I thank all of them in a separate acknowledgment section. I am also thankful to my wife, Ruglin, and my daughter, Ada, for their patience with me.

Acknowledgments This book was fully revised with the help of the faculty members of the School of Computer Science and Engineering (SCSE) at the Chongqing Three Gorges University (CTGU) in Wanzhou, China. I paid three visits to CTGU, which were extraordinary in terms of academic exchange and personal experience. I want to thank the President of CTGU, Prof. Wei Zhang, and the Dean of SCSE, Prof. Yuming Feng. I distributed a crude version of this book to the faculty members of SCSE, who gave valuable feedback, which turned this book into its current form. My heartiest thank you to the faculty members of SCSE!

This book originated during my six-month sabbatical in China. The Xidian University (XDU) in Xi'an was my main workplace in the Spring of 2024. Professor Zhiwu Li of the Systems Control and Automation (SCA) group at the School of Mechano-Electronic Engineering was my host. Also, I was lucky to have discussions with Dr. Jiafeng Zhang and Dr. Ding Liu. The research assistants, Jing Wu and Bingrun Chen were also very helpful. I sincerely thank the SCA group and XDU for the funding and facilities they offered.

Professor Liang Zhang of Fudan University invited me for a week-long visit; Prof. Liang Zhang is an ardent user of GPenSIM and was kind enough to write the Foreword for this book. I had long discussions with Prof. Liang Zhang and his students. Chapter 6, "Processor Files as Interfaces", of this book was written due to the conversation with Prof. Liang Zhang; my sincere thanks to him!

From publisher Springer's side, I would like to thank the "Asset Analytics" series editor, Prof. Ajit Kumar Verma, for encouraging me to submit the book to the series. My sincere thanks also go to Ms. Kamiya Khatter, Springer Nature's Senior Editor.

Competing Interests The author has no competing interests to declare that are relevant to the content of this manuscript.

Contents

About the Author

Reggie Davidrajuh has a master's degree in control systems and a Ph.D. in industrial engineering (awarded by the Norwegian University of Science and Technology). Also, he has a D.Sc. (habilitation) degree in information science (AGH University of Science and Technology) and one more Ph.D. in mechanical engineering (Silesian University of Technology). He is presently a professor of informatics at the University of Stavanger, Norway, and holds a visiting professor position at the Silesian University of Technology, Poland. Dr. Davidrajuh has published three books so far. *Modeling Discrete-Event Systems with GPenSIM: An Introduction* in 2018, *Petri Nets for Modeling of Large Discrete Systems* in 2022, and *Colored Petri Nets for Modeling of Discrete Systems* in 2023. Springer published all three books. He is a senior member of IEEE. He is also a member of the Norwegian Academy of Technical Sciences.

Part I
Interfacing with GPenSIM

Chapter 1
File Structure in GPenSIM

This chapter presents some basic details on the file structure of Petri net models implemented with GPenSIM. Modeling a discrete-event system with GPenSIM usually ends up with the following files: one Main Simulation File (MSF), one or more Petri net Definition Files (PDFs), and Processor Files (or, simply, "processors").

The first section, Sect. 1.1, discusses the file systems in monolithic (non-modular) Petri net models, and the following section, Sect. 1.2, is on modular Petri net models. Section 1.3 summarizes the differences between processor files in monolithic versus modular Petri net models. Finally, Sect. 1.4 present some details about the data packets "**`global_info`**" and "**`PN`**", which are accessible in the processor files.

The material presented in this chapter is a compact summary of the file structure of GPenSIM discussed in Davidrajuh [1, 3, 4]. Davidrajuh [1, 4] present the basics of model building with GPenSIM using non-modular ("**monolithic**" in GPenSIM literature) Petri nets, whereas Davidrajuh [3] presents **modular** Petri net model building, especially for large discrete systems.

1.1 Files of a Monolithic Petri Net Model

Let us consider a simple monolithic (non-modular) Petri net shown in Fig. 1.1. The Petri net is composed of three functional parts: a driver on the left end that creates and supplies the tokens ("D" in the element names stands for the driver), the middle part that processes the tokens, and the part on the right is a stub (or a sink) that removes the tokens from the net ("S" stands for stub or sink).

R. Davidrajuh, *Petri Nets for Modeling Complex Discrete-Event Systems*, Asset Analytics,
https://doi.org/10.1007/978-981-96-6396-5_1

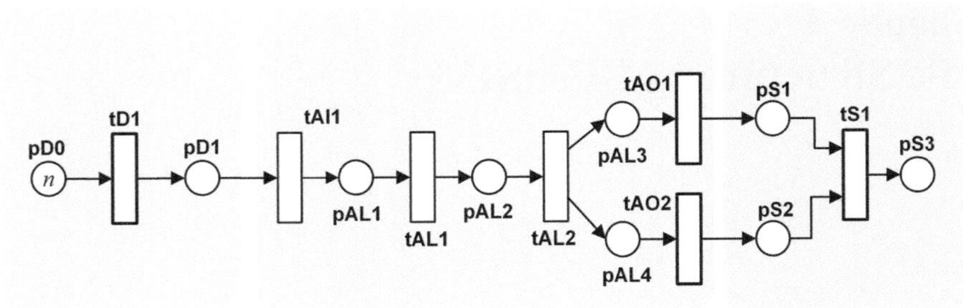

Fig. 1.1 A simple monolithic Petri net

1.1.1 Example 01: Max. One Token in pALx

Let us imagine that the Petri net (shown in Fig. 1.1) is a model of a real-life discrete system in which the middle part—the processing part consisting of places **pAL1** to **pAL4** (buffers) has a limitation, which is they can hold a maximum of one token only. In this example, we will imitate the limitation of the buffers by the use of:

1. "MUTEX"—a global variable that will be declared in the main simulation file (MSF).
2. Logic conditions (restrictions for firing) in the pre-processor of transition **tAI1**.
3. Post-firing actions in the post-processors of transitions **tAO1** and **tAO2**.

1.1.2 Petri Net Definition File (PDF)

Petri net Definition File (PDF) defines a *static* (also, no dynamics) *Petri net graph*, meaning the set of places, transitions, and arcs. The PDF file is displayed below as Listing 1.1. The PDF first declares a name or label for the Petri net, followed by the declarations of the set of places, transitions, and arcs.

Listing 1.1 The PDF (Example 01)

```
function [png] = ex_01_pdf()
global global_info

png.PN_name = 'simple monolithic Petri net';    % a name ...
    or label
% set of places (Ps), transitions (Ts), and arcs (As)
png.set_of_Ps = {'pD0','pD1','pAL1','pAL2', 'pAL3', ...
    'pAL4', 'pS1','pS2','pS3'};
png.set_of_Ts = {'tD1','tAI1','tAL1','tAL2', 'tAO1', ...
    'tAO2', 'tS1'};
png.set_of_As = {...
    'pD0','tD1',1, 'tD1','pD1',1, ...% tD1
```

```
    'pD1','tAI1',1, 'tAI1','pAL1',1, ...    % tAI1
    'pAL1','tAL1',1, 'tAL1','pAL2',1, ... % tAL1
    'pAL2','tAL2',1, ... % tAL2 inputs
    'tAL2','pAL3',1, 'tAL2','pAL4',1, ... % tAL2 output
    'pAL3','tAO1',1, 'tAO1','pS1',1, ... % tAO1
    'pAL4','tAO2',1, 'tAO2','pS2',1, ... % tAO2
    'pS1','tS1',1, 'pS2','tS1',1, 'tS1','pS3',1 ... % tS1
           };
```

1.1.3 Main Simulation File (MSF)

As the name indicates, the Main Simulation File (MSF) is the one that the user directly executes. MSF, in turn, will pull all other files (PDF and processor files) as needed. Listing 1.2, shown below, is a sample code for the main simulation file of Fig. 1.1.

Listing 1.2 Main Simulation File (MSF) (Example 01)

```
clear all;
global global_info
global_info.STOP_AT = 50;
global_info.MUTEX = 2;
global_info.INITIAL_TOKENS = 5;

spng = pnstruct('ex_01_pdf');
dyn.ft = {'allothers', 1};
dyn.m0 = {'pD0',global_info.INITIAL_TOKENS};
pni = initialdynamics(spng, dyn);

sim_results = gpensim(pni);
prnss(sim_results);
subplot(4,1,1), plotp(sim_results, {'pAL1'});
subplot(4,1,2), plotp(sim_results, {'pAL2'});
subplot(4,1,3), plotp(sim_results, {'pAL3'});
subplot(4,1,4), plotp(sim_results, {'pAL4'});
%subplot(5,1,5), plotp(sim_results, {'pS3'});
```

The MSF starts with a header block in which some compiler options and global variables are set. Note that in Listing 1.2, "**`global_info`**" is used to set the compiler option `STOP_AT` to stop simulation after 50 time units (TU). Also, assign a value of 2 to the global variable "MUTEX" and initial tokens (in **pD0**) to be five. In GPenSIM, "`global_info`" is used for two purposes:

1. To set compiler options, and
2. To pass user-defined global variables between files (e.g., between MSF and processor files).

In the second block, we start with the declaration of the PDF file. In this example, we use only one PDF. From this PDF, we create the structure for the static Petri net graph (‘`spng`’) using the function ‘`pnstruct`’. Then, the assignments of initial dynamics, and finally, the combination of the static Petri net graph (`spng`) and initial dynamics to form the structure representing the Petri net structure with initial dynamics (‘`pni`’).

The third block calls the function ‘`gpensim`’ to run the simulations. Once the simulations are complete, the results can be studied using the functions ‘`prnss`’ and ‘`plotp`’.

The functions ‘`prncolormap`’ and ‘`prnfinalcolors`’ are also used if colors are involved (Colored Petri net). The function ‘`cotree`’ is the one to be used to establish the reachability tree.

1.1.4 TU: Time Unit

In this book, **TU** stands for time unit, a unit of time that is any particular time interval used as a standard way of measuring or expressing duration. For example, for a specific application, 1 TU can be taken as an hour (1 TU = 1 h); for another application, 1 TU can be taken as a day (1 TU = 24 h). For non-real-time applications, GPenSIM, and in this book, the firing times and start and stop times of simulation are given in TU.

However, for real-time applications, all timing becomes seconds (1 TU = 1 s), and GPenSIM uses the CPU clock; see Sect. 8.4, “Interfacing with External Hardware” of Davidrajuh [1]).

1.1.5 Processor Files

There are **two groups of processor files** based on **time line** (when they will be called):

1. Pre-processors.
2. Post-processors.

A pre-processor file will be called when a transition is enabled (to start firing). Only when a pre-processor file returns logic true for firing will the transition be allowed to begin firing.

A post-processor will be automatically called when a transition completes firing. A post-processor implements code for post-firing actions.

Also, there are **three classes of processor files** based on the **transitions’ visibility**:

1. Specific pre-processors and specific post-processors.
2. Modular pre-processors and modular post-processors: Only valid for modular Petri nets, as discussed in the next section, Sect. 1.2.
3. Common processors: COMMON_PRE and COMMON_POST.

1.1.6 Specific Processors

All transitions are visible in their own specific processor files. For example, transition **tAI1** is visible in its pre-processor "tAI1_pre" and post-processor "tAI1_post". Whenever **tAI1** becomes enabled, its pre-processor "tAI1_pre" will be automatically executed, if "tAI1_pre" exists. Only if "tAI1_pre" returns logic true for firing **tAI1** will it be allowed to start firing. When **tAI1** completes firing, its post-processor "tAI1_post" will be automatically executed if "tAI1_post" exists.

As an example for a specific pre-processor, Listing 1.3 shows the specific pre-processor of transition **tD1**. Whenever **tD1** is enabled, its specific pre-processor "tD1_pre" is run in which the number of tokens in the place **pD0** is checked. A warning message will be displayed if there is only one token (because the source **pD0** is running out of tokens to supply).

Listing 1.3 Specific pre-processor "tD1_pre" (Example 01)

```
function [fire, transition] = tD1_pre (transition)

npD0 = ntokens('pD0'); % number of tokens in "pD0"
if eq(npD0, 1)
     disp('"tD1" is taking the last token from ...
          "pD0"');
end
fire = 1; % always fire, if enabled
```

As an example for a specific post-processor, Listing 1.4 shows the "tS1_post". Whenever **tS1** completes firing, its specific post-processor checks the number of tokens in **pS3**. If this number equals the initial tokens assigned to **pD0**, then all the tokens from **pD0** have reached **pS3** so that the simulation can be stopped (by setting the option "`STOP_SIMULATION`" to true). Even though we wanted the simulation to run for 50 TU in the MSF (because the option "`STOP_AT`" was set to 50), now the simulations are stopped at 22 TU.

Listing 1.4 Specific post-processor "tS1_post" (Example 01)

```
function [] = tS1_post (transition)
global global_info

npS3 = ntokens('pS3'); % number of tokens in "pS3"
if eq(npS3, global_info.INITIAL_TOKENS)
```

```
    disp('all tokens have reached "pS3"');
    global_info.STOP_SIMULATION = true;
end
```

1.1.7 Common Processors

Common processors (COMMON_PRE and COMMON_POST) work differently for monolithic Petri nets and modular Petri nets:

- **Monolithic (non-modular) Petri nets**: **all transitions** are visible in common processors.
- **Modular Petri nets**: Only the transitions of **IMC**s and the **Input Ports** and **Output Ports** of **Petri Modules** are visible in common processors (Sect. 1.2).

The Petri net in Fig. 1.1 is a monolithic Petri net consisting of seven transitions; all of these seven transitions are visible in the common processors.

Listing 1.5 presents *a template* for COMMON_PRE for the Petri net in Fig. 1.1. This template shows all the transitions that are visible in COMMON_PRE.

Listing 1.5 COMMON_PRE: A template for Petri net in Fig.1.1 (Example 01)

```
function [fire, transition] = COMMON_PRE (transition)

global global_info

% Visibility of transitions of a monolith Petri net
%     in COMMON_PRE
% All transitions in a monolith Petri net are visible here
% Example 01: (tD1, tAI1, tAL1, tAL2, tAO1, tAO2, tS1)

switch transition.name
    case 'tD1'  %
        % check some conditions before firing
        % fire = true or false?

    case 'tAI1' %
        % check some conditions before firing
        % fire = true or false?

    case 'tAL1' %
        % check some conditions before firing
        % fire = true or false?

    case 'tAL2' % output port of Alfa
        % check some conditions before firing
        % fire = true or false?

    case 'tAO1' % output port of Alfa
        % check some conditions before firing
```

```
        % fire = true or false?

    case 'tAO2' % IMC transition
        % check some conditions before firing
        % fire = true or false?

    case 'tS1' % IMC transition
        % check some conditions before firing
        % fire = true or false?
end
```

Listing 1.6 presents a *template* for COMMON_POST for the Petri net in Fig. 1.1. This template also shows all the transitions that are visible in COMMON_POST.

Listing 1.6 COMMON_POST: A template for Petri net in Fig. 1.1 (Example 01)

```
function [fire, transition] = COMMON_PRE (transition)

global global_info

% Visibility of transitions of a monolith Petri net
%      in COMMON_POST
% All transitions in a monolith Petri net are ...
    visible here
% Example 01: (tD1, tAI1, tAL1, tAL2, tAO1, tAO2, ...
    tS1)

switch transition.name
    case 'tD1' % IMC transition
        % some post-firing actions

...
...

    case 'tS1'  % IMC transition
        % some post-firing actions
end
```

1.1.8 *Common Processors in a Monolithic Petri Net*

Coming back to Example 01, what is the use of "MUTEX" in the main simulation file shown in Listing 1.2? As stated before, the places **pAL1**, **pAL2**, **pAL3**, and **pAL4** can hold only a maximum of one token each. In this case, we can add some conditions to the transition **tAI1**, as this transition allows token flow into the processing section. Also, we are going to add some post-firing actions to **tAO1** and **tAO2**:

- In MSF, we assign the global variable MUTEX a value of 2. Whenever **tAI1** is enabled in the pre-processor (e.g., COMMON_PRE), the compiler will check

whether the value of MUTEX is 2; if it is, then **tAI1** is allowed to fire, and at the same time, MUTEX is reduced to zero so that **tAI1** will not fire again.
- The token that enters through **tAI1** reaches **tAO1** and **tAO2** as two tokens; when these two transitions fire, in the post-processor (e.g., COMMON_POST), each of them increases the MUTEX value by one so that MUTEX becomes 2, and in turn, will allow **tAI1** to fire again.
- Also, rather than adding the post-actions to the individual post-processors tAO1_post and tAO2_post, which will require duplication, we can add the post-actions to COMMON_POST as common code.

Listings 1.7 and 1.8 present COMMON_PRE and COMMON_POST, respectively.

Listing 1.7 COMMON_PRE (Example 01)

```
function [fire, transition] = COMMON_PRE (transition)

global global_info

% if enabled transition is "tAI1"
if strcmp(transition.name, 'tAI1')
    if eq(global_info.MUTEX, 2)
        fire = 1;
        global_info.MUTEX = 0;
    else
        fire = 0;
    end
    return
end

% if enabled transition is NOT "tAI1"
fire = 1; % allow it to fire
```

Listing 1.8 COMMON_POST (Example 01)

```
function [] = COMMON_POST (transition)

global global_info

% if the fired transition is either "tAO1" or "tAO2"
if ismember(transition.name, {'tAO1', 'tAO2'})
    % increase mutex value by one
    global_info.MUTEX = global_info.MUTEX + 1;
end
```

Figure 1.2 shows the simulation results in which the places **pAL1** to **pAL4** possess a maximum of one token each.

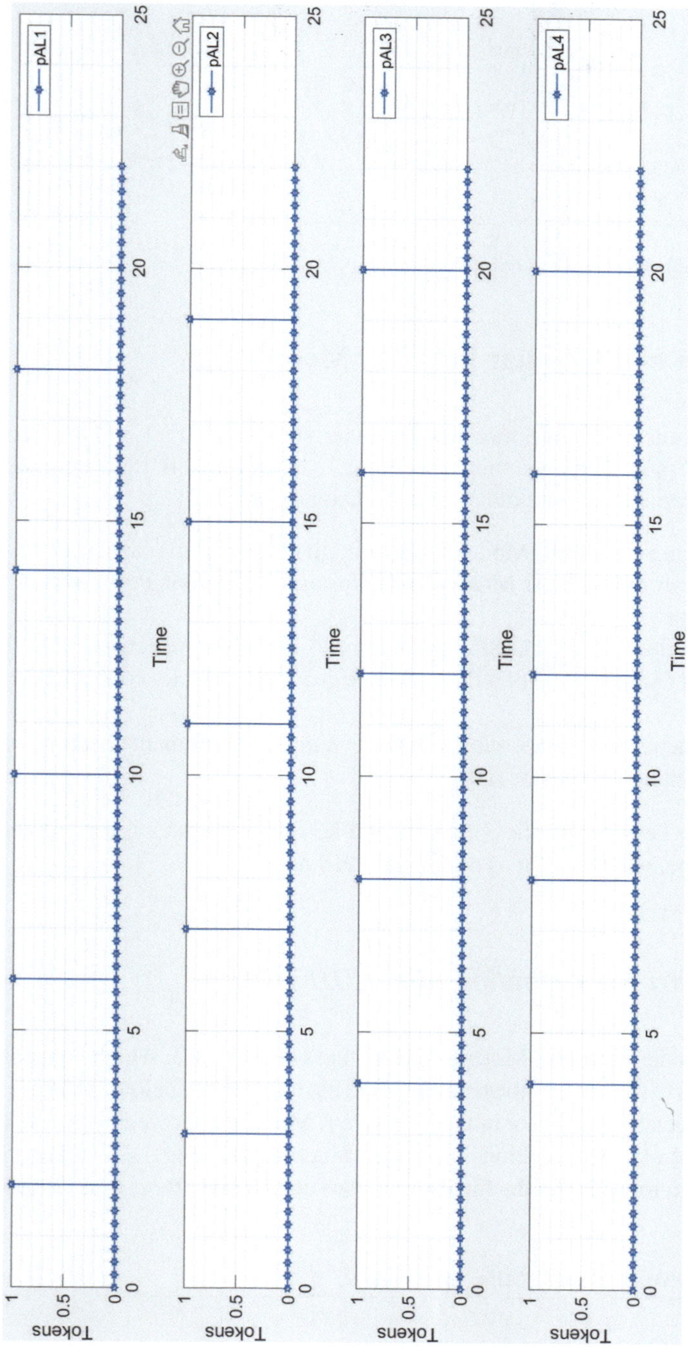

Fig. 1.2 Places **pAL1** to **pAL4** possess a maximum of one token each

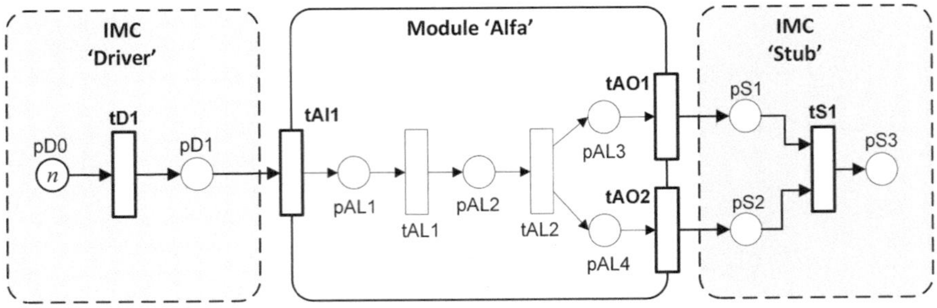

Fig. 1.3 Simple modular Petri net

1.2 Files of a Modular Petri Net Model

Let us consider a simple modular Petri net shown in Fig. 1.3. This Petri net is exactly the same Petri net shown in Fig. 1.1. However, this Petri net satisfies the strict requirements of a modular Petri net Davidrajuh [2, 3]:

- Tokens can enter a Petri Module only through its Input Ports, which are transitions.
- Tokens can exit a Petri Module only through its Output Ports, which are also transitions.
- Internal ("local" in GPenSIM terminology) elements (which exclude the Input Ports and Output Ports) of a Petri Module cannot be directly connected to external elements.
- The elements that do not satisfy the above three requirements become part of an Inter-Modular Connector (IMC).

Since the Petri net satisfies (Figs. 1.1 and 1.3) the requirements for a modular Petri net, this time, we declare it as a modular Petri net.

1.2.1 Petri Net Definition Files (PDFs)

Let us consider the **Petri Module "Alfa"** shown in Fig. 1.3, which consists of four places and five transitions, the resulting PDF file is displayed below as Listing 1.9. The PDF first declares a name or label for the Petri Module, followed by the declarations of the set of places, transitions, and arcs. Since **Alfa** in Fig. 1.3 is a Petri Module, **the last statement is the declaration of the set of Input Ports and Output Ports**.

Listing 1.9 PDF of Module "Alfa" (Example 02)

```
function [png] = PDF_Alfa()
global global_info
```

```
png.PN_name = 'Alfa';   % module name
% set of places (Ps), transitions (Ts), and arcs (As)
png.set_of_Ps = {'pAL1','pAL2','pAL3','pAL4'};
png.set_of_Ts = {'tAI1','tAL1','tAL2','tAO1','tAO2'};
png.set_of_As = {'tAI1','pAL1',1, ...    % tAI1
    'pAL1','tAL1',1, 'tAL1','pAL2',1, ... % tAL1
    'pAL2','tAL2',1, ... % tAL2 inputs
    'tAL2','pAL3',1, 'tAL2','pAL4',1,... % tAL2 ...
      output
    'pAL3','tAO1',1, ... % tAO1
    'pAL4','tAO2',1 ... % tAO2
    };

% set of input and output ports
png.set_of_Ports = {'tAI1','tAO1','tAO2'};
```

Listings 1.10 and 1.11 show the PDFs for **Inter-Modular Connectors (IMCs)** "Driver" and "Stub", respectively. Since these are IMCs and not Petri Modules, they don't have statements that declare Input Ports and Output Ports.

Listing 1.10 PDF of IMC "Driver" (Example 02)

```
global global_info
% IMC's name
png.PN_name = 'IMC Driver';

% set of places, transitions, and arcs
png.set_of_Ps = {'pD0', 'pD1'};
png.set_of_Ts = {'tD1'};
png.set_of_As = {...
    'pD0','tD1',1, 'tD1','pD1',1, ... % tD1
    'pD1','tAI1',1, ... % IMC connection
    };
```

Listing 1.11 PDF of IMC "Stub" (Example 02)

```
function [png] = PDF_Stub()
global global_info

% IMC's name
png.PN_name = 'IMC Stub';

% set of places, transitions, and arcs
png.set_of_Ps = {'pS1','pS2','pS3'};
png.set_of_Ts = {'tS1'};
png.set_of_As = {...
    'pS1','tS1',1, 'pS2','tS1',1, ... % tS1 inputs
    'tS1','pS3',1, ... % tS1 output
    'tAO1','pS1',1, ... % imc connection
    'tAO2','pS2',1 ... % imc connection
    };
```

1.2.2 Main Simulation File (MSF)

Listing 1.12, shown below, is a sample code for the main simulation file of Fig. 1.3. The MSF is almost the same as the one shown in Listing 1.2, except the new MSF declares a set of PDFs rather than a single PDF.

Listing 1.12 Main Simulation File (MSF) (Example 02)

```
clear all;
global global_info
global_info.STOP_AT = 50;
global_info.MUTEX = 2;
global_info.INITIAL_TOKENS = 5;

spng = pnstruct({'PDF_Driver', 'PDF_Alfa', ...
    'PDF_Stub'});
dyn.ft = {'allothers', 1};
dyn.m0 = {'pD0',global_info.INITIAL_TOKENS};
pni = initialdynamics(spng, dyn);

sim_results = gpensim(pni);
prnss(sim_results);
subplot(4,1,1), plotp(sim_results, {'pAL1'});
subplot(4,1,2), plotp(sim_results, {'pAL2'});
subplot(4,1,3), plotp(sim_results, {'pAL3'});
subplot(4,1,4), plotp(sim_results, {'pAL4'});
% subplot(5,1,5), plotp(sim_results, {'pS3'});
```

The MSF starts with a header block in which some compiler options and global variables are set.

In the second block, we start with the declaration of the PDF files. In this MSF, we use three PDFs, one PDF for the Petri Module **Alfa**, and the other two for the IMCs “Driver” and “Stub”. For further study on modular Petri nets, Davidrajuh [3] is suggested. From these three PDFs, we create the structure for the static Petri net graph (“`spng`”) using the function “`pnstruct`”. Then, the assignments of initial dynamics, and finally, the combination of the static Petri net graph (`spng`) and initial dynamics to form the structure representing the Petri net with initial dynamics (“`pni`”).

The third block calls the function “`gpensim`” to run the simulations. Once the simulations are complete, the results can be studied using the functions “`prnss`” and “`plotp`”.

1.2.3 Processor Files in Modular Petri Nets

As already mentioned in Sect. 1.1.5, there are **two groups of processor files** based on **time line** (when they will be called):

1. Pre-processors: A pre-processor file will be called when a transition is enabled (to start firing). Only when a pre-processor file returns logic true for firing conditions (if there are any) will the transition be allowed to start firing.
2. Post-processors: A post-processor will be automatically called when a transition completes firing. A post-processor implements code for post-firing actions, if there are any.

Also, there are **three classes of processor files** based on the **transitions' visibility**:

1. Specific pre-processors and specific post-processors: Just as in a monolithic Petri net, every transition can have its specific pre-processor and specific post-processor in a modular Petri net.
2. Modular pre-processors and modular post-processors: Each Petri Module can have its modular pre-processor and modular post-processor; only the transitions of a Petri Module (Input Ports, local transitions, and Output Ports) are visible in the modular processors.
3. Common processors (COMMON_PRE and COMMON_POST): Unlike in a monolithic Petri net, in a modular Petri net, every transition is ***not*** visible in the common processors. Only the Input Ports and Output Ports of Petri Modules and the IMC transitions are visible on the common processors.

1.2.4 Modular Processors

Modular processors are only available for modular Petri nets, not monolithic (non-modular) Petri nets. Modular processors are for the transitions of a Petri Module. For example, for the modular Petri net in Fig. 1.3, transitions in Petri Module **Alfa** (such as **tAI1**, **tAL1**, **tAL2**, **tAO1**, and **tAO2**) are visible in their modular pre-processor named "MOD_Alfa_PRE" and post-processor named "MOD_Alfa_POST". If any of these transitions of the Petri Module becomes enabled the modular pre-processor MOD_Alfa_PRE will be executed. It should return logic true for the transition to start firing. When this transition completes firing, the modular post-processor MOD_Alfa_POST will be executed.

*1.2.5 Example 02: Modular Version: Max. One Token in pAL**x***

Let us revisit the modular Petri net with the goal of restricting a maximum of one token only in **pAL1** to **pAL4**. In this example, just like in Example 01, we will use the following:

1. "MUTEX"—a global variable that will be declared in the MSF.
2. Logic conditions (restrictions for firing) in the pre-processor of transition **tAI1**.
3. Post-firing actions in the post-processors of transitions **tAO1** and **tAO2**.

tAI1 is visible in three processors (its specific processors, Modular **Alfa** processors, and common processors); hence, we can leave the conditions in COMMON_PRE as shown in Listing 1.7 or move them to MOD_Alfa_PRE, as shown in Listing 1.3. We can also move the conditions to tAI1_pre; however, specific processors are sparsely used in modular models.

Listing 1.13 Modular pre-processor "MOD_Alfa_PRE" (Example 02)

```
function [fire, transition] = MOD_Alfa_PRE ...
    (transition)

global global_info

% Only the transitions of "Alfa" are visible here:
switch transition.name
    case 'tAI1'  % input port of Alfa
        if eq(global_info.MUTEX, 2)
            fire = 1;
            % dont fire again until tAO1 and tAO2 ...
                fire
            global_info.MUTEX = 0;
        else
            fire = 0;
        end

    case {'tAO1', 'tAO2'}  % Output Ports of Alfa
        fire = 1;

    case {'tAL1', 'tAL2'} % local transitions of Alfa
        fire = 1;
end
```

tAO1 and **tAO2**—Output Ports of **Alfa** are visible in Modular **Alfa** processors and common processors (in addition to their specific processors). Hence, the code shown in COMMON_POST in Listing 1.8 for **tAO1** and **tAO2** is still valid, as these two transitions are also visible in common processors. We can also move this code to the post-processor MOD_Alfa_POST, as shown in Listing 1.14.

Listing 1.14 Modular post-processor "MOD_Alfa_POST" (Example 02)

```
function [] = MOD_Alfa_POST (transition)

global global_info

% Only the transitions of "Alfa" are visible here:
switch transition.name
    case 'tAI1'  % Input Port of Alfa
        % do nothing

    case {'tAO1', 'tAO2'}  % Output Ports of Alfa
        % increase mutex value by one
```

```
        global_info.MUTEX = global_info.MUTEX + 1;

    case {'tAL1', 'tAL2'} % local transitions of Alfa
        % do nothing
end
```

1.3 Summary of Processor Files

We now know that there are two groups of processors based on the timeline (pre and post) and three classes based on the visibility (specific, modular, and common).

On the timeline (pre and post):

- **Pre-processors**: Pre-processors will be executed when a transition becomes enabled to fire. This transition can only fire if all the existing pre-processors (in which this transition is visible) return logic true for firing.
- **Post-processors**: Post-processors will be executed when a transition completes firing.

On the visibility (specific, modular, and common):

- **Specific processors**: All transitions are visible in their own specific pre- and post-processors.
- **Modular processors**: All transitions within a Petri Module are visible in their modular pre- and post-processors.
- **Common processors**:
  - **Monolithic (non-modular) Petri net**: All transitions are visible in the common processors (COMMON_PRE and COMMON_POST).
  - **Modular Petri net**: Only transitions in the IMCs (IMC transitions) and transitions that function as Input Ports and Output Ports of Petri Modules are visible in the common processors (COMMON_PRE and COMMON_POST).

1.4 "global_info" and "PN"

From the code listings shown above, we see that many listings declare "**`global_info`**" as a global variable to read and modify user data. In addition to facilitating the exchange of user data between files, `global_info` is also used to set the compiler options, as shown in the MSF (Listing 1.2).

Similarly, the run-time details can be accessed by declaring "**`PN`**"—**the Petri net run-time structure**—as a global variable. If we do so, we can access the Petri net's run-time properties and change any of the details (e.g., names of places, transitions, priorities, and virtually anything). However, it is strongly recommended **not to declare PN** as a global variable in the processor files **to change the run-time values**; instead, use GPenSIM built-in functions; all GPenSIM built-in functions mentioned in the reference manual Davidrajuh [5]. If we find that the functionality we want is not among the GPenSIM functions, we need to create a new function as a MATLAB file (just like the rest of GPenSIM built-in functions) and should not directly change **PN** to achieve the result.

> **CAUTION:**
> **Directly changing PN in the processor files causes expected results!!!!**

However, you are welcome to declare **PN** as a global variable in processor files just to inspect some of its run-time values at the time of inspection.

Listing 1.15 shows a COMMON_PRE. In this COMMON_PRE, whenever a transition (visible in common processors) is enabled, this file will print all the firing transitions at that moment in time. To achieve this result, we declare **PN** as a global variable and access its field "`Firing_Transitions`". Since we are not changing any values of **PN**, it is OK to do this.

Listing 1.15 COMMON_PRE that accesses "PN"

```
function [fire, transition] = COMMON_PRE (transition)

global PN

% total number of transitions
Ts = PN.No_of_transitions;
currently_Firing = ''; % currently firing ...
    transitions

for i = 1:Ts
    if PN.Firing_Transitions(i) % is this trans ...
        firing?
         currently_Firing = [currently_Firing, ' ...
             ', tname(i)];
    end
end

disp(['These transitions are currently firing: ',...
      currently_Firing]);

fire = 1;
```

However, Listing 1.16 shows a better way to achieve the same result. This time, we are using the GPenSIM built-in functions "`ntrans`" (instead of **PN**.`No_of_transitions`) and "`is_firing`" (instead of **PN**.`Firing_Transitions`) as an alternative (and a better way than accessing **PN** directly).

Listing 1.16 COMMON_PRE that does not access "PN"

```
function [fire, transition] = COMMON_PRE (transition)

Ts = ntrans(); % total number of transitions
currently_Firing = ''; % currently firing ...
    transitions

for i = 1:Ts
    if is_firing(i) % is this trans firing?
        currently_Firing = [currently_Firing, ' ...
            ', tname(i)];
    end
end

disp(['These transitions are currently firing: ',...
      currently_Firing]);

fire = 1;
```

The structure of **PN** is further discussed in Sect. 2.6.

References

1. Davidrajuh R (2018) Modeling discrete-event systems with GPenSIM. Springer International Publishing, Cham
2. Davidrajuh R (2021a) Literature review on modular petri nets. Petri nets for modeling of large discrete systems, pp 77–85
3. Davidrajuh R (2021b) Petri nets for modeling of large discrete systems. Springer, Berlin
4. Davidrajuh R (2023) Colored petri nets for modeling of discrete systems: a practical approach with GPenSIM. Springer Nature
5. Davidrajuh R (2024) GPenSIM reference manual. University of Stavanger

Chapter 2
Data Structures in GPenSIM

This chapter presents the data structures in GPenSIM. Some of the data structures are simple as they represent the basic elements such as a place, transition, token, token colors, and resource. The other data structures are large (and sometimes complex) as they represent static Petri net graph ('`spng`'), Petri net structure with initial dynamics ('`pni`'), and Petri Net run-time structure ('`PN`'); these structures combine the basic Petri net structure with colors and resources (in Colored Petri nets) and Modules (in Modular Petri nets).

2.1 Data Structure of a Place

A simple data structure represents each place, consisting of a name, the number of tokens in it, and a token bank that describes the details of each token. For example, place **pBUFFER2** may possess the following data structure:

- name: 'pBUFFER2'
- tokens: 3
- `token_bank`: [1–3 struct]

Since **pBUFFER2** possesses three tokens, `token_bank` will be a series of 3 substructures. For example, the structure of the `token_bank` of **pBUFFER2**:

1. token_bank(1)
    - `tokID`: 77
    - `creation_time`: 101
    - `color`: {}
    - `cost`: 600

R. Davidrajuh, *Petri Nets for Modeling Complex Discrete-Event Systems*, Asset Analytics,
https://doi.org/10.1007/978-981-96-6396-5_2

2. `token_bank(2)`
   - `tokID`: 79
   - `creation_time`: 111
   - `color`: {'CNC1', 'Robot1'}
   - `cost`: 801
3. `token_bank(3)`
   - `tokID`: 104
   - `creation_time`: 302
   - `color`: {'Robot1','Robot2'}
   - `cost`: 680

2.2 Data Structure of a Transition

Since transitions are the most active element, they possess dynamic data structures; a transition's data changes depending on its status, whether it is *enabled*, *firing*, or *has fired*. Also, a transition can request (and thus reserve) resources, use resources during firing (acquired, as the transition is firing), or release resources after the completion of firing. All these details will be recorded in the transition's data structure.

The basic data structure of a transition:

- `name`: Name of the transition.
- `firing_time`: Firing time of the transition.
- `times_fired`: Number of times this transition has fired so far.

Additional data in a data structure of a transition:

- `absorbed_tokens`: when this transition is firing, how many tokens it is holding (*aka* 'virtual tokens' in Chap. 3).
- `firing_cost_fixed`: fixed firing cost.
- `firing_cost_variable`: variable firing cost.
- `resources_reserved`: when a pre-processor is active, a transition may have requested (reserved) some resources. If the pre-processors return the logic true, this transition will be allocated the requested resources.
- `resources_owned`: when a transition is firing, it owns (uses) some resource.

Note that `absorbed_tokens` is a vector of natural numbers in which each index (column) represents a place, and the value denotes the number of tokens. For example, if a Petri net has four places named **p1** to **p4**, and if the value of `absorbed_tokens` is [1 0 0 3], it means a transition is currently holding one token from **p1** and three tokens from **p4**. `absorbed_tokens` are further discussed in Chap. 3 as "**virtual tokens**".

`resources_reserved` and `resources_owned` are vectors of natural numbers in which each index (column) represents a resource, and the value denotes the number of resource instances the transition has reserved or owned. For example, if a Petri net has five resources named **res1** to **res5**, and if the value of `resources_owned` is [1 0 1 0 3], it means this transition is currently using one instance of **res1**, one instance of **res3**, and three instances of **res5**.

2.3 Extended Incidence Matrix

GPenSIM does not offer any data structure for an arc (that connects a place to transition or vice versa). However, the **Extended Incidence Matrix** ($\mathbf{A_e}$) represents all the details of the connection between places and transitions. From the topological information in the PDF file(s), the function `pnstruct` computes $\mathbf{A_e}$ and adds it as an element to the **`spng`** structure as a field named '**`incidence_matrix`**'.

Figure 2.1 shows a simple Petri net. The *input incidence matrix* $\mathbf{A_i}$ of this Petri net represents the arcs from the input places to the transitions. Rows of $\mathbf{A_i}$ represent transitions, and the columns the places:

$$\mathbf{A_i} = \begin{array}{c} \\ t1 \\ t2 \\ t3 \end{array} \begin{array}{c} \begin{array}{ccc} p1 & p2 & p3 \end{array} \\ \begin{pmatrix} 2 & 0 & 0 \\ 0 & 1 & 1 \\ 1 & 0 & 1 \end{pmatrix} \end{array}$$

The *output incidence matrix* $\mathbf{A_o}$ represents the arcs from transitions to the output places.

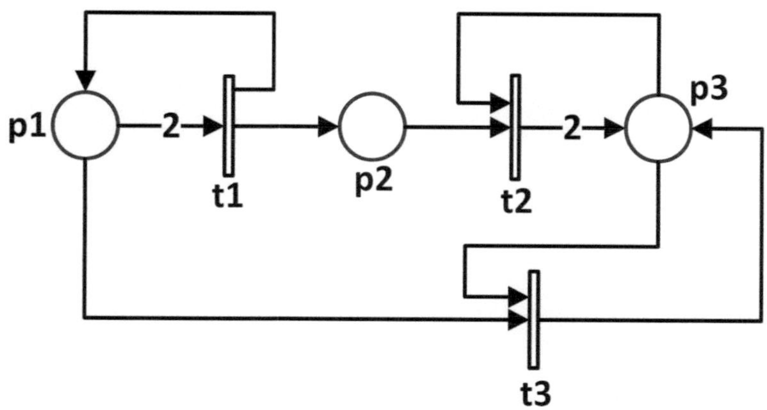

Fig. 2.1 A small static Petri Net graph

$$\mathbf{A_o} = \begin{array}{c} \\ t1 \\ t2 \\ t3 \end{array} \begin{array}{c} \begin{array}{ccc} p1 & p2 & p3 \end{array} \\ \begin{pmatrix} 1 & 1 & 0 \\ 0 & 0 & 2 \\ 0 & 0 & 1 \end{pmatrix} \end{array}$$

GPenSIM's **extended incidence matrix** ($\mathbf{A_e}$) is a combination of $\mathbf{A_i}$ and $\mathbf{A_o}$:

$$\mathbf{A_e} = [\mathbf{A_i} \mid \mathbf{A_o}]$$

For the Petri net in Fig. 2.1, $\mathbf{A_e}$:

$$\mathbf{A_e} = \begin{array}{c} \\ t1 \\ t2 \\ t3 \end{array} \begin{array}{c} \begin{array}{ccccccc} p1 & p2 & p3 & | & p1 & p2 & p3 \end{array} \\ \begin{pmatrix} 2 & 0 & 0 & | & 1 & 1 & 0 \\ 0 & 1 & 1 & | & 0 & 0 & 2 \\ 1 & 0 & 1 & | & 0 & 0 & 1 \end{pmatrix} \end{array}$$

Davidrajuh [3, 5] present interesting applications of $\mathbf{A_e}$, such as the classification of Petri nets and generating random Petri nets.

2.4 Example 03: Place, Transition Data Structures

Figure 2.2 shows a simple Petri net for inspecting place and transition data structures. Transition **tGen** ('Gen' stands for generator) produces tokens for the net. In this example, **tGen** does not possess firing cost. Whereas **tA** and **tB** are assigned with some firing costs.

We will simulate for 15 TU so that at the end, there will be seven, three, and two tokens left in places **pGen**, **pAB**, and **pEnd**, respectively.

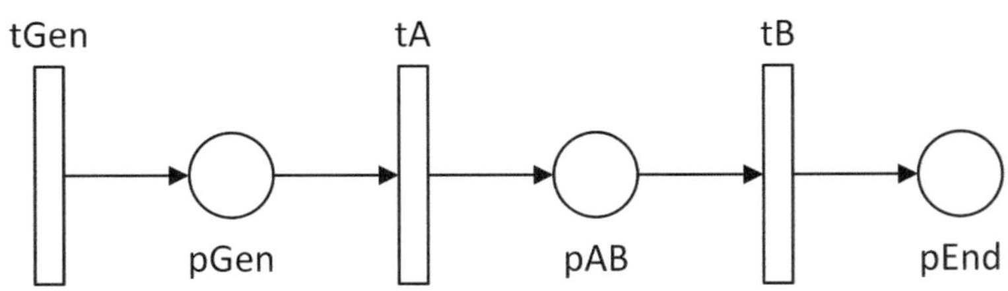

Fig. 2.2 Inspecting place and transition data structures

Listing 2.1 Main Simulation File (Example 03)

```
global global_info
global_info.STOP_AT = 15;

spng = pnstruct('ex_03_pdf');

dyn.m0 = {};    % no initial tokens
dyn.ft = {'tGen',1, 'tA',2, 'tB',5}; dyn.fc_fixed ...
    = {'tA',100,
'tB',200}; dyn.fc_variable = {'tA',10, 'tB',20};

pni = initialdynamics(spng, dyn);

sim = gpensim(pni);

% print details of each place and tokens
print_tokens();

% print details of each transition
print_trans_struct();
```

In COMMON_PRE (Listing 2.2), transitions **tA** and **tB** add their own name as color (namely, 'tA' and 'tB') to the deposited tokens.

Listing 2.2 COMMON_PRE (Example 03)

```
function [fire, transition] = COMMON_PRE(transition)
switch transition.name
    case 'tGen'
        % do nothing
    case {'tA', 'tB'}
        transition.new_color = transition.name;
end
% let the enabled transition fire
fire = 1;
```

2.4.1 Structure of a Place

Let us inspect the structure of places and tokens with the help of the function `print_tokens`.

Listing 2.3 print_tokens() (Example 03)

```
function [] = print_tokens()

Ps = nplaces(); % Number of places
```

```
for i = 1:Ps  % for each place
    % print the current place's name
    disp(['**** Place: ', pname(i), '   *****']);

    % get the current place's structure
    placeI = get_place(i);

    % display place structure
    disp(placeI);

    % get all the tokens in the current place
    tokens = get_tokens(i);

    % print tokens' structure one by one
    for j = 1:length(tokens)
        disp(tokens(j)); disp(' ');
    end
end
```

Structure of the place **pGen** shows that it had seven tokens when the simulation was complete:

```
name: 'pGen'
tokens: 7
token_bank: [1-7 struct]
```

Tokens in **pGen** do not have any colors or costs as **tGen** did not add any; structure of the token bank at **pGen**:

```
tokID: 2
creation_time: 2
color: {0-1 cell}
cost: 0

tokID: 5
creation_time: 4
color: {0-1 cell}
cost: 0
...
...
```

Structure of the place **pAB** shows that it had three tokens when the simulation was complete; structure of the place **pAB**:

```
 name: 'pAB'
tokens: 3
token_bank: [1-3 struct]
```

However, tokens in **pAB** possess a color 'tA' (as **tA** added this color) and bear some costs; structure of these tokens at **pAB**:

```
 tokID: 7
creation_time: 5
color: {'tA'}
cost: 120

tokID: 14
creation_time: 9
color: {'tA'}
cost: 120
...
...
```

Note that the cost of the token in **pAB** is 120 CU (cost units). Because the token cost is equal to: (fixed firing cost of **tA**) + [(firing time of **tA**) × (variable firing cost of **tA**)] = 100 + (2 × 10) = 120.

Finally, the structure of the place **pEnd** shows that it had two tokens when the simulation was complete:

```
 name: 'pEnd'
tokens: 2
token_bank: [1-2 struct]
```

Also, the details of these two tokens:

```
 tokID: 12
creation_time: 8
color: {'tA' 'tB'}
cost: 420

tokID: 21
creation_time: 13
color: {'tA' 'tB'}
cost: 420
```

The tokens colors in **pEnd** are now {'tA' 'tB'}; this is because **tB** adds a color 'tB' to the tokens it took from **pAB** that already possessed color 'tA'. Also, the structure of the tokens in **pEnd** shows that the cost of each token is 420 CU. This is because the cost of this token = (cost of a token in **pAB**) + (fixed firing cost of **tB**) + [(firing time of **tB**) × (variable firing cost of **tB**)] = 120 + 200 + (5 × 20)] = 420.

2.4.2 *Structure of a Transition*

Let us check the transitions and their structures with the help of the function `print_trans_struct()`:

Listing 2.4 print_trans_struct() (Example 03)

```
Ts = ntrans();  % number of transitions

% for each transition
for i = 1:Ts

    % display the name of the current transition
    disp(['**** Structure of ', tname(i), '  ****']);

    % get the current transition's structure
    tStructure = get_trans(i);

    % display the transition's structure
    disp(tStructure);
end
```

Structure of the transition **tGen**:

```
name: 'tGen'
firing_time: 1
firing_cost: 0
times_fired: 14
absorbed_tokens: [0 0 0]
firing_cost_fixed: []
firing_cost_variable: []
```

Structure of the transition **tA**:

```
 name: 'tA'
firing_time: 2
firing_cost: 0
times_fired: 6
absorbed_tokens: [0 0 1]
firing_cost_fixed: 100
firing_cost_variable: 10
```

Structure of the transition **tB**:

```
 name: 'tB'
firing_time: 5
firing_cost: 0
times_fired: 2
absorbed_tokens: [1 0 0]
firing_cost_fixed: 200
firing_cost_variable: 20
```

2.5 Data Structure of a Resource

Each resource in GPenSIM is represented by a simple data structure that consists of six fields:

- `name`: Name of the resource.
- `max_instances`: Number of instances of this resource.
- `MAX_CAP`: Life cycle time (how long it can be used without a break).
- `rc_fixed`: Fixed cost of this resource.
- `rc_variable`: Variable cost of this resource.
- `instance_usage`: (a substructure) how each instance is used so far.

`instance_usage` is a matrix of dimension ($4 \times n_{ri}$), four rows and n_{ri} columns, where n_{ri} equals the number of resource instances. Let us take a resource with three instances.

- The first row of `instance_usage` shows which instances are under use and by which transition. For example, if this resource's first and third instances are used by transitions with indices 11 and 22 (the second instance is unused), then the first row of the matrix will be [11 0 22].
- The second row of `instance_usage` shows the start time of using a resource instance. If the transition with index 11 starts using an instance at time 34 and the transition with index 22 at time 36, then the second row becomes the vector [34 0 36].
- The third row reveals how long each instance will be used; if the firing times of these two transitions are 10 and 20 TU, the third row becomes [10 0 20].
- (The fourth row of `instance_usage` is unused)

2.6 PN Structure

PN structure is already mentioned in Sect. 1.4. `PN` (short for "**Petri Net run-time structure**") is the run-time details that can be accessed by declaring "`PN`" as a global variable in most of the files (MSF and processor files) to access the Petri net's run-time properties.

Various forms of PN:

1. **spng**: The starting point of PN is the Main Simulation File (MSF), in which PN is formed as spng—**structure for the static Petri net graph**—using the function 'pnstruct'.
2. **pni**: the static Petri net graph spng is combined with the initial dynamic details (using the function 'initialdynamics') to form the **Petri net structure with initial dynamics** ('pni').
3. **PN**: Finally, pni is passed to the function 'gpensim' to run the simulations; during simulation, PN is accessible in any of the processor files as long as we declare it as a global variable these files.
4. **Simulation results**: when the simulation is completed, gpensim will output the simulation result. The first part of this simulation result is the final run-time values of PN; the second part of the simulation result is the log files that keep all states and token color information.

When the function gpensim starts running, the only way to interact with the ongoing simulation is through the processor files. These files are called whenever a transition is enabled and a firing transition completes. Hence, we can use GPenSIM built-in functions in the processor files to understand and modify the run-time parameters (or use PN to do the same; however, accessing PN to change its values directly is not recommended).

The data structure of PN consists of more than 40 fields; in essence, PN contains all the run-time details.

2.6.1 Example 04: Inspecting PN Structure

This example uses a modular Petri net that is shown in Fig. 2.3; Davidrajuh [2] described the basics of modular Petri nets. This Petri net is composed of two Petri Modules, **Alfa** and **Zeta**, which are joined together by the IMC 'Driver'. Petri Module **Alfa** possesses two inhibiting arcs, (**pAL1**, **tAI1**) and (**pAL2**, **tAL1**). Since the source **tD1** has a higher firing rate (shorter firing time) than all other transitions, there will be many tokens in places. These two inhibiting arcs are to make sure that the local places of **Alfa**, **pAL1** and **pAL2**, would possess a maximum of one token anytime.

Listing 2.5 shows the PDF for Petri Module **Alfa**, which now includes a declaration of inhibiting arcs ('png.**set_of_Is**').

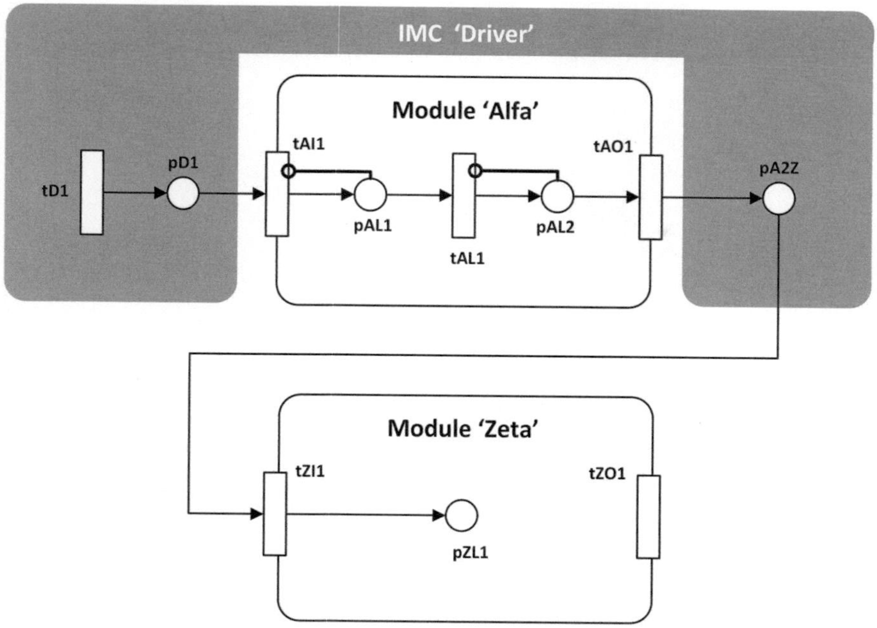

Fig. 2.3 Petri Net with two Petri Modules

Listing 2.5 PDF of Alfa (Example 04)

```
function [png] = PDF_Alfa()

png.PN_name = 'Alfa';    % module name

% set of places (Ps), transitions (Ts), and arcs (As)
png.set_of_Ps = {'pAL1','pAL2'}; png.set_of_Ts =
{'tAI1','tAL1','tAO1'}; png.set_of_As = {...
     'tAI1','pAL1',1, ...    % tAI1
     'pAL1','tAL1',1, 'tAL1','pAL2',1, ... % tAL1
     'pAL2','tAO1',1 ... % tAO1 inputs
     };

% inhibiting arcs
png.set_of_Is = {'pAL1','tAI1',1, 'pAL2','tAL1',1};

% set of input and output ports
png.set_of_Ports = {'tAI1','tAO1'};
```

Listing 2.6 shows the PDF for Petri Module **Zeta**, which includes a "dummy" transition **tZO1**. This dummy transition doesn't do anything other than always firing; it is included here for further expansion of the module **Zeta** later; hence, it is called a "dummy" in GPenSIM literature.

Listing 2.6 PDF of Zeta (Example 04)

```
function [png] = PDF_Zeta()

% Module's name
png.PN_name = 'Zeta';

% set of places, transitions, and arcs
png.set_of_Ps = {'pZL1'}; png.set_of_Ts = ...
    {'tZI1', 'tZO1'};
png.set_of_As = {'tZI1','pZL1',1}; % tZI1; tZO1 ...
    is dummy

% set of input and output ports
png.set_of_Ports = {'tZI1','tZO1'};
```

Listing 2.7 shows the main simulation file (MSF). In MSF, we add some costs (fixed and variable) to transitions **tAL1** and **tD1**. Also, we declare two resources ('Printer-A' and 'Printer-B'), which will be used by **tAI1** and **tZI1**, respectively. Also, the resources cost money (fixed and variable).

In the main simulation file, we remove the semicolon at the end of some of the statements so that MATLAB prints the output of that line (`spng`, `pni`, and sim_results) to the screen.

Listing 2.7 Main Simulation File (Example 04)

```
clear all; clc;

global global_info
global_info.STOP_AT = 100;
global_info.MUTEX = 2;
global_info.TOKENS_TO_PRODUCE = 5;

spng = pnstruct({'PDF_Driver','PDF_Alfa','PDF_Zeta'})
dyn.ft = {'tD1',1,'tAI1',1, 'allothers', 5};
dyn.m0 = {}; % no intial tokens
dyn.ip = {'tAI1',2 'tZI1',1};

dyn.fc_fixed = {'tAL1',50, 'tD1',100};
dyn.fc_variable = {'tAL1',20, 'tD1',25};

dyn.re = {'Printer-A', 1,inf, 'Printer-B',1,inf};
dyn.rc_fixed = {'Printer-A',10, 'Printer-B',10};
dyn.rc_variable = {'Printer-A',2, 'Printer-B',1};
pni = initialdynamics(spng, dyn)

sim_results = gpensim(pni)

%prnss(sim_results);
subplot(5,1,1), plotp(sim_results, {'pD1'});
subplot(5,1,2), plotp(sim_results, {'pAL1'});
subplot(5,1,3), plotp(sim_results, {'pAL2'});
```

```
subplot(5,1,4), plotp(sim_results, {'pA2Z'});
subplot(5,1,5), plotp(sim_results, {'pZL1'});
```

COMMON_PRE (Listing 2.8) shows that **tAI1** and **tZI1** request resources 'Printer-A' and 'Printer-B', respectively, before they start firing. COMMON_POST (Listing 2.9) shows that **tAI1** and **tZI1** releases their resources at the completion of firing.

Listing 2.8 COMMON_PRE (Example 04)

```
function [fire, transition] = COMMON_PRE(transition)

switch transition.name
    case 'tAI1'
        granted = requestSR({'Printer-A',1});
    case 'tZI1'
        granted = requestSR({'Printer-B',1});

    otherwise
        granted = 1;
end
fire = granted; % fire if resource aquired
```

Listing 2.9 COMMON_POST (Example 04)

```
% Example-04: COMMON_PRE
function [] = COMMON_POST(transition)

release();
```

And finally, we add a specific pre-processor to **tD1** so that it will fire only five times; see Listing 2.10.

Listing 2.10 Specific Pre-processor of "tD1" (Example 04)

```
function [fire, trans] = tD1_pre (trans)

global global_info

ntD1 = timesfired('tD1'); fire = lt(ntD1,
global_info.TOKENS_TO_PRODUCE); if fire
    disp(['"tD1" is firing for the ', ...
        int2str(ntD1+1), ' time!']);
end
```

2.6.2 *Structure of* **spng**

```
name: 'IMC Driver + Alfa + Zeta'
global_places: [1-5 struct]
No_of_places: 5
global_transitions: [1-6 struct]
No_of_transitions: 6
global_Vplaces: [1-5 struct]
incidence_matrix: [6-10 double]
Inhibited_Transitions: [1 1 0 0 0 0]
Inhibitors_exist: 1
inhibitor_matrix: [6-5 double]
No_of_modules: 2
module_membership: [2-6 double]
module_names: {'Alfa' 'Zeta'}
```

spng is a compact representation of **the static Petri net graph**. There are 13 fields in spng:

1. name: Since we declared three PDFs (named 'Alfa', 'Zeta', and 'IMC Driver') in the main simulation file, the compiler will take all three labels of the PDFs and put them as the name of the resulting Petri net ('IMC Driver + Alfa + Zeta').
2. global_places: this is a structure array in which each structure represents a place initialized with the place name given in PDFs.
3. No_of_places (n_p): Total number of places (5 in Example 04) in the Petri net.
4. global_transitions: this is a structure array in which each structure represents a transition initialized with the transition name given in the PDF.
5. No_of_transitions (n_t): Total number of transitions (6, in Example 04) in the Petri net.
6. global_Vplaces: place structures for all the places, initialized with the place names given in PDFs; these places represent the tokens consumed by firing transitions.
7. incidence_matrix: the extended incidence matrix ($A_e = [A_i|A_o]$). Dimension is ($n_t \times 2 \cdot n_p$).
8. Inhibitors_exist: (Boolean value) Whether or not we have inhibiting arcs in the Petri net (in Example 04, we have).
9. Inhibited_Transitions: A vector of Boolean values (length n_t) indicating which transitions are inhibited (identified by the transition index). (in Example 04, the value of Inhibited_Transitions is [1 1 0 0 0 0], meaning transition **tAI1**, and **tAL1** are inhibited; their indices are 1 and 2).
10. inhibitor_matrix: A matrix that represents the inhibiting arcs. Dimension: ($n_t \times n_p$). Each row represents a transition, and each column a place. In Example 04:

$$
\begin{array}{c} tAI1 \\ tAL1 \\ tAO1 \\ tD1 \\ tZI1 \\ tZO1 \end{array}
\overset{\begin{array}{ccccc} pA2Z & pAL1 & pAL2 & pD1 & pZL1 \end{array}}{\begin{pmatrix}
\text{inf} & 1 & \text{inf} & \text{inf} & \text{inf} \\
\text{inf} & \text{inf} & 1 & \text{inf} & \text{inf} \\
\text{inf} & \text{inf} & \text{inf} & \text{inf} & \text{inf} \\
\text{inf} & \text{inf} & \text{inf} & \text{inf} & \text{inf} \\
\text{inf} & \text{inf} & \text{inf} & \text{inf} & \text{inf} \\
\text{inf} & \text{inf} & \text{inf} & \text{inf} & \text{inf}
\end{pmatrix}}
$$

inhibitor_matrix for Example 04 shows that there are two inhibiting arcs (**pAL1**, **tAI1**) and (**pAL2**, **tAL1**), with arc weight of one.

11. No_of_modules (n_M): How many Petri Modules are there in the Petri net? In Example 04, we have two Petri Modules.
12. module_membership: A matrix of dimension $(2 - n_t)$. The first row of the matrix shows the membership of each transition. The second row indicates whether a transition is an input or output port. module_membership in Example 04:

$$
\begin{array}{c} membership \\ IOPort? \end{array}
\overset{\begin{array}{cccccc} tAI1 & tAL1 & tAO1 & tD1 & tZI1 & tZO1 \end{array}}{\begin{pmatrix}
1 & 1 & 1 & 0 & 2 & 2 \\
1 & 0 & 1 & 0 & 1 & 1
\end{pmatrix}}
$$

- The first row of module_membership in Example 04 shows transitions **tAI1**, **tAL1**, and **tAO1** are members of Petri Module **Alfa** (**Alfa** has module index 1), and transitions **tZI1** and **tZO1** are members of Petri Module **Zeta** (**Zeta** has module index 2). Whereas, being a member of an IMC, **tD1** does not belong to any modules (value 0 for module index).
- The second row shows that the Petri net has the following Input and Output Ports: **tAI1** and **tAO1** (input and output ports of **Alfa**), and **tZI1** and **tZO1** (input and output ports of **Zeta**).

13. module_names: Set of all the module names. In Example 04, the modules' names are **Alfa** and **Zeta**.

2.6.3 *Structure of* `pni`

The function initialdynamics combines the structure spng representing the static Petri net graph, and the initial dynamics to create the **Petri net structure with initial dynamics** (**pni**). **pni** possesses 37 fields that are divided into two parts.

The first 13 fields of pni are the same as spng (in other words, the first block of pni is the spng). For Example 04, the rest 24 fields of pni:

```
delta_T: 0.2500
REAL_TIME: 0
HH_MM_SS: 0
current_time: 0
STOP_TIME: 100
X: [0 0 0 0 0]
initial_marking: [0 0 0 0 0]
VX: [0 0 0 0 0]
token_serial_numer: 0
Set_of_Firing_Costs_Fixed: [0 50 0 100
0 0]
Set_of_Firing_Costs_Variable: [0 20 0
25 0 0]
Firing_Costs_Enabled: 1
COST_CALCULATIONS: 1
Set_of_Firing_Times: [1 5 5 1 5 5]
priority_list: [2 0 0 0 1 0]
system_resources: [1-2 struct]
No_of_system_resources: 2
Resource_usage_LOG: []
PRE_exist: [0 0 0 1 0 0]
POST_exist: [0 0 0 0 0 0]
MOD_PRE_exist: [0 0]
MOD_POST_exist: [0 0]
COMMON_PRE: 1
COMMON_POST: 1
```

14. `delta_T`: this is the sampling frequency, which is the one-fourth of the least firing time of any transition. For Example 04, it is one-fourth of the firing time of **tD1**, equal to 0.25 TU.
15. `REAL_TIME`: (Boolean value) whether the simulation uses GPenSIM's simulated clock or the computer's real-time clock. In Example 04, we are not using a real-time clock; hence, the value is false.
    To activate the real-time clock, we must set the OPTION '`REAL_TIME`' to true in the main simulation file.
16. `HH_MM_SS`: (Boolean value) whether the simulation uses the hourly (business) clock using time in HH:MM:SS format. In Example 04, we are not using the hourly clock; therefore, the value is false (0).
17. `current_time`: at the start, the current time will be 0, unless the start time is assigned a different value using the OPTION `START_AT`.
18. `STOP_TIME`: we can set the compiler OPTION `STOP_TIME` in the main simulation file to declare the simulation stop time. For Example 04, it is 100 TU. If the stop time is not given, then the default stop time is 200 TU.
19. `X`: `X` is the current state. At the start, `X` is the same as the `initial_marking`.

20. `initial_marking`: a vector of n_p natural numbers, representing the initial tokens in various places. In Example 04, the vector is a set of zeros, as we did not assign any initial marking.
21. `VX`: virtual tokens, a vector of n_p natural numbers, representing the virtual tokens in various places; see Chap. 3 for details. Initially, this vector will be all zeros.
22. `token_serial_numer`: Compiler add a new token identification number (`tokID`) starting from 1. `token_serial_numer` shows how many tokens have been created so far. The next token created will get the `tokID` equals `token_serial_numer` + 1. In Example 04, since there are no initial tokens created, `token_serial_numer` is equal to 0.
23. `Set_of_Firing_Costs_Fixed`: This is a vector of real numbers (of length n_t) that represents the fixed firing costs of all transitions. In Example 04, we assigned fixed costs to **tAL1** and **tD1**, with costs 50 and 100 cost units (CU). Hence, the vector is [0 50 0 100 0 0].
24. `Set_of_Firing_Costs_Variable`: This is a vector of real numbers (of length n_t) that represents the variable firing costs of all transitions. In Example 04, we assigned variable costs to **tAL1** and **tD1**, with costs 20 and 25 cost units per TU (CU/TU). Hence, the vector is [0 20 0 25 0 0].
25. `Firing_Costs_Enabled`: (Boolean value) whether or not the transitions are assigned costs; since we assigned costs to some transitions in Example 04, the value is true, meaning the compiler will perform cost calculations automatically.
26. `COST_CALCULATIONS`: (Boolean value) whether or not the resources are assigned costs; since we assigned costs to the two resources in Example 04, the value is true, meaning the compiler will perform cost calculations automatically.
27. `Set_of_Firing_Times`: This is a vector of real numbers (of length n_t) that represents the firing times of all transitions. In Example 04, we assigned a firing time of 1 TU to **tAI1** and **tD1**, and all other transitions got 5 TU. Therefore, the vector becomes [1 5 5 1 5 5].
28. `priority_list`: This is a vector of natural numbers (of length n_t) that represents the priority levels of each transitions. By default, each transition has 0 priority, and the higher the number, the better priority. Since we assigned higher priorities to **tAI1** (of value 2) and **tZI1** (value 1), the vector becomes [2 0 0 0 1 0].
29. `No_of_system_resources` (n_R): The number of resources; in Example 04, it is two ('Printer-A' and 'Printer-B').
30. `system_resources`: This is a structure array (array length is n_R number of structures), and each structure represents a resource. Since we declared two resources in Example 04, `system_resources` will be a [1–2 structures]. Let us inspect these two structures:
    `system_resources(1):`

```
name: 'Printer-A'
max_instances: 1
MAX_CAP: Inf
rc_fixed: 10
rc_variable: 2
instance_usage: [4-1 double]
```

`system_resources(2):`

```
name: 'Printer-B'
max_instances: 1
MAX_CAP: Inf
rc_fixed: 10
rc_variable: 1
instance_usage: [4-1 double]
```

(a) `max_instances` is the number of instances of each resource.
(b) `MAX_CAP` is the cycle time of the resource, meaning how long we can use the resource without a break.
(c) `rc_fixed` and `rc_variable` are fixed and variable costs of the resource.
(d) `instance_usage`: this is a $(4 \times n_{ri})$ dimensional matrix, n_{ri} is number of instances of a particular resource. See Sect. 2.5 "Data structure of a Resource", for details. In `pni`, `instance_usage` will be a matrix $(4 \times n_{ri})$ of all zeros, as none of the resources are used yet (the simulation has not started yet).

31. `Resource_usage_LOG`: This is log file that will filled during the simulation. See Chap. 4 for details.
32. `PRE_exist`: This is a vector of Boolean values (of length n_t) that represents whether we have specific pre-processors for transitions. In Example 04, only transition **tD1** has a specific pre-processor; hence the vector becomes [0 0 0 1 0 0] as the index of **tD1** is 4.
33. `POST_exist`: This is a vector of Boolean values (of length n_t) that represents whether we have specific post-processors for transitions. In Example 04, none of the transitions have specific pre-processors; hence, the vector becomes all zeros, [0 0 0 0 0 0].
34. `MOD_PRE_exist`: This is a vector of Boolean values (of length n_M, number of Petri Modules) that represents whether we have modular pre-processors for Petri Modules. In Example 04, none of the Petri Modules have modular pre-processors; hence, the vector becomes all zeros, [0 0].
35. `MOD_POST_exist`: This is a vector of Boolean values (of length n_M, number of Petri Modules) that represents whether we have modular post-processors for Petri Modules. In Example 04, none of the Petri Modules have modular post-processors; hence, the vector becomes all zeros [0 0].
36. `COMMON_PRE`: (Boolean value) whether or not there is a COMMON_PRE processor; since we have a COMMON_PRE in Example 04, the value is true.
37. `COMMON_POST`: (Boolean value) whether or not there is a COMMON_POST processor; since we have a COMMON_POST in Example 04, the value is true.

2.6.4 *Structure of* **PN**

The function gpensim takes pni as the input argument and renames it as PN. As the simulation progresses, gpensim will continue to change the values of the fields in PN. In PN, there are two types of fields:

- **Static fields**: fields whose values will not be changed during the simulation. For these fields, the values in pni and PN will be the same.
- **Dynamic fields**: the values for these fields will be updated as the simulation progresses.

Static fields of PN:

- OPTIONS fields (delta_T, REAL_TIME, and HH_MM_SS).
- Initial Marking (initial_marking).
- Cost fields (Set_of_Firing_Costs_Fixed, Set_of_Firing_Costs_Variable, Firing_Costs_Enabled, and COST_CALCULATIONS).
- Firing Times (Set_of_Firing_Times).
- Number of Resource (No_of_system_resources).
- File existence (PRE_exist, POST_exist, MOD_PRE_exist, MOD_POST_exist, COMMON_PRE, and COMMON_POST).

Dynamic fields of PN:

- Current Time (current_time).
- Current State (X, VX, and token_serial_numer)
- Priorities of Transitions (priority_list).
- Resource Usage (a sub-field of system_resources, and Resource_usage_LOG).

2.6.5 *Structure of Simulation Result*

When function gpensim completes the simulation, PN will be updated with the final values. Also, gpensim will add the simulation result as LOG matrices (e.g., LOG, Firing_Trans_Set, and Enabled_Trans_Set) to PN; the LOG matrices are discussed in Chap. 4.

In Example 04, 'sim_results'—the simulation output from gpensim may look like the following:

```
...
%%% PN with final values is the first
block
...
%%% following fields are the
additional ones
State: 44
LOG: [487-16 double]
Firing_Trans_SET: [443-7 double]
Enabled_Trans_SET: [443-7 double]
color_map: []
completion_time: 100
overall_no_of_tokens_used: 25
```

Structure of simulation output by`gpensim`:

- *[the first block of the simulation result will be the `PN` with final values].*
- `State`: Total number of states in the result.
- `LOG`: The state space (all the states and the times; discussed in Chap. 4).
- `Firing_Trans_SET`: At each state, which transitions were firing?
- `Enabled_Trans_SET`: At each state, which transitions were enabled?
- `color_map`: for Colored Petri net, a LOG file that contains all the colors of tokens at various states (discussed in Chap. 4).
- `completion_time`: Simulation completion time; this can be different from `STOP_AT`, as a pre-processor or a post-processor may force simulations to stop abruptly (by setting on the OPTION `STOP_SIMULATION`).
- `overall_no_of_tokens_used`: The total number of tokens used.

2.7 Concluding Remarks

The scope of this chapter is to present the details of data structures in GPenSIM. For a complete understanding of the basic theories, the following books are suggested:

- Davidrajuh [1] for the basics of GPenSIM.
- Davidrajuh [2] for modular Petri nets.
- Davidrajuh [4] for Colored Petri nets that include tokens colors, resources, and cost calculations.
- Finally, Davidrajuh [6] presents details of GPenSIM built-in functions.

References

1. Davidrajuh R (2018) Modeling discrete-event systems with GPenSIM. Springer International Publishing, Cham
2. Davidrajuh R (2021) Petri nets for modeling of large discrete systems. Springer
3. Davidrajuh R (2023a) A classifier of petri nets for GPenSIM environment. In: 2023 7th International symposium on multidisciplinary studies and innovative technologies (ISMSIT). IEEE, pp 1–6
4. Davidrajuh R (2023b) Colored Petri Nets for modeling of discrete systems: a practical approach with GPenSIM. Springer Nature
5. Davidrajuh R (2023c) Generating random petri nets for GPenSIM environment. In: 2023 9th International conference on systems and informatics (ICSAI). IEEE, pp 1–6
6. Davidrajuh R (2024) GPenSIM reference manual. University of Stavanger

Chapter 3
Virtual Tokens and Virtual State

In P/T Petri nets, transitions take zero firing time [3]. Thus, these transitions are called "primitive" transitions as they cannot represent real-life events (real-life events do take time). This chapter describes "non-primitive" transitions that take non-zero time to fire. A "non-primitive" transition keeps the consumed tokens inside during the firing time, creating the concept of "virtual tokens" and "virtual state".

Note that "consumed tokens", "absorbed tokens", and "virtual tokens" refer to the same thing, and we will use them interchangeably. When a transition starts firing, tokens are "consumed" from input places and these are "absorbed" into the transition to become "virtual tokens" (meaning not visible outside). Most of the literature uses the word "consumed", whereas GPenSIM literature uses all three.

3.1 Primitive and Non-primitive Transitions

When a primitive transition fires, it performs three actions:

1. It consumes tokens from input places.
2. It starts firing, and
3. At the end of the firing, it deposits newer tokens onto its output places.

In primitive transitions, these three steps take zero time, called the "atomicity" property.

GPenSIM is designed to model real-life systems and thus works in two modes [1]:

1. Untimed mode: all transitions are primitive and take zero time to fire.
2. Timed mode: all transitions are non-primitive, taking finite time ("firing time") to fire.

In timed mode, when a non-primitive transition fires, it also performs three actions:

R. Davidrajuh, *Petri Nets for Modeling Complex Discrete-Event Systems*, Asset Analytics,
https://doi.org/10.1007/978-981-96-6396-5_3

1. At the start of firing: it consumes tokens from input places.
2. Firing: until the firing is complete, all the consumed tokens are inside the transition (the transition is working on these tokens).
3. Completion of firing: when a transition completes firing, instantaneously, the consumed tokens are transformed into output tokens, and the transition deposits newer tokens onto their output places.

These three steps take non-zero time, which is equal to the transition's firing time. In GPenSIM, when a transition is firing, the consumed tokens confined inside the transition are known as the "virtual tokens", and the set of virtual tokens as a vector is called the "virtual state" (or virtual marking). "virtual tokens" are described as "`absorbed_tokens`" in Sect. 2.4.2.

Figure 3.1 shows a **non-primitive transition** as an aggregate of two **primitive transitions** ("**Starter**" and "**Stopper**") and two places. One of the places is the **virtual place**, which keeps the virtual tokens during the firing of the transitions. The other place, "**pme**" is for mutual exclusion: once the non-primitive transition starts firing, transition **starter** consumes the token from **pme** so that **starter** will not consume any more input tokens until **stopper** releases the token when the non-primitive transition completes firing [1, 2].

The "Atomicity" property in P/T Petri net is to make sure that all tokens are accountable when a primitive transition fires. In GPenSIM, the atomicity property is preserved differently, as shown in Fig. 3.2.

In Fig. 3.2b, when the transition is working on the consumed tokens (transition is still firing), the tokens inside the virtual place (except the token for locking) are called the virtual tokens. A set of all these tokens form the virtual state.

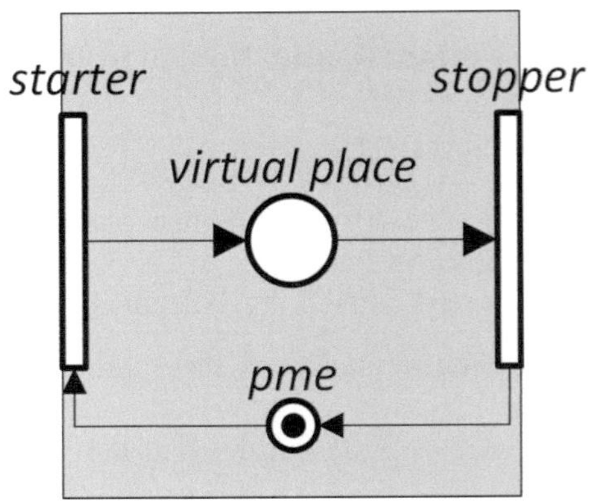

Fig. 3.1 A non-primitive transition. *Source* Davidrajuh [1]

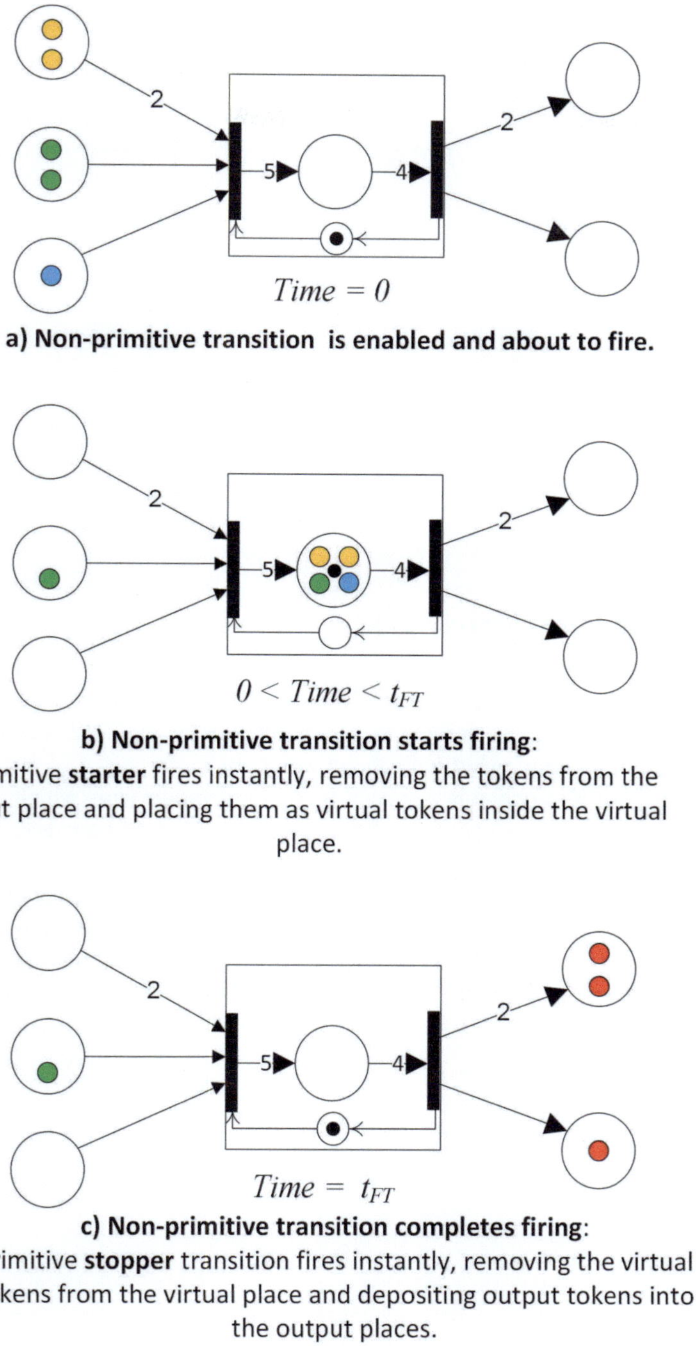

Fig. 3.2 Preserving the "Atomicity" property in GPenSIM. *Source* Davidrajuh [1]

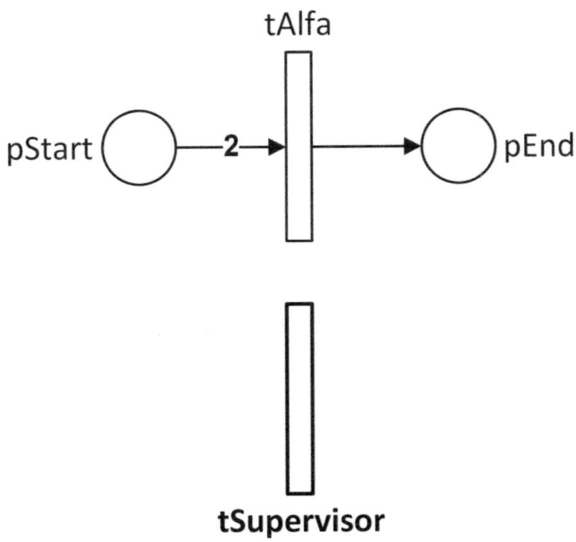

Fig. 3.3 A tiny Petri net for understanding virtual tokens and virtual states

3.2 Example 05: Virtual Tokens

Figure 3.3 shows a tiny Petri net for testing the virtual tokens and the virtual state. In this Petri net, **tAlfa** has an input place **pStart**, and the input arc weight is 2. The output place of **tAlfa** is **pEnd** with an arc weight of 1.

The Petri net also contains a special transition **tSupervisor**, which neither has input nor output places. The lack of input places makes **tSupervisor** fire at will without causing any changes to the existing state (because it neither consumes nor deposits tokens). Also, **tSupervisor** usually has the shortest firing time than all other transitions, so it often fires; hence, we can use its pre- and pro-processors, `tSupervisor_pre` and `tSupervisor_post`, for the system-wide inspection.

Listing 3.1 shows the PDF; In this PDF, **tSupervisor** doesn't possess any input or output places.

Listing 3.1 PDF (Example 05)

```
function [png] = virtual_pdf()
png.PN_name = 'Example 05: virtual tokens';
png.set_of_Ps = {'pStart', 'pEnd'};
png.set_of_Ts = {'tAlfa', 'tSupervisor'};
png.set_of_As = {'pStart','tAlfa',2,...
    'tAlfa','pEnd',1};
```

Listing 3.2 shows the main simulation file.

Listing 3.2 Main Simulation File (Example 05)

```
clear all;
global global_info
global_info.STOP_AT = 8;

spng = pnstruct('ex_05_pdf');
dyn.m0 = {'pStart',4};
dyn.ft = {'tAlfa',3, 'tSupervisor',1};
pni = initialdynamics(spng, dyn);

disp('In the beginning ....');
disp([' Time: [', int2str(current_time), ']: ']);
prnstate('State : ');
prnVirtualState('Virtual state :');

sim = gpensim(pni);
subplot(2,1,1), plotp(sim, {'pStart'});
subplot(2,1,2), plotp(sim, {'pEnd'});
```

For testing, we will use only one processor, which will be COMMON_POST (Listing 3.3).

Listing 3.3 COMMON_POST (Example 05)

```
function [] = COMMON_POST(transition)

tname = transition.name;
% number of times this trans has fired so far
nt = timesfired(tname);

disp(' ');
disp(['after ', int2str(nt), ' firings of "', ...
    tname, '" ...']);
disp([' Time: [', int2str(current_time), ']: ']);
prnstate('State : ');
prnVirtualState('Virtual state :');
disp(' '); disp(' ');
```

Figure 3.4 shows how tokens in **pStart** and **pEnd** change with time. At the start, we have four tokens in **pStart** (initial tokens). Though **tSupervisor** fires often (firing time is 1 TU), it doesn't impact in Fig. 3.4.

```
In the beginning ....
Time: [0]:
State : 4pStart
Virtual state : (no tokens)
```

When **tAlfa** starts at time 0, it consumes two tokens, and these two consumed tokens become virtual tokens. Thus, the current state (marking) is two tokens in **pStart** and 0 tokens in **pEnd**; the virtual state is 2 tokens from **pStart** are now inside

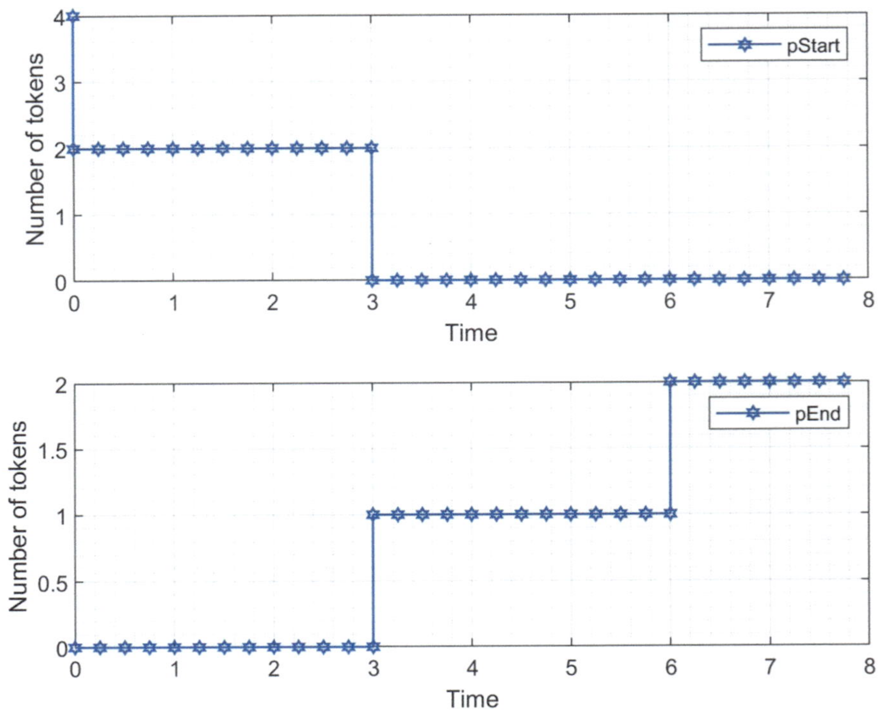

Fig. 3.4 Tokens in **pStart** and **pEnd**

tAlfa.

```
after 1 firings of"tSupervisor" ...
Time: [1]:
State : 2pStart
Virtual state : 2pStart
```

At time 1, **tSupervisor** completes firing for the first time; **tAlfa** is still firing (its firing time is 3 TU), holding the virtual tokens inside.

At time 2, **tSupervisor** completes the second firing; **tAlfa** is still firing (its firing time is 3 TU), holding the virtual tokens inside. Thus, there is no change in the state and virtual state.

```
after 2 firings of "tSupervisor" ...
Time: [2]:
State : 2pStart
Virtual state : 2pStart
```

At time 3, **tSupervisor** completes firing for the third time yet makes no change in the state and virtual state. However, **tAlfa** also completes firing, transforming the two virtual tokens into an output token and depositing it on **pEnd**.

```
After 3 firings of "tSupervisor" ...
Time: [3]:
State : 2pStart
Virtual state : 2pStart

After 1 firings of "tAlfa" ...
Time: [3]:
State : 1pEnd + 2pStart
Virtual state : (no tokens)
```

After completing the firing (and depositing a token into **pEnd**), **tAlfa** is enabled again and thus starts firing by consuming two new tokens from **pStart**. (**tSupervisor** starts firing again but doesn't cause any change in the state)

At time 4, **tSupervisor** fires for the fourth time, and **tAlfa** is still on the second firing, holding the virtual tokens inside.

```
after 4 firings of "tSupervisor" ...
Time: [4]:
State : 1pEnd
Virtual state : 2pStart
```

At time 5 TU, **tSupervisor** fires for the fifth time, making no change. However, at time 6 TU, both **tSupervisor** and **tAlfa** complete firing.

```
after 2 firings of "tAlfa" ...
Time: [6]:
State : 2pEnd
Virtual state : (no tokens)
```

From now on, **tSupervisor** will continue to fire at every whole TU but will not make any change. And, **tAlfa** is disabled due to lack of tokens in **pStart**.

References

1. Davidrajuh R (2018) Modeling discrete-event systems with GPenSIM. Springer International Publishing, Cham
2. Davidrajuh R (2021) Petri nets for modeling of large discrete systems. Springer, Berlin
3. Peterson JL (1981) Petri net theory and the modeling of systems. Prentice Hall PTR

Chapter 4
Log Files

This chapter presents formats (compositions) of simulation results. For example, the function 'gpensim' returns the simulation result, which is used by functions 'prnss' (print state space) and 'plotp' (plot tokens in places). Suppose the user wants to circumvent the GPenSIM functions for printing and plotting the results and create a new function. However, this new function still has to use the result output by 'gpensim'. Hence, the user needs to understand the composition of the resulting output by 'gpensim'.

4.1 Example 06: Simulation Result Output by 'gpensim'

Let us consider a simple Petri net shown in Fig. 4.1 (this example is adapted from Davidrajuh [1]). The transitions **tAlfa** and **tBeta** are supposed to fire alternatively (not simultaneously). We can use a semaphore (*aka* 'mutex') to achieve this alternating firing, as shown in the Listings 4.1, 4.2, and 4.3.

Listing 4.1 Main Simulation File (Example 06)

```
clear all;
global global_info
global_info.STOP_AT = 100; % stop simulations after 100 TU.
global_info.semaphore = 'tAlfa';  % "tAlfa" to fire first

spng = pnstruct('alternate_pdf');
dyn.m0 = {'pStart',9};
dyn.ft = {'tAlfa',10, 'tBeta',20};
pni = initialdynamics(spng, dyn);

sim_results = gpensim(pni);
% print LOG on screen
disp(sim_results.LOG);
```


R. Davidrajuh, *Petri Nets for Modeling Complex Discrete-Event Systems*, Asset Analytics,
https://doi.org/10.1007/978-981-96-6396-5_4

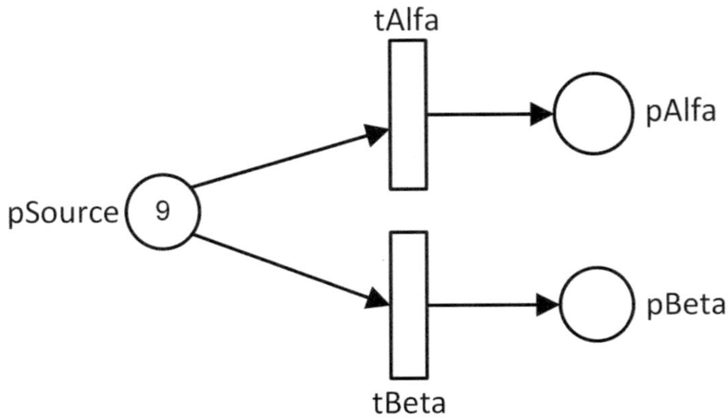

Fig. 4.1 Petri net for Example 06

```
prnss(sim_results);

TOKEN = plotp(sim_results, {'pAlfa', 'pBeta'});
% print TOKEN matrix on screen
disp(TOKEN);
```

Listing 4.2 COMMON_PRE (Example 06)

```
function [fire, trans] = COMMON_PRE(trans)
global global_info

if strcmp(trans.name, 'tAlfa')
    % tAlfa fires if semaphore == "tAlfa"
    fire = strcmp(global_info.semaphore, 'tAlfa');

else % this is tBeta
    % tBeta fires if semaphore == "tBeta"
    fire = strcmp(global_info.semaphore, 'tBeta');
end
```

Listing 4.3 COMMON_POST (Example 06)

```
function [] = COMMON_POST(transition)
global global_info

if strcmp(transition.name, 'tAlfa')
    % tAlfa releases semaphore to "tBeta"
    global_info.semaphore = 'tBeta';

else     % transition.name 'tBeta'
    % tBeta releases semaphore to "tAlfa"
    global_info.semaphore = 'tAlfa';
end
```

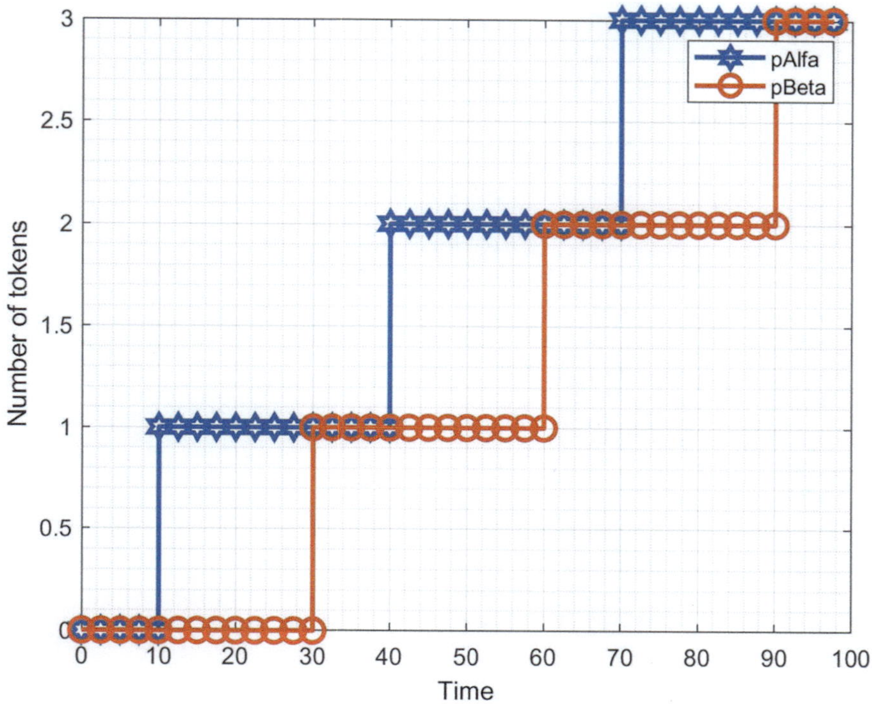

Fig. 4.2 Plot of tokens in places versus time

Figure 4.2 shows the plot of tokens in places versus time, using the function `plotp`. The function `prnss` will display similar results on the screen, which is not shown here due to brevity. As seen in the Listing 4.1, both `plotp` and `prnss` use the simulation result ('sim_results') output by the function `gpensim`.

4.1.1 Composition of the Simulation Result

The screen dump shown below shows 49 fields of the simulation output 'sim_results' structure. The first part of this simulation result is the final run-time values of **PN** (the Petri Net run-time structure; see Sect. 2.6). The second part of the simulation result is the fields (named '**LOG**', '**Firing_Trans_SET**', '**Enabled_Trans_SET**', and '**color_map**') that keeps all the information that are necessary for printing and plotting the results.

```
No_of_modules: 0
Name: 'Alternating Fire'
global_places: [1×3 struct]
No_of_places: 3
global_transitions: [1×2 struct]
No_of_transitions: 2
global_Vplaces: [1×3 struct]
incidence_matrix: [2×6 double]
Inhibited_Transitions: [0 0]
Inhibitors_exist: 0
inhibitor_matrix: []
module_membership: [2×2 double]
module_names:
delta_T: 2.5000
REAL_TIME: 0
HH_MM_SS: 0
current_time: 100
STOP_TIME: 100
X: [3 3 2]
initial_marking: [0 0 9]
VX: [0 0 1]
token_serial_numer: 15
Set_of_Firing_Costs_Fixed: [0 0]
Set_of_Firing_Costs_Variable: [0 0]
Firing_Costs_Enabled: 0
COST_CALCULATIONS: 0
Set_of_Firing_Times: [10 20]
FORCED_DELAYS: 0
priority_list: [0 0]
system_resources: []
No_of_system_resources: 0
Resource_usage_LOG: []
PRE_exist: [0 0]
POST_exist: [0 0]
MOD_PRE_exist: [1×0 double]
MOD_POST_exist: [1×0 double]
COMMON_PRE: 1
COMMON_POST: 1
Firing_Transitions: [1 0]
Enabled_Transitions: [1 1]
```

```
State: 6
attempting_trans: 2
completing_trans: 2

LOG: [53×12 double]
Firing_Trans_SET: [47×3 double]
Enabled_Trans_SET: [47×3 double]
color_map: []

completion_time: 100
overall_no_of_tokens_used: 15
```

4.2 Composition of ETS and FTS

`Enabled_Trans_SET` (**ETS**, for short) and `Firing_Trans_SET` (**FTS**, for short) are matrices that show the set of enabled and firing transitions during each sampling. In the Petri net of example 06 (Listing 4.1), the least firing time is 10 TU (firing time of **tAlfa**). Hence, the sampling frequency is 10/4 = 2.50 TU. Since the simulation was stopped at 100 TU, there will be 100/2.5 = 40 sampling points.

At each of these 40 sampling points, the simulator collects the set of enabled and firing transitions and adds this information to ETS and FTS, respectively. In addition, whenever a transition firing is completed, the simulator also collects the set of enabled and firing transitions. In example 06, there were six firings of **tAlfa** and **tBeta** (Fig. 4.2), making six more checks of enabled and firing transitions. Finally, before the simulation is stopped when the clock hits 100 TU, the simulator will do one more final checking of the enabled and firing transitions, resulting in $40 + 6 + 1 = 47$ samples. This is the reason that both ETS and FTS possess 47 rows, one row for each sampling. These two matrices possess $(1 + n_t)$ columns; the first column is the sampling time, and the second to last column represents each transition. Since we have just two transitions in example 06, both ETS and FTS possess 3 columns: the first column represents the sampling time, the second column represents **tAlfa**, and the third **tBeta**.

Let us look into the first few rows of ETS:

```
0.0000        1       1
2.5000        1       1
5.0000        1       1
7.5000        1       1
10.0000        1       1
10.0000        1       1
12.5000        1       1
15.0000        1       1
```

The screen dump shown above shows that both **tAlfa** (second column) and **tBeta** (third column) are always enabled at the sampling times 0.0000, 2.5000, 5.0000, etc., as there are plenty of enabling tokens in **pSource**. However, at the sampling time of 10.0000, in addition to the usual sampling, one more check was done as **tAlfa** just completed a firing at the time equal to 10.0000 TU.

Also, let us look into the first few rows of FTS:

```
0.0000      1       0
2.5000      1       0
5.0000      1       0
7.5000      1       0
10.0000      1       0
10.0000      0       1
12.5000      0       1
15.0000      0       1
17.5000      0       1
20.0000      0       1
22.5000      0       1
25.0000      0       1
27.5000      0       1
30.0000      0       1
30.0000      1       0
```

The screen dump shown above shows that only **tAlfa** (second column) was firing during the period 0.0000 to 10.0000, and then, only **tBeta** (third column) was firing during the period 10.0000 to 30.0000.

4.3 Composition of LOG

LOG is a matrix in which each row has the following eight elements:

1. **New state** (new marking, a vector of natural numbers): the length of the vector is the number of places (n_p).
2. **Fired transition** (a natural number): the transition index is given.
3. **State number** (a natural number): the state number increases from zero (zero is the state number of the initial state).
4. **Parent state's number** (a natural number): the current (new) state's parent state number.
5. **FTS index** (a natural number): this index points to the relevant row in `Firing_Trans_SET` to show the set of firing transitions at the start of the new state.
6. **Start time of the fired transition** (a real number).
7. **Completion time (finishing time) of the fired transition** (a real number).

8. **The virtual state** (`absorbed_tokens`, a vector of natural numbers): the length of the vector is the number of places (n_p).

Let us print out of the LOG file (`sim_results.LOG` in the main simulation file, Listing 4.1):

<u>**Row-01**</u>:

```
9, 0, 0, 0, 0, 0, 0, 0, 0, 0, 0, 0
```

Row-01 represents the initial state, and nothing has started yet:

1. The first three numbers, "[9, 0, 0]", are the initial tokens (9 tokens in **pStart**, and zeros in the other two places).
2. The fourth number, "0", represents that no transitions have been fired yet.
3. The fifth number is the current state number, which is 0.
4. The sixth number is the parent state number, which is also 0 as we are still in the initial state.
5. The seventh number of FTS-index, which is zero at the beginning.
6. The eighth and ninth numbers are the starting and finishing times of the current state "[0, 0]".
7. The tenth to twelfth numbers represent the virtual tokens, "[0, 0, 0]"; since we are still in the initial state, there are no virtual tokens.

<u>**Row-02**</u>:

```
8, 0, 0, 0, 0, 0, 0, 0, 0, 1, 0, 0
```

Row-02 represents the "take off" from the initial state, as the timer has started to tick, but we are still at time = 0 (or time is equal to $0 + \delta$, more precisely).

1. The first three numbers, "[8, 0, 0]", are the current tokens (8 tokens in **pStart**, and zeros in the other two places, as **tAlfa** has consumed a token from **pStart**).
2. The fourth number, "0", represents that no transitions have been fired yet.
3. The fifth number is the current state number, which is 0.
4. The sixth number is the parent state number, which is also 0 as we are still in the initial state.
5. The seventh number of FTS-index, which is still zero.
6. The eighth and ninth numbers are starting and finishing times of the current sampling "[0, 0]".
7. The tenth to twelfth numbers represent the virtual tokens, "[**1**, 0, 0]"; **tAlfa** has consumed a token from **pStart**; **pStart**'s place index is 1).

Row-03 to **Row-06**:

```
8, 0, 0, 0, 0, 0, 0, 2.50, 2.50, 1, 0, 0
8, 0, 0, 0, 0, 0, 0, 5.00, 5.00, 1, 0, 0
8, 0, 0, 0, 0, 0, 0, 7.50, 7.50, 1, 0, 0
8, 0, 0, 0, 0, 0, 0, 10.0, 10.0, 1, 0, 0
```

Row-03 to **Row-06** represent the sampling at every 2.5 time units, as the sampling rate is one-fourth of the least firing time Davidrajuh [1].

Row-07:

```
8, 1, 0, 1, 1, 0, 5, 0, 10.0, 0, 0, 0
```

Row-07, a transition has fired at last, moving the system to a new state from the initial state.

1. The first three numbers represent the current state, "[8, 1, 0]"; 8 tokens in **pStart**, and one token in **pAlfa**.
2. Fired transition: the fourth number, "1", represents that the fired transition is **tAlfa** (**tAlfa**'s transition index is 1).
3. The fifth number is the **current state number**, which is 1 (one more from the initial state).
4. The sixth number is the **parent state number**, which is 0 as the initial state's number is 0.
5. The seventh number, the FTS-index, which is 5, indicates that the fifth row of `Firing_Trans_SET` represents the set of firing transitions at this state.
6. The eighth and ninth numbers are **starting** and **finishing times** of the current state, which is "[0, 10]".
7. The tenth to twelfth numbers represent the virtual tokens, "[0, 0, 0]"; These are all zeros as none of the transitions has started to fire yet.

4.4 Composition of TOKEN matrix

Sometimes, the **LOG** file (output by `gpensim`) in the previous section is too detailed. We may want a simpler file that shows the time and the state (marking), just as Fig. 4.2 shows. Luckily, the function `plotp` not only displays Fig. 4.2 but also returns the **TOKEN** matrix with only time versus (partial) state info. Note that to get the full state info (tokens in all the places), we must enter the complete set of place names as the input parameter to function `plotp`.

In the main simulation file (Listing 4.1), the last statement is to display the `TOKEN` matrix. Let us look into the displayed `TOKEN` matrix.

Row-01 of TOKEN matrix:

```
0 2 3
```

The first element of this row is always zero (or not used); the following elements are the place indices (place indices of **pAlfa** and **pBeta** are 2 and 3, respectively).

Row-02 of TOKEN matrix:

```
0 0 0
```

After the first row, the successive rows show the time and markings. For example, row-02 shows that when time equals 0, the state was [0, 0], meaning no tokens in either **pAlfa** or **pBeta**.

Row-03 to Row-06 of TOKEN matrix:

```
2.50 0 0
5.00 0 0
7.50 0 0
10.00 0 0
```

Row-03 to row-06 show that when the timer was incremented by 2.50 time units at each step (sampling rate), nothing changed.

Row-07 of TOKEN matrix:

```
10.00 1 0
```

Row-07 represents the state change when the time was equal to 10 TU; at this time, **tAlfa** fired, depositing one token into **pAlfa**.

4.5 COTREE Matrix

GPenSIM function '`cotree`' generates a Petri net's reachability (and coverability) tree. The reachability tree will be displayed as:

1. A graphical plot (for example, the plot in Fig. 4.4) and
2. An ASCII (text) printout on screen.

In addition to displaying the reachability tree, the function `cotree` will also return a matrix, known as the **COTREE matrix**, that will be equivalent to the displayed plot. Hence, a user can manipulate this COTREE matrix for further analysis.

We will go through a simple example (Example 07) to understand the composition of the COTREE matrix.

4.5.1 Example 07: COTREE Matrix

Figure 4.3 shows a Petri net for which we will generate the reachability tree. Figure 4.4 shows the reachability tree.

Listing 4.4 shows the main simulation file. We don't need any processor files for this example. Note that in the main simulation file, we generate the reachability tree and get a copy of the COTREE matrix from the function `cotree`. As said before, in terms of contents, the COTREE matrix is equivalent to Fig. 4.4 in the information portrayed.

Listing 4.4 Main Simulation File (Example 07)

```
clear all;
spng = pnstruct('ex_07_pdf');
dyn.m0 = {'p1',2, 'p4',1};
pni = initialdynamics(spng, dyn);

% plot reachability tree graphically,
% and as text on screen
% and get a copy of COTREE matrix
COTREE = cotree(pni, 1, 1);

disp('print COTREE matrix on screen:')
disp(COTREE);
```

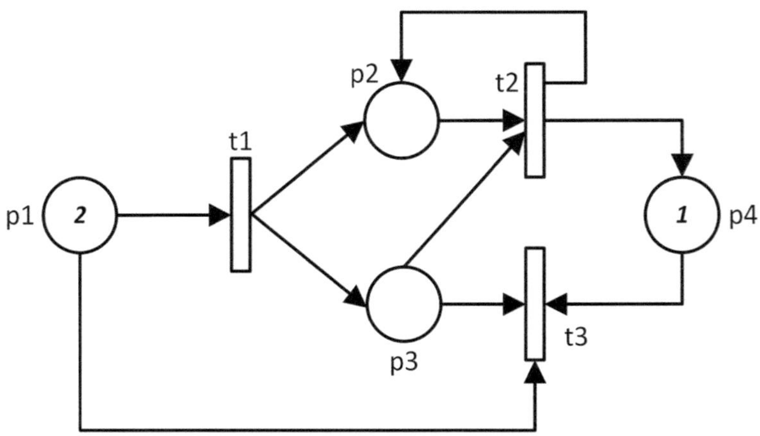

Fig. 4.3 Petri net for understanding COTREE matrix

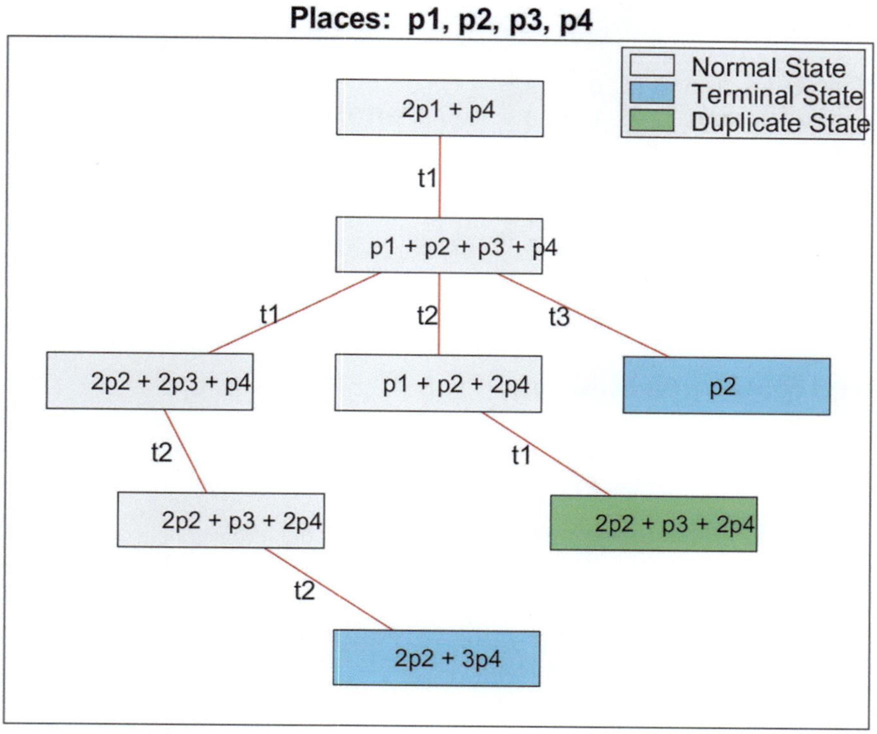

Fig. 4.4 Reachability tree of Petri net in Fig. 4.3

COTREE matrix consists of several rows equal to the number of states. **In each row**:

1. The first element (a vector of natural numbers) is the state (marking), and the length will equal the number of places.
2. The second element (a natural number) is the index of the fired transition.
3. The third element (a natural number) is the state number of the parent state.
4. Finally, the fourth element (a natural number) is an indicator of the state:

   - 82 is the ASCII value of the character "R," meaning this is a Root (initial) state.
   - 68 is the ASCII value of the character "D," meaning this is a Duplicate state.
   - 84 is the ASCII value of the character "T," meaning this is a Terminal (dead) state.

Let us inspect the COTREE matrix:

```
Row-1: 2 0 0 1 0 0 82
Row-2: 1 1 1 1 1 1 0
Row-3: 0 2 2 1 1 2 0
Row-4: 1 1 0 2 2 2 0
Row-5: 0 1 0 0 3 2 84
Row-6: 0 2 1 2 2 3 0
Row-7: 0 2 1 2 1 4 68
Row-8: 0 2 0 3 2 6 84
```

Row-1 represents the initial state:

```
Row-1: 2 0 0 1 0 0 82
```

1. The first element (first four integers), [2 0 0 1], is the initial state, two tokens in **p1** and one in **p4**.
2. The second element (fifth integer), 0, is the fired transition (0 represents none).
3. The third element (sixth integer), 0, is the parent state number (for the initial state, the parent state is none).
4. Finally, the fourth element (seventh integer), 82, stands for "R", meaning this is the "Root" state.

Row-2 represents the second state due to the firing of t1:

```
Row-2: 1 1 1 1 1 1 0
```

1. The first element (first four integers), [1 1 1 1], is the second state, one token in each place, **p1** to **p4**.
2. The second element (fifth integer), 1, is the fired transition (1 is the index of **t1**).
3. The third element (sixth integer), 1, is the parent state number, which is the initial state.
4. Finally, the fourth element (seventh integer), 0, stands for normal state (*aka* interior state, according to Peterson [3]).

Let us skip states 3 and 4 and jump to state 5. **Row-5 represents the fifth state due to the firing of t3**:

```
Row-5: 0 1 0 0 3 2 84
```

1. The first element (first four integers), [0 1 0 0], is the fifth state, one token in **p2**.
2. The second element (fifth integer), 3, is the fired transition (3 is the index of **t3**).
3. The third element (sixth integer), 2, is the parent state number.
4. Finally, the fourth element (seventh integer), 84, stands for "Terminal" state.

Finally, let us inspect a duplicate state. **Row-7 represents the seventh state due to the firing of t1**:

```
Row-7: 0 2 1 2 1 4 68
```

1. The first element (first four integers), [0 2 1 2], is the seventh state, with two tokens in **p2**, one token in **p3**, and two more in **p4**.
2. The second element (fifth integer), 1, is the fired transition (1 is the index of **t1**).
3. The third element (sixth integer), 4, is the parent state number.
4. Finally, the fourth element (seventh integer), 68, stands for "Duplicate" state.

4.6 COTREE_TC Matrix

The reachability (coverability) tree generated by the function `cotree` and discussed in the previous section (Sect. 4.5) possesses four shortcomings:

1. It does not include time, even if the transitions have firing times.
2. It does not include costs, even if the transitions are assigned with firing costs.
3. It does not consider the preprocessors (the enabling conditions).
4. It does not allow parallel firings of transitions; only one transition is allowed to fire at a time.

The function `cotreeTC` (short for "coverability tree with cost and timed") fixes the first two shortcomings of the function `cotree`:

1. The function `cotreeTC` considers the firing times of transitions (if transitions are timed)
2. The function `cotreeTC` considers the firing costs of transitions (if transitions are assigned with firing costs).

However, as a function to generate the reachability tree, the function `cotreeTC` still has the other two issues: It does not consider preprocessors and allows only one transition to fire at a time.

The function `cotreeTC` returns a matrix known as the `COTREE_TC`. In this matrix (`COTREE_TC`), each row corresponds to a state. In a row, the first part (vector of n_p elements) is the marking, followed by the fired transition (transition index), parent state (root state number stats with 0), the time of the state (real number), and the cost of the state (real number).

Note: The function '`cotreeTC`' does not produce a graphical output; it only prints ASCII text info on the screen. Also, this function takes an additional (optional) input as the number of states to be printed. For example, if the number of states is too large, we can ask the function to output only a limited number of states that are generated from the initial state.

4.6.1 Example 07-II: COTREE_TC Matrix

Let us continue with the previous example (Example 07, Sect. 4.5.1). However, this time, we shall add time and cost to the transitions, as shown in Listing 4.5.

Listing 4.5 Main Simulation File (Example 07-II)

```
clear all; clc; close all;

spng = pnstruct('ex_07_II_pdf');
dyn.m0 = {'p1',2, 'p4',1};
dyn.ft = {'t1',1, 't2',2, 't3',3};
dyn.fc_fixed = {'t1',100, 't2',200, 't3',300};
dyn.fc_variable = {'t1',10, 't2',20, 't3',30};
pni = initialdynamics(spng, dyn);

% generate Only three states, in addition to the root
COTREE_TC = retree(pni, 3);
disp('COTREE_TC matrix:'); disp(COTREE_TC);
```

We can see from the following printout that the state space now lists the costs of the state and the time.

```
======= Extended Reachability Tree
=======
State no.: 1 ROOT node
2p1 + p4

State no.: 2 Firing event: t1
Time of the state: 1
Cost of the state: 110
State: p1 + p2 + p3 + p4
Node type: ' ' Parent state: 1

State no.: 3 Firing event: t1
Time of the state: 2
Cost of the state: 220
State: 2p2 + 2p3 + p4
Node type: ' ' Parent state: 2

State no.: 4 Firing event: t2
Time of the state: 3
Cost of the state: 350
State: p1 + p2 + 2p4
Node type: ' ' Parent state: 2

State no.: 5 Firing event: t3
Time of the state: 4
Cost of the state: 500
State: p2
Node type: 'T' Parent state: 2
```

The printout of COTREE_TC is given below. If we look at the third row (the third state):

```
0 2 2 1 1 2 0 2 220
```

The first element (first four integers) represents the state, {2**p2** + 2**p3** + **p4**}. The second element (fifth integer) is the fired transition (**t1**, which has an index of 1). The third element (sixth integer) is the parent state, which is 2. The fourth element (seventh integer), 0, indicates that this is a normal state.

The fifth and sixth elements are new to the COTREE_TC matrix, as they lack in the COTREE matrix. The fifth element (eighth integer) indicates that the state's time is 2, as it is reached by two firings of **t1**, and a firing of **t1** takes one TU. The sixth and final element (last integer) indicates that the cost of reaching this state is 220 CU.

```
COTREE_TC matrix:
2 0 0 1 0 0 82 0 0
1 1 1 1 1 1 0 1 110
0 2 2 1 1 2 0 2 220
1 1 0 2 2 2 0 3 350
0 1 0 0 3 2 84 4 500
0 2 1 2 2 3 0 4 460
0 2 1 2 1 4 68 4 460
0 2 0 3 2 6 84 6 700
```

4.7 DURATION and OCCUPANCY Matrices

In GPenSIM, transitions represent active elements such as machines, events, CPU, humans, etc. Places are passive, and they just keep the tokens. Hence, we may want to extract how active some transitions were during a simulation. Since the simulation output from gpensim is heavy (loaded with a lot of details), we may want a simple structure that clearly states the transitions' activities. DURATION and OCCUPANCY matrices exactly do that.

Function 'extractt' extracts transitions and their activation times from the simulation result. The output of the function extractt is the DURATION matrix. The function 'occupancy' returns a much simpler matrix known as the OCCUPANCY matrix (function occupancy returns DURATION matrix too in addition to the OCCUPANCY matrix).

4.7.1 Composition of DURATION Matrix

The number of rows in DURATION matrix is equal to the total number of times the transitions have fired, and each row represents a firing. In each row:

1. The first element (a natural number) is the index of the transition that has fired.
2. The second element (a positive real number) is the start time of the firing.
3. The third element (a positive real number) is the finishing time (completion time) of the firing.

4.7.2 Composition of OCCUPANCY Matrix

The function `occupancy` calls the function `extractt` to obtain the DURATION matrix from which the OCCUPANCY matrix is computed.

In the OCCUPANCY matrix, each column is about a transition (e.g., column 1 is for **t1**, column 2 is for **t2**, and so on). The OCCUPANCY matrix possesses two rows:

1. The first row: the total activation times of each transition.
2. The second row: the total activation times of each transition in the percentage of the total time.

4.7.3 Example 08: Total Firing Times

Let us take the same Petri net that we used in Example 06 in Sect. 4.1. The Petri net is shown in Fig. 4.1. As in Example 06, we will allow transitions **tAlfa** and **tBeta** to fire alternatively (not simultaneously); alternative firing is achieved by manipulating a semaphore in the common processor files as discussed in Sect. 4.1.

In the main simulation file (Listing 4.6), we will call only the function `occupancy` as this function will return both DURATION and OCCUPANCY matrices.

Listing 4.6 Main Simulation File (Example 08)

```
clear all;
global global_info
global_info.STOP_AT = 150; % stop simulations after 100 TU.
global_info.semaphore = 'tAlfa';  % allow "tAlfa" to fire first

spng = pnstruct('ex_08_pdf');
dyn.m0 = {'pStart',5};
dyn.ft = {'tAlfa',10, 'tBeta',20};
pni = initialdynamics(spng, dyn);
Sim_Results = gpensim(pni);
```

```
[OCCUPANCY, DURATION] = ...
        occupancy(Sim_Results, {'tAlfa','tBeta'});
disp('**** DURATION matrix ****');
disp(DURATION);
disp('**** OCCUPANCY matrix ****');
disp(OCCUPANCY);
```

The function `occupancy` outputs the following on screen:

```
 Occupancy analysis ....
Simulation Completion Time: 150
occupancy tAlfa:
total time: 30
Percentage time: 20%
occupancy tBeta:
total time: 40
Percentage time: 26.6667%
```

The DURATION matrix:

```
1 0 10
1 30 40
1 60 70
2 10 30
2 40 60
```

The first three rows are for transition **tAlfa** (as it has the index "1"). **tAlfa** has fired three times during the time intervals (0, 10), (30, 40), and (60, 70). Thus, **tAlfa** was active for a total of 30 TU.

The final two rows are for **tBeta**, as it has the index "2". **tBeta** has fired two times during the time intervals (10, 30) and (40, 60). Thus, **tBeta** was active for a total of 40 TU.

The OCCUPANCY matrix:

```
30.0000 40.0000
20.0000 26.6667
```

From the DURATION matrix, we know that **tAlfa** and **tBeta** have fired for a total of 30 and 40 TU, respectively. Since the simulation time is 150 TU (set in the main simulation file), **tAlfa** has taken 30/150 = 20% of the total simulation time. Whereas **tBeta** has taken 40/150 = 26.67% of the total simulation time. These findings are confirmed in the OCCUPANCY matrix. In the OCCUPANCY matrix, the first column is for **tAlfa** (as **tAlfa** has index 1), and the second column is for **tBeta**.

4.8 Transition Indices and Place Indices

A note on transition and place indices:
LOG, TOKEN, COTREE, DURATION, OCCUPANCY, etc., are all matrices. Thus, we can only have numerals (integers, natural numbers, and real numbers) as elements of these matrices. Hence, places and transitions are represented by their indices.

When GPenSIM function pnstruct creates the spng—the static Petri net graph structure—from the PDF files, GPenSIM usually allocates indices based on alphabetical order. For example, if a Petri net has three places **p1**, **p2**, and **p3**, **p1** will be given place index 1, **p2** place index 2, and so on. If there are three transitions **tAlfa**, **tBeta**, and **tGamma**, then **tAlfa** will get transition index 1, **tBeta** will get 2, and so on.

> **CAUTION:**
> **However, this indexing based on alphabetical order is NOT GUARANTEED.**
> **We need to get the index of a transition using the function 'is_trans' and the index of a place using the function 'is_place'.**

On the other hand, if we want the name of a transition (res. place) identified only by the transition index (res. place index), then we use the function 'tname' (res. 'pname'). Note that functions is_trans, is_place, tname, and pname are GPenSIM's built-in function Davidrajuh [2].

4.9 Color Map

When tokens carry colors (in Colored Petri nets), simulation output by function 'gpensim' also contains a field known as 'color_map.' This field, color_map, carries all the information needed for the functions prncolormap and prnfinalcolors to printout complete information about how the token colors changed during the simulation. We will study about color_map through Example 09.

4.9.1 Example 09: Color Map

This example is the same as Example 03. However, its details are presented here for convenience.

Figure 4.5 shows the Petri net for producing color_map. **tGen** (generator) produces tokens for the net.

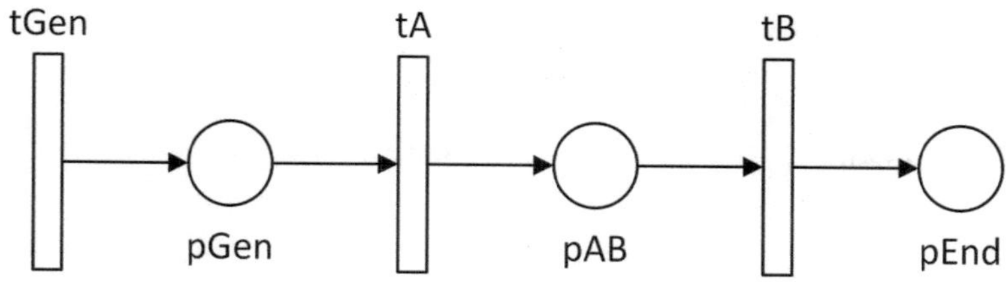

Fig. 4.5 Petri net for producing '`color_map`'

Listing 4.7 Main Simulation File (Example 09)

```
clear all; clc; close all;

global global_info global_info.STOP_AT = 10;

spng = pnstruct('ex_09_pdf');

dyn.ft = {'tGen',1, 'tA',2, 'tB',5}; pni = initialdynamics(spng,
dyn);

sim = gpensim(pni); plotp(sim, {'pGen', 'pAB', 'pEnd'});

% display structure of color_map
sim.color_map

% display details of each struct
for i = 1:length(sim.color_map)
    disp(int2str(i)), sim.color_map(i)
end
```

In COMMON_PRE (Listing 4.8), **tA** and **tB** add their own name as color (namely, 'tA' and 'tB') to the deposited tokens.

Listing 4.8 COMMON_PRE (Example 09)

```
function [fire, transition] = COMMON_PRE(transition)
switch transition.name
    case 'tGen'
        % do nothing
    case {'tA', 'tB'}
        transition.new_color = transition.name;
end
% let the enabled transition fire
fire = 1;
```

In this Petri net, **tGen** produces colorless tokens every 1 TU. **tA** consumes a colorless token from **pGen** and adds its name 'tA' to the deposited token into **pAB**, taking 2 TU. Finally, **tB** consumes a token from **pAB** (which possesses color 'tA') and adds its name 'tB' to the deposited token into **pEnd**, taking 5 TU.

After the simulations, we can see that `color_map` is a part of the simulation output 'sim_results.'

4.9.1.1 How the `color_map` Is Created?

When a transition completes firing, the compiler will deposit output tokens into the transition's output places. After that, the compiler will scan each place in the Petri net. If a token possesses some colors, then the time, this token's tokID, and colors, will be added as a new structure to `color_map`. If the token is colorless, then it will be ignored. Hence, 'sim_results.`color_map`' is an array of structures in which each structure represents tokens' colors at different places.

In Example 09, 'sim_results.`color_map`' is an array of 16 structures. Each structure has the following fields:

- time: the time a place was checked.
- place: the place identified its index.
- color: summation of all the colors of all the tokens in that place.
- tokID: token's identification number.

Figure 4.6 shows the `plotp` output, showing the number of tokens in all three places. Table 4.1 summarizes the contents of 16 structures of `color_map`.

- At time = 3 TU (Structure-01): **tA** fires for the first time and deposits a token with color 'tA' in **pAB**.

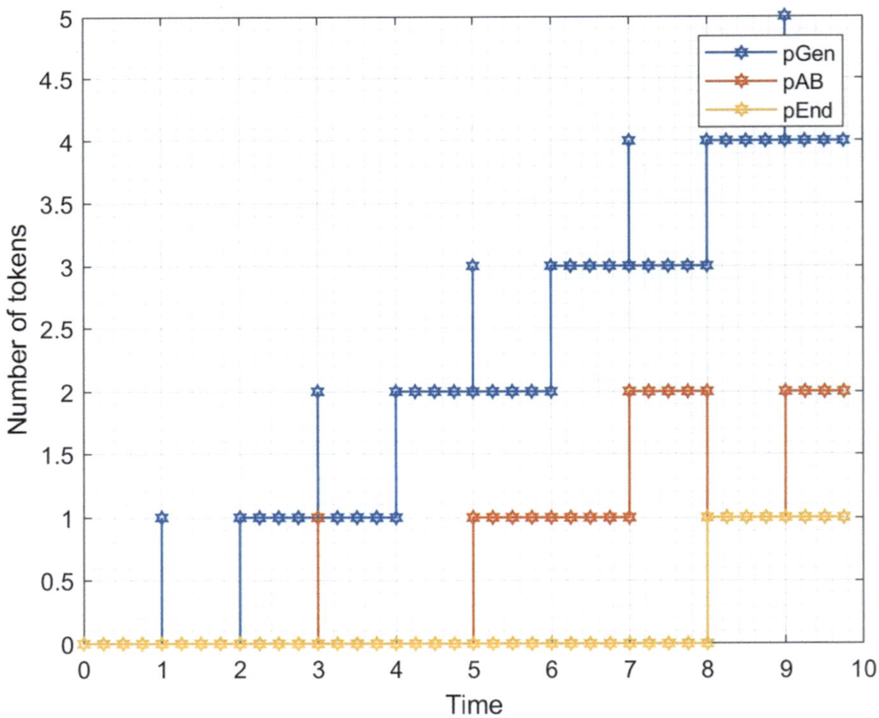

Fig. 4.6 `Plotp` showing the number of tokens in places

Table 4.1 Sample 'color_map' from Example 09

Structure no.	Time	Place	Token colors
1	3	**pAB**	{'tA'}
2	5	**pAB**	{'tA'}
3	6	**pAB**	{'tA'}
4	7	**pAB**	{'tA'}
5	7	**pAB**	{'tA'}
6	7	**pAB**	{'tA'}
7	8	**pAB**	{'tA'}
8	8	**pAB**	{'tA'}
9	8	**pAB**	{'tA'}
10	8	**pAB**	{'tA'}
11	8	**pEnd**	{'tA', 'tB'}
12	9	**pAB**	{'tA'}
13	9	**pEnd**	{'tA', 'tB'}
14	9	**pAB**	{'tA'}
15	9	**pAB**	{'tA'}
16	9	**pEnd**	{'tA', 'tB'}

- At time = 4 TU, **tGen** fires; the compiler finds no tokens with color (there are two colorless tokens in **pGen**); thus, no new structure is made.
- At time = 5 TU (Structure-02): **tGen** and **tA** fire; the compiler finds a token with color 'tA' in **pAB**.
- At time = 6 TU (Structure-03): **tGen** fires; the compiler finds a token with color 'tA' in **pAB**.
- At time = 7 TU (Structures 04–06): **tGen** and **tA** fire; when **tGen** fires, the compiler finds a token (tokID: 7) with color 'tA' in **pAB**. when **tA** fires, the compiler finds two tokens (tokID: 7 and 10) with color 'tA' in **pAB**. Thus, there are three separate structures, though two of them are identical (with tokID 7).
- At time = 8 TU (Structures 07–11): **tGen**, **tA**, and **tB** fire.
  - when **tGen** fires, the compiler finds one token (tokID: 7) with color 'tA' in **pAB**.
  - when **tA** fires, the compiler finds the two tokens (tokIDs 7 and 10) with color 'tA' in **pAB**.
  - Finally, when **tB** fires for the first time and deposits a token (tokID: 12) with colors {'tA', 'tB'} into **pEnd**; when the compiler scans the places, **tB** has already consumed a token from **pA** (tokID:7); thus, the compiler finds one token (tokID: 10) in **pAB** with color 'tA' and one more (tokID: 12) in **pEnd** with colors {'tA', 'tB'}.

Thus, at time = 8 TU, there are five structures for the tokens with tokIDs 7, 10, 7, 10, and 12. Tokens with tokIDs 7 and 10 possess only one color, namely 'tA'; Token with tokID 12 in **pEnd** possesses two colors, namely {'tA', 'tB'}.

4.10 Resource_usage_LOG

When resources are used in a Petri net, then function `gpensim` outputs `Resource_usage_LOG` as a field of the simulation results. `Resource_usage_LOG` is a matrix of natural and real numbers.

The number of rows of `Resource_usage_LOG` is equal to the total number of resource instances used. In other words, each row of `Resource_usage_LOG` represents a resource's instant usage. `Resource_usage_LOG` has five columns. The columns are:

- Column-1: the index of resource used.
- Column-2: the index of transition that used the resource.
- Column-3: Start time of resource usage.
- Column-4: End time of resource usage.
- Column-5: the index of the resource instance used.

Let us study the composition of `Resource_usage_LOG` through Example 10.

4.10.1 Example 10: Resource_usage_LOG

Figure 4.7 shows the Petri net for Example 10. The Petri net models manufacturing activities to make a product:

- The production processes involve two steps: Step 1 and Step 2.
- Step 1 uses a CNC machine and a Robot. Step 1 takes 2 TU.
- When Step 1 is completed, Step 2 uses a Cutter and a Robot. Step 2 takes 5 TU.
- In a day, the facility is expected to make three products.

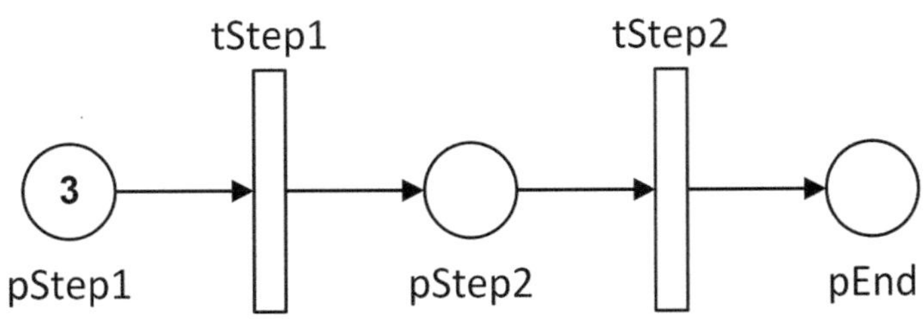

Fig. 4.7 Petri net modeling a two-step manufacturing process

Listings 4.9, 4.10, and 4.11 show the main simulation file, COMMON_PRE, and COMMON_POST, respectively.

Listing 4.9 Main Simulation File (Example 10)

```
clear all;
global global_info
global_info.STOP_AT = 30;

spng = pnstruct('ex_10_pdf');

dp.m0 = {'pStep1', 3};
dp.ft = {'tStep1',2, 'tStep2',5};
dp.re = {'CNC M/C',1,inf, 'Robot',2,inf, 'Cutter',1,inf};
pni = initialdynamics(spng, dp);

sim_results = gpensim(pni);
prnschedule(sim_results);
sim_results.Resource_usage_LOG
```

Listing 4.10 COMMON_PRE (Example 10)

```
function [fire, trans] = COMMON_PRE(trans)
switch trans.name
    case 'tStep1'
        granted = requestSR({'CNC M/C',1,'Robot',1});

    case 'tStep2'
        granted = requestSR({'Cutter',1, 'Robot',1});
end
fire = granted;
```

Listing 4.11 COMMON_POST (Example 10)

```
function [] = COMMON_POST(transition)
release();
```

At the end of the simulation, the screen output of `prnschedule` is shown below (only a part is shown).

```
RESOURCE USAGE:

RESOURCE INSTANCES OF ***** CNC M/C
*****
tStep1 [0 : 2]
tStep1 [2 : 4]
tStep1 [4 : 6]
Resource Instance: CNC M/C:: Used 3
times. Utilization time: 6

RESOURCE INSTANCES OF ***** Robot
*****
(Robot-1): tStep1 [0 : 2]
(Robot-1): tStep1 [2 : 4]
(Robot-1): tStep1 [4 : 6]
(Robot-2): tStep2 [2 : 7]
(Robot-1): tStep2 [7 : 12]
(Robot-1): tStep2 [12 : 17]
Resource Instance: (Robot-1):: Used 5
times. Utilization time: 16
Resource Instance: (Robot-2):: Used 1
times. Utilization time: 5

RESOURCE INSTANCES OF ***** Cutter
*****
tStep2 [2 : 7]
tStep2 [7 : 12]
tStep2 [12 : 17]
Resource Instance: Cutter:: Used 3
times.Utilization time: 15
```

Also, the screen dump of sim_results.`Resource_usage_LOG` is shown below:

```
1 1 0 2 1
2 1 0 2 1
1 1 2 4 1
2 1 2 4 1
1 1 4 6 1
2 1 4 6 1
2 2 2 7 2
3 2 2 7 1
2 2 7 12 1
3 2 7 12 1
2 2 12 17 1
3 2 12 17 1
```

Let us look into the first three rows of sim_results.`Resource_usage_LOG`, one row at a time.

Row-1:

```
1 1 0 2 1
```

CNC M/C (resource index 1) was used by **tStep1** (transition index 1) from 0 to 2 TU, and it was the first instance of CNC M/C (this resource has only one instance, anyway).

Row-2:

```
2 1 0 2 1
```

Robot (resource index 2) was used by **tStep1** (transition index 1), from 0 to 2 TU, and it was the first instance of Robot (Robot has two instances).

Row-3:

```
1 1 2 4 1
```

CNC M/C (resource index 1) was used by **tStep1** (transition index 1) from 2 to 4 TU, and it was the first instance of Robot (Robot has two instances).

The information displayed by `prnschedule` is identical to the information in the matrix sim_results.`Resource_usage_LOG`.

However, `Resource_usage_LOG` is chronological (follows the timer), whereas `prnschedule` categorizes usage based on resources.

References

1. Davidrajuh R (2018) Modeling discrete-event systems with GPenSIM. Springer International Publishing, Cham
2. Davidrajuh R (2024) GPenSIM reference manual. University of Stavanger
3. Peterson JL (1981) Petri net theory and the modeling of systems. Prentice Hall PTR

Chapter 5
Retention of Tokens in Input Places

In GPenSIM, by default, whenever a transition becomes enabled and the conditions in the pre-processor files are satisfied, the transition is allowed to consume the input tokens and start firing immediately. However, sometimes, we may want the input tokens in the input places visible for some time before the enabled transition consumes these tokens. In other words, we may want the tokens to be held (retained) in the input places for a while. This chapter introduces two techniques: (1) "Time Windows," a function that can be used in the pre-processor. (2) "Delayed Enabled Transitions" is a new functionality that was introduced in version 11.

5.1 Time and Petri Nets

Popova-Zeugmann [4] classifies the association of time and Petri Nets under three classes of time-dependent Petri nets:

1. Time Petri Nets.
2. Timed Petri Nets.
3. Petri Nets with Time Windows.

Time Petri nets are classic Petri nets where each transition $\mathbf{t_j}$ is associated with a time interval [*eft*, *lft*]. When $\mathbf{t_j}$ becomes enabled, it cannot fire before *eft* (earliest firing time), and it has to fire no later than *lft* (latest firing time) time units after being enabled; note that after enabled, when a transition waits for firing, it can become disabled by the firing of another transition. Here, *eft* and *lft* are relative to the point in time when $\mathbf{t_j}$ was last enabled. As in the case of classical (P/T) Petri nets, the firing of a transition itself does not take up any time; in other words, unlike transitions in GPenSIM, $\mathbf{t_j}$ is primitive, and its firing time is zero. The interval bounds (*eft* and *lft*) are non-negative rational numbers or ∞.

R. Davidrajuh, *Petri Nets for Modeling Complex Discrete-Event Systems*, Asset Analytics,
https://doi.org/10.1007/978-981-96-6396-5_5

In **Timed Petri nets**, a firing time (duration) is incorporated with each transition; all transitions in Petri net implemented with GPenSIM are either timed (Timed Petri net) or zero-timed (Untimed Petri net). In a Timed Petri net, GPenSIM does not allow assigning zero time duration to transitions.

Petri Nets with Time Windows allows delays between events by assigning retention times for tokens in the places. It is noteworthy that, unlike the previous two classes in which time is attached to transitions, in Petri nets with Time Windows, time is attached to tokens in places.

5.2 Time and GPenSIM

GPenSIM realizes Timed Petri nets, as non-zero firing times (duration) are attached to transitions. Using GPenSIM, holding (retention of) tokens in places can be done in two different approaches:

1. "**Time Windows**:" The function **`timeWindow`** can be used in the pre-processor. Note that this function is used **inside a pre-processor** to check whether an input token has waited enough in the input place. Section 5.4 presents the details of the approach "Time Windows" and the details of the function `timeWindow`.
2. "**Delayed Enabled Transitions**" is a new functionality that was introduced in version 11. **In the main simulation file**, when we declare initial dynamics like firing times of transitions, we can also declare delay times for enabled transitions. By forcing the enabled transitions to wait, we indirectly force the input tokens to wait in the input places. Section 5.3 presents the details of "Delayed Enabled Transitions."

Note that these two approaches are different in many ways:

1. Time Windows is applied inside a pre-processor; thus, checking whether an input token has waited long enough is one of the enabling conditions, as there can be several other enabling conditions coded in the pre-processor. Also, this approach of using a function (to check whether an input token has waited long enough) is a simple and robust approach.
2. Delayed Enabled Transitions are declared in the main simulation file. Delayed Enabled Transitions force an enabled transition to wait, and its pre-processor will not be executed. Only after the retention time is passed, and if the transition is still enabled, its pre-processor will be executed. Note that Delayed Enabled Transitions is a new functionality that was introduced in version 11. This functionality was tested using some simple examples, and three of these examples are given in this chapter. Though this approach is also simple, whether it is robust is yet to be verified.

5.3 Delayed Enabled Transitions

GPenSIM realizes Timed Petri nets in which non-zero firing times (duration) are attached to transitions. From version 11, GPenSIM supports the delayed enabled transitions—in which only *eft* (earliest firing time) is defined. When a transition is enabled, it can be delayed by a duration *eft*. Only after the time has passed and the transition is still enabled (it can happen that this transition is disabled due to other firing transitions) will the pre-processor files be checked for additional conditions to satisfy.

However, *lft*, which is defined in Time Petri nets (Sect. 5.1), is not supported in GPenSIM, and it is assumed that *lft* (latest firing time) = *eft*, meaning the enabled transition should fire immediately after the forced delay.

5.3.1 Declaring Delayed Enabled Transitions

In GPenSIM, all transitions are not delayed by default. Hence, we must declare the delayed enabled transitions in the main simulation file.

Suppose a Petri net consists of five transitions, **tA** to **tE**. Let us also assume that **tA** and **tE** are not delayed (start firing when enabled and the pre-processor files are checked), but **tB**, **tC**, and **tD** are delayed. The following code snippet shows how to declare delayed enabled transitions in the main simulation file.

```
% in the Main Simulation File
spng = pnstruct('ex_delayed_pdf');  % PDf file
dyn.m0 = {'pStart', 10};     % initial tokens
dyn.ft = {'tA', 10, 'tB', '5', 'allothers',1};  % firing times

% delayed enabled transitions
dyn.delayed = {'tB', 5.3,  'tC', 'unifrnd(8,10)', 'tD', ...
    'myDelayFunction(1,10)'};

pni = initialdynamics(spng, dyn);
sim_results = gpensim(pni);
```

In the code snipped shown above, **tB** is delayed by a deterministic 5.3 TU, meaning after becoming enabled, **tB** will be forced to wait for 5.3 more TU before its enability is checked again. **tC**'s delay is declared as a random number with uniform distribution and **tD** with a user-defined delay function.

Declaring delays:

- **A constant (deterministic) time**: For example, 12.7 TU.
- **A random number**: A random number which is declared in MATLAB format, e.g., Gaussian random function (normrnd(1,0.1)), Binomial random function (binornd(10,0.9)), Poisson random function, Uniform random function (unifrnd(8,10)).

- **A simple user-defined delay**: Listing 5.1 shows a simple user-defined delay function that will return a delay time every time it is invoked.

Listing 5.1 Sample user-defined delay function

```
function [delayVal] = myDelayFunction(addVal, divVal)
6
nt = ntrans(); % number of transitions
ct = current_time(); % current time

delayVal = (ct + nt + addVal)/divVal;
```

Note: the delay value—whether it is a constant, a random number, or returned by a user-defined function—must be zero or a positive number. **If the delay value is negative, the compiler will ignore it and take it as zero**.

'allothers':
Let us consider another example. This time, too, there are five transitions, **t1** to **t5**. **t1** is delayed by a large delay, a random duration of 10–15 TU (unifrnd(10,15)), **t5** by a shorter delay, (unifrnd(5,7)), whereas the rest of the transitions (**'allothers'**) are delayed by a small duration of 1–3 TU (unifrnd(1,3)). The code snippet given below shows how we can program these delays. Note that 'allothers' is a reserved word in GPenSIM that is used for declaring firing times and for delay times of delayed enabled transitions.

```
% in the Main Simulation File
dyn.m0 = {'pStart', 10};     % initial tokens

% firing times
dyn.ft = {'t1', 10, 't2', '5', 'allothers',1};

% delayed enabled transitions
dyn.delayed = {'t1','unifrnd(10,15)', 't5','unifrnd(5,7)', ...
    'allothers','unifrnd(1,3)'};

pni = initialdynamics(spng, dyn);
```

5.3.2 *OPTION 'DELTA_TIME'*

GPenSIM automatically sets the sampling rate to one-fourth of the shortest firing time Davidrajuh [1]. For example, if there are three transitions **tA**, **tB**, and **tC**, with firing times 5, 10, and 15 TU, then the sampling rate will be set to 5/4 = 1.25 TU. If we want a better sampling rate, the default sampling rate can be overridden by setting the OPTION DELTA_TIME Davidrajuh [1].

Suppose we want to use delayed enabled transitions, **we must manually set the sampling rate if the minimum delay is less than the minimum firing time**. For example, the firing times of transitions **tA**, **tB**, and **tC** are 5 TU, and they are delayed by unifrnd(2,5), unifrnd(3,5), and 8, respectively. In this case, the minimum delay is 2, which is less than the minimum firing time (which is 5). Hence, we must assign 2/4 = 0.50 to the sampling rate using the OPTION `DELTA_TIME` in the main simulation file.

5.3.3 Example 11: Delayed Enabled Transitions I

Figure 5.1 shows a simple Petri net with three transitions, **tA**, **tB**, and **tC**, all of which are delayed by constant (deterministic) time. Listing 5.2 shows the main simulation file, with the declaration of the delays.

Listing 5.2 Main Simulation File (Example 11)

```
clear all; clc; close all;
global global_info
% minimum delay is 2, which is less than the minimum
% firing time (10). Hence, set DELTA_TIME to 0.5
global_info.DELTA_TIME = 0.5;
global_info.STOP_AT = 50;

spng = pnstruct('ex_10_pdf');
dyn.m0 = {'p0', 20};
dyn.ft = {'allothers',10};

%%%%%%%% simulation - 1: without delay
```

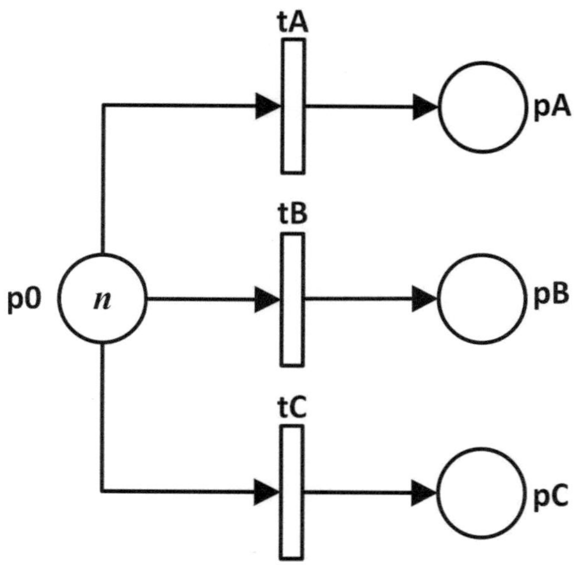

Fig. 5.1 Petri net for Example 11

```
pni1 = initialdynamics(spng, dyn);
sim1 = gpensim(pni1);

%%%%%%%% simulation - 2: with delay
dyn.delayed = {'tA',2, 'tB',5, 'tC', 10};
pni2 = initialdynamics(spng, dyn);
sim2 = gpensim(pni2);

subplot(2,1,1), plotp(sim1, {'pA'});
title('"tA" without delay');
subplot(2,1,2), plotp(sim2, {'pA'});
title('"tA" with delay');
```

We are running two simulations in Example 11. In the first simulation, none of the transitions endure delay. In the second simulation, all the transitions are delayed.

In Fig. 5.2, we focus only on **tA**'s firings. In the first subplot, whenever **tA** is enabled, it consumes a token from **p0** and starts firing. At the end of firing (10 TU), **tA** deposits a token into **pA**. Hence, there will be an additional token in **pA** every 10 TU. In the second subplot, whenever **tA** is enabled, it will be forced to wait for 2 TU; after that, it will be allowed to start firing. Hence, it will take 2 (waiting time) + 10 (firing time) = 12 TU per every token deposited in **pA**.

5.3.4 Example 12: Delayed Enabled Transitions II

Petri net for this example (shown in Fig. 5.3) is different because **p0** possesses only one token, so all three transitions compete for this token. At the start (time equals zero), all three transitions, **tA** to **tC**, are enabled but were forced to wait 2, 5, and 10 TU, respectively. **tA** will be out of the waiting period as it has the shortest delay. Hence, **tA** will consume the token from **p0** and start firing. At the completion of firing, **tA** will deposit a token into **p0**. Again, all three transitions become enabled and will be forced to wait. Again, **tA** will be the first out of the waiting period, consume the token in **p0**, and start firing.

Listing 5.3 Main Simulation File (Example 12)

```
clear all; clc; close all;
global global_info

global_info.STOP_AT = 75;

% minimum delay is 3, which is less than the minimum
% firing time (10). Hence, defult "Δ_T" is NOT ok.
global_info.DELTA_TIME = 0.5; % (= 2/4)

spng = pnstruct('ex_12_pdf');

dyn.m0 = {'p0', 1};
dyn.ft = {'allothers',10};
dyn.delayed = {'tA',2, 'tB',5, 'tC',10};
```

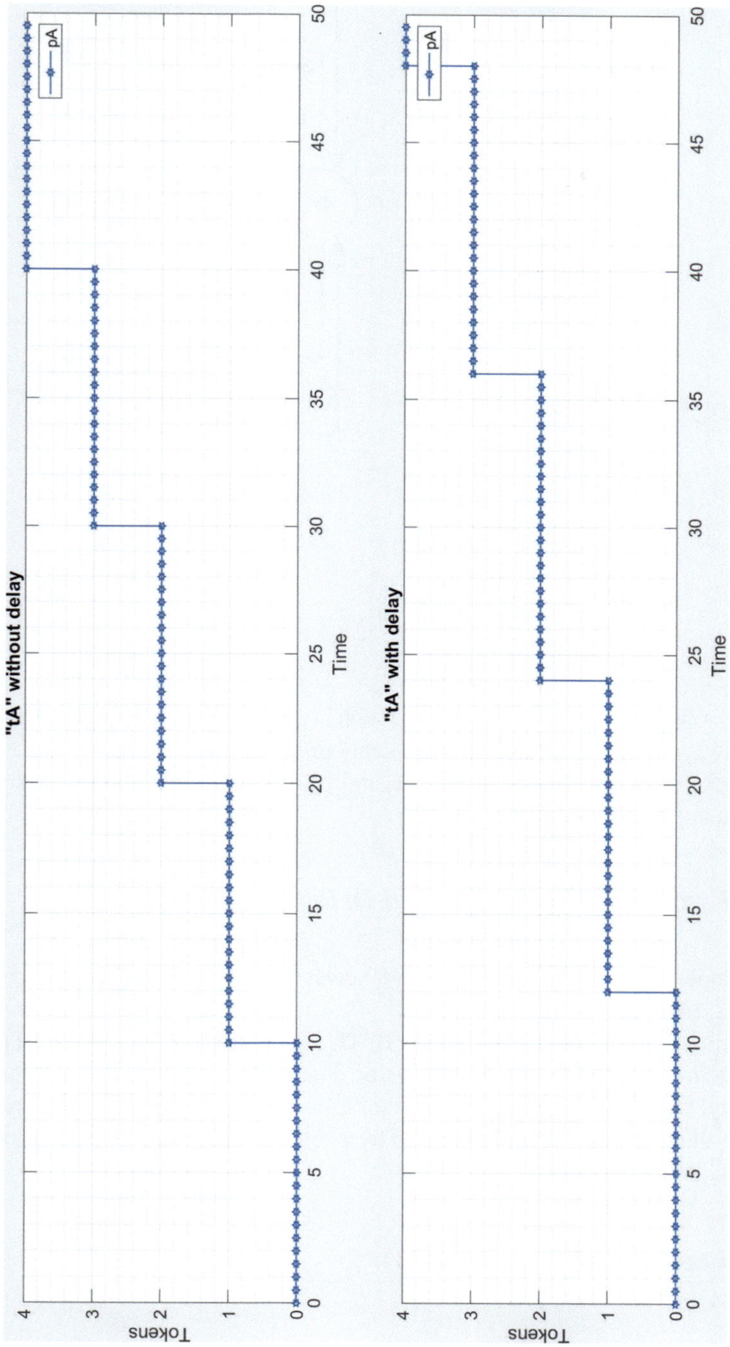

Fig. 5.2 Number of tokens in **pA**, when **tA** fires with or without delay

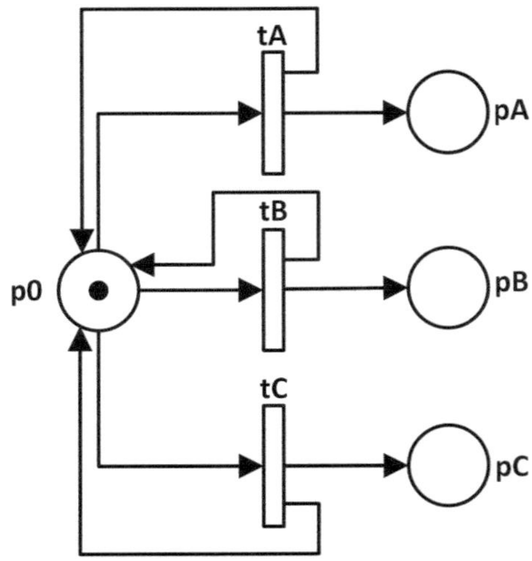

Fig. 5.3 Petri net for Example 12

```
pni = initialdynamics(spng, dyn);

sim = gpensim(pni);
subplot(3,1,1), plotp(sim, {'p0'});
subplot(3,1,2), plotp(sim, {'pA'});
subplot(3,1,3), plotp(sim, {'pB'});
```

In this example, it doesn't matter how much higher priorities **tB** and **tC** may have; **tA** will always win as it has the shortest delay time.

Figure 5.4 shows the tokens in **p0**, **pA**, and **pB** (tokens in **pC** will be the same as the tokens in **pB**, always zero).

5.3.5 Example 13: User-Defined Delay Functions

This example is similar to Example 11; however, in this example, we have six transitions, **tA** to **tF**; see Fig. 5.5.

The firing times of all transitions are 10 TU. Transition **tA** is delayed 0 TU (not delayed as in the default case), by **tB** a value determined by a user-defined function ("myDelayFunction_B"), and **tD** by another user-defined function ("myDelayFunction_D"); all other transitions are delayed by a deterministic 2 TU. Listing 5.4 shows the main simulation file.

Listing 5.4 Main Simulation File (Example 13)

```
clear all; clc; close all;
global global_info

global_info.STOP_AT = 40;
```

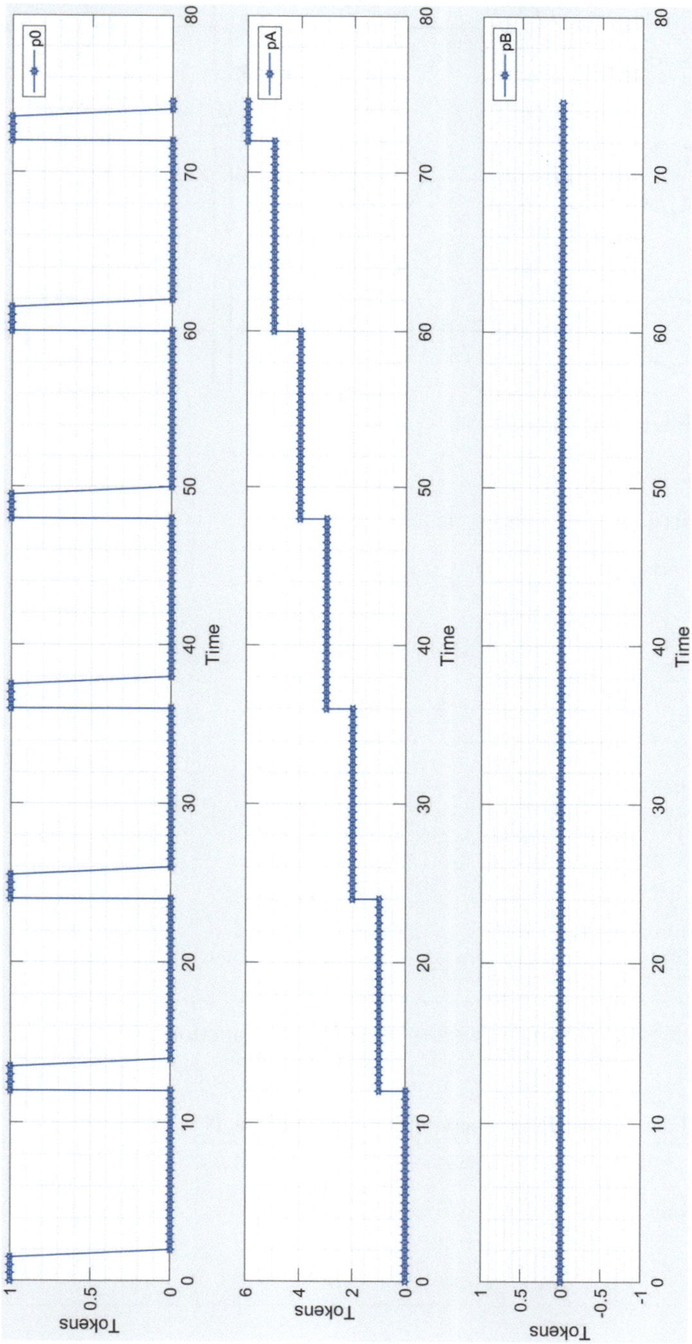

Fig. 5.4 Number of tokens in places **p0**, **pA**, and **pB**, when transitions compete for common token in **p0**

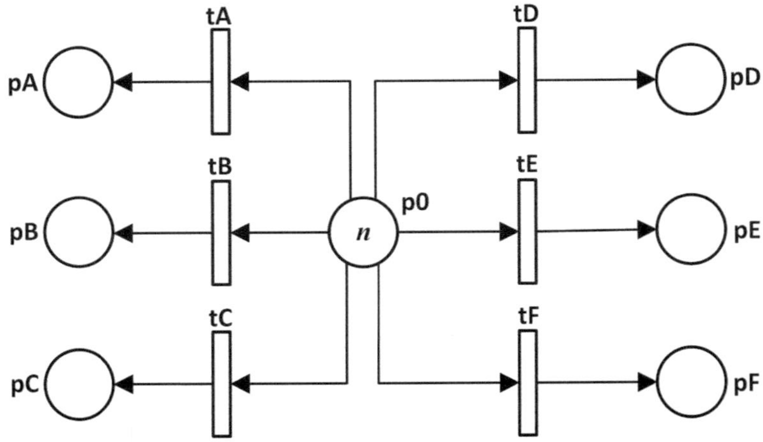

Fig. 5.5 Petri net for Example 13

```
global_info.DELTA_TIME = 0.1;

spng = pnstruct('ex_13_pdf');

dyn.m0 = {'p0', 18};
dyn.ft = {'allothers',10};
dyn.delayed = {'tA',0, 'tB','myDelayFunction_B(1,10)',...
    'tD','myDelayFunction_D(5)', 'allothers', 2};

pni = initialdynamics(spng, dyn);

sim = gpensim(pni);
subplot(4,1,1), plotp(sim, {'pA'});
subplot(4,1,2), plotp(sim, {'pC'});
subplot(4,1,3), plotp(sim, {'pE'});
subplot(4,1,4), plotp(sim, {'pF'});

figure, subplot(3,1,1), plotp(sim, {'pA'});
subplot(3,1,2), plotp(sim, {'pB'});
subplot(3,1,3), plotp(sim, {'pD'});
```

Listings 5.5 and 5.6 show the user-defined delay functions.

Listing 5.5 User-defined delay function "myDelayFunction_B"

```
function [delayVal] = myDelayFunction_B(addVal, divVal)

nt = ntrans(); % number of transitions
ct = current_time(); % current time

delayVal = (ct + nt + addVal)/divVal;
```

Listing 5.6 User-defined delay function "myDelayFunction_D"

```
function [delayValue] = myDelayFunction_D(a)
delayValue = 5 + a;
```

Figure 5.6 shows the plotp of **pC**, **pE**, and **pF**, which were input by the transitions delayed by the same deterministic value of 2 TU.

Figure 5.7 shows the plotp of **pA**, **pB** and **pD**; **pA** is input by **tA** which is not delayed (delay value is assigned to zero TU). However, even though **tA** should not be delayed, the compiler processing adds some offset values. Hence, it is better not to mention **tA** is the assignment as it will get default 0 delays (more accurate). Places **pB** and **pD** were input by the transitions **tB** and **tD** that were delayed by specific user-defined functions.

5.4 Time Windows

Even though delayed enabled transitions are implemented only in GPenSIM version 11, "Time Windows" (retaining tokens in a place for an amount of time) can be simulated even in older versions of GPenSIM as well as in version 11. In this approach, checking whether a token in an input place has waited long enough becomes yet another condition in the pre-processor file.

Note that the function `timeWindow` introduced in this section has a **limitation** as it assumes:

1. **The enabled transition has only one input place**, and
2. **the input arc weight is also one**.

If the enabled transition has multiple input places or the arc weights are larger than one, then the user needs to extend this function.

5.4.1 Example 14: Time Windows

Figure 5.8 shows a simple Petri net with four places and six transitions. Places **p1** and **p3** have one initial token each. Let the firing times of the transitions be 1 TU. Let us assume that the enabled transitions are allowed to fire freely; hence, there is no need for pre-processors. Figure 5.9 shows the simulation results, showing that there are two tokens in some places.

Let us imagine that the Petri net is a mini-version of the classical "Cat and Mouse" problem that is used in some books on supervisory control (e.g., Moody and Antsaklis [3]); the initial token in **p1** represents the cat, and the initial token in **p3** represents the mouse.

In the "Cat and Mouse" problem, the cat and the mouse must not stay in the same room to avoid the death of the mouse. However, GPenSIM will keep these two

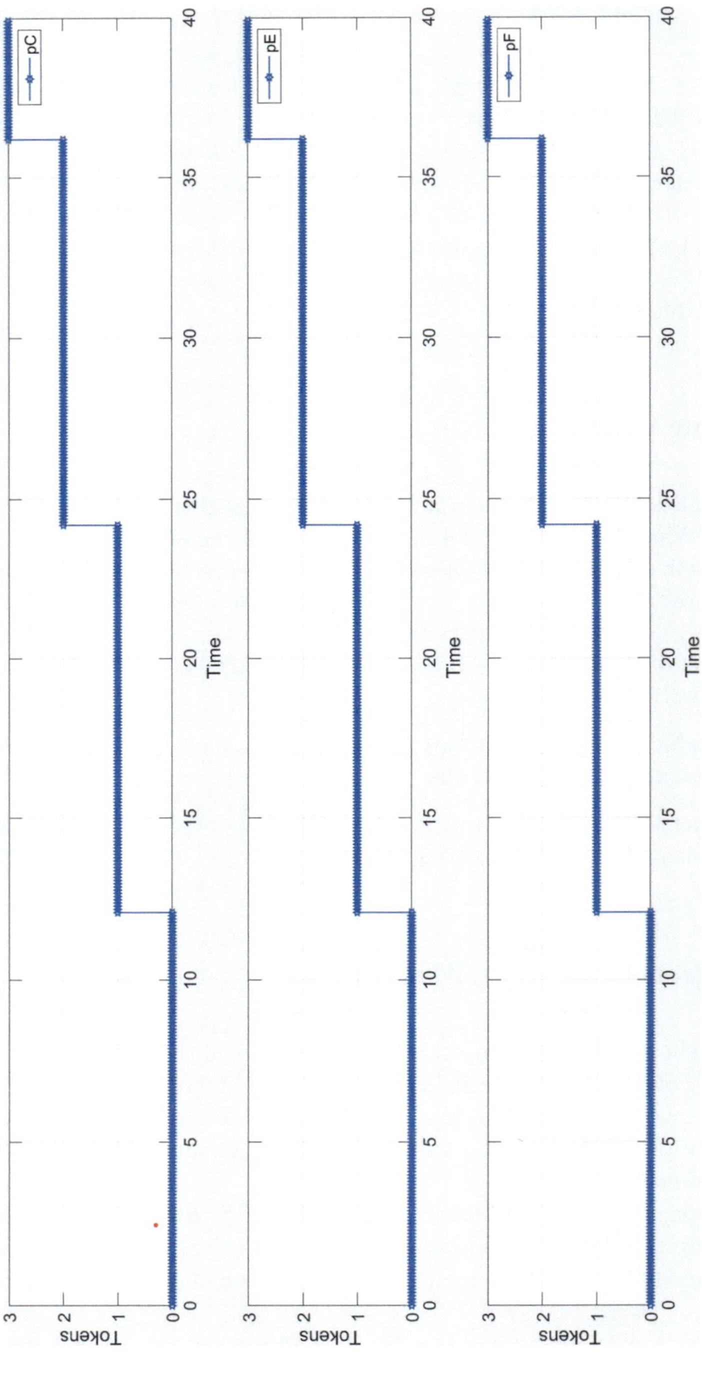

Fig. 5.6 Number of tokens in places **pC**, **pE**, and **pF**, which were fed by transitions delayed by deterministic value (2 TU)

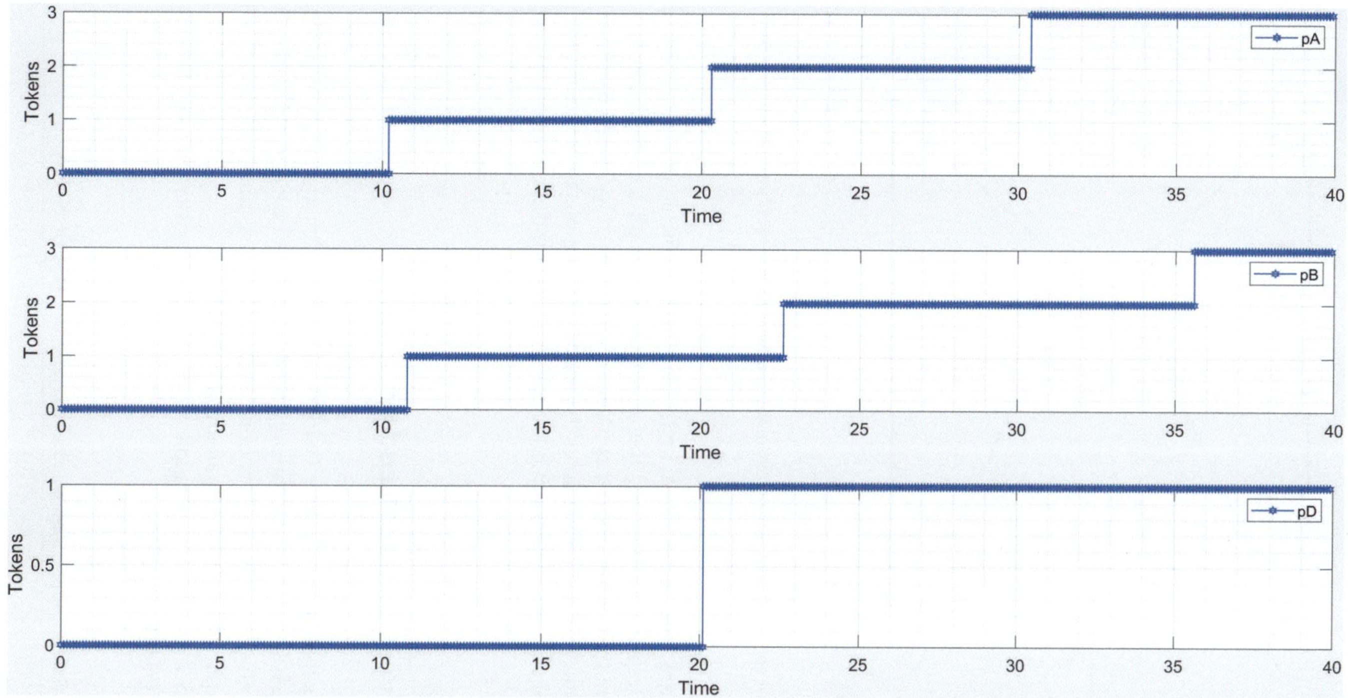

Fig. 5.7 Number of tokens in places **pA**, **pB**, and **pD**; **pA** was fed by **tA**, which should not be delayed; **pB** and **pD** were fed by transitions delayed by user-defined delay functions

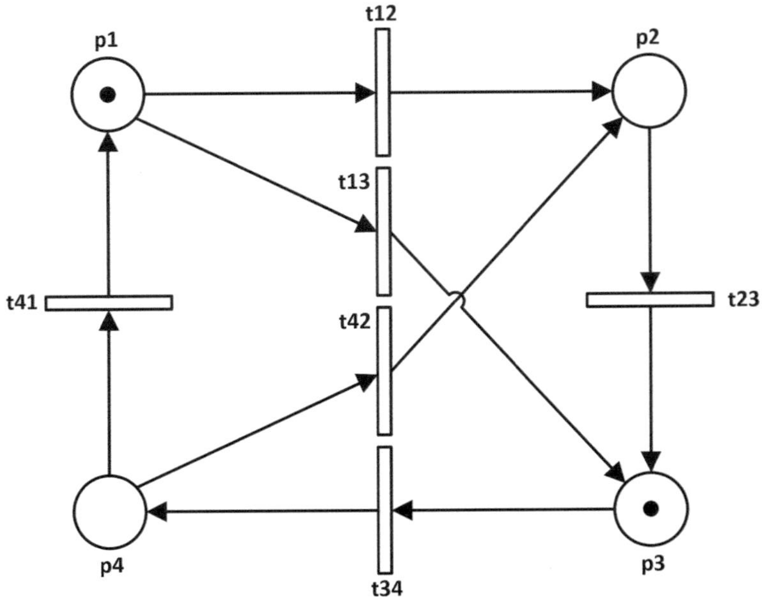

Fig. 5.8 Petri net for Example 14 (Miniature "Cat and Mouse" problem)

animals in any place **only for an instant of time**, as visible in Fig. 5.9. For example, when time equal to 21 and 31, these animals are in **p2** for an instant before they depart to another place. Also, they meet momentarily in **p3** when the time is equal to 14, 53, and 78. GPenSIM allows the enabled transitions to immediately consume the input tokens, which does not allow enough time for the cat and mouse to interact in any place.

5.4.2 *Function* `timeWindow`

Let us introduce "Time Window" with the help of the function `timeWindow`. Note: This function `timeWindow` can only be used in a pre-processor file (specific, modular, or common). Also, this function fundamentally assumes that the transition has only one input place and the input arc weight is one.

Listing 5.7 shows a typical application of `timeWindow` in a pre-processor, this time in a COMMON_PRE.

Listing 5.7 Sample application of `timeWindow` in COMMON_PRE

```
function [fire, transition] = COMMON_PRE(transition)

global global_info
```

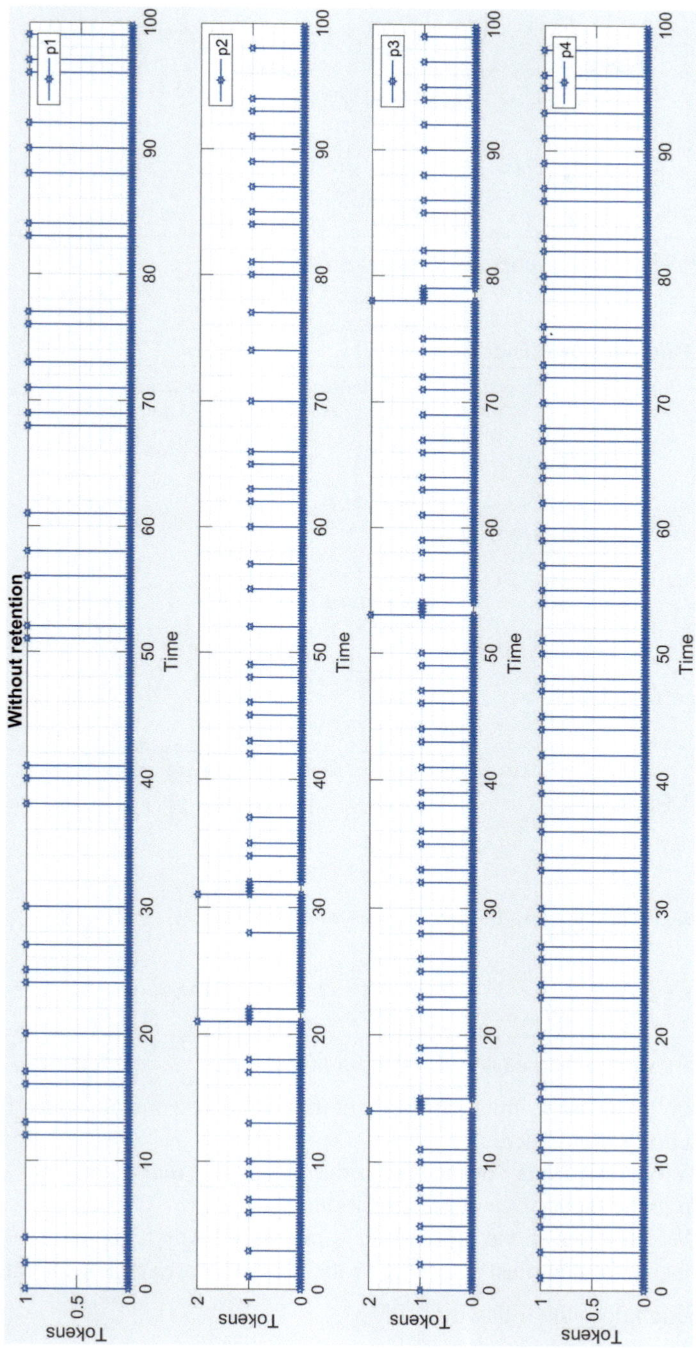

Fig. 5.9 The cat and the mouse stay in one place only for an instant of time

```
% minimum retention time (TIME_WINDOW) of a token
% in an input place.
% TIME_WINDOW is declared in the main simulation file
% as an element of the global_info packet
TIME_WINDOW = global_info.TIME_WINDOW;

% enabled transition is not allowed to fire
% until the token has stayed for at least
% the minimum retention time in the input place
[fire, transition] = timeWindow(transition, TIME_WINDOW, 'any');
```

Listing 5.8 shows the function `timeWindow`.

Listing 5.8 Function `timeWindow`

```
function [fire, transition] = timeWindow(transition,...
                  TIME_WINDOW, policy)
%         Simulating "Petri Nets with Time Window"
%

% if policy is not given, assume 'any' token
if eq(nargin,2), policy = 'any'; end

% identify the input place
pid = get_inputplace(transition.name);
placeName = pname(pid);

% chose the appropriate token from the input place
switch policy
    case 'any', tokID = tokenAny(placeName, 1);
    case 'early', tokID = tokenArrivedEarly(placeName, 1);
    case 'late', tokID = tokenArrivedLate(placeName, 1);
    otherwise
end

% get the time this token was deposited
% into the input place
tokCreationTime = get_tokCT (placeName, tokID);

% fire, only if this token has stayed long enough
fire = ge(current_time, tokCreationTime + TIME_WINDOW);
transition.selected_tokens = tokID;
```

Function `timeWindow` takes three input arguments:

1. "transition": This is the input parameter of the pre-processor from which function `timeWindow` was called.
2. TIME_WINDOW: (delay or retention time) A positive real number for keeping the token in the input place of the transitions.
3. Policy: Which token in the input place is preferred? Any token is fine ("any"), the one that arrived earliest ("early"), or the token that arrived latest ("late")?

This function does the following:

- If the policy ("any", "early", or "late") is not given, then any token will be considered.

- o Based on the policy, a token in the input place is identified (using functions `tokenAny`, `tokenArrivedEarly`, or `tokenArrivedLate`).
- o Then, using the token's identification number (`tokID`) and the function `get_tokCT`, the time this token was deposited into the input place (the token creation time) is extracted.
- o Finally, the current time is compared with the token creation time plus the delay time (TIME_WINDOW). If the current time has surpassed the token creation time plus the delay time, then the transition is allowed to start firing.

The output arguments of the function `timeWindow`:

1. "fire": Boolean value; the transition can fire or not, as the token has stayed in the input place long enough or not.
2. "transition": this is the output parameter of the pre-processor from which function `timeWindow` was called.

Note: Functions `tokenAny`, `tokenArrivedEarly`, `tokenArrivedLate`, and `get_tokCT` are GPenSIM built-in functions Davidrajuh [2].

5.4.3 Files for Example 14

Listings 5.9 and 5.10 show the main simulation file and the PDF.

Listing 5.9 Main Simulation File (Example 14)

```
global global_info
global_info.STOP_AT = 100;

%%% retention time for tokens %%%%%%%%%%%
global_info.TIME_WINDOW = 5;

%%% Petri Net
spng = pnstruct('ex_14_pdf');
dyn.m0 = {'p1',1, 'p3',1};
dyn.ft = {'allothers', 1};
pni = initialdynamics(spng, dyn);

%%% Simulation and results
sim = gpensim(pni);

subplot(4,1,1), plotp(sim, {'p1'});
title('Firings with Time Windows');
subplot(4,1,2), plotp(sim, {'p2'});
subplot(4,1,3), plotp(sim, {'p3'});
subplot(4,1,4), plotp(sim, {'p4'});
```

Listing 5.10 PDF (Example 14)

```
function [png] = ex_14_pdf()

png.PN_name = 'Example 14: Petri Nets with Time Windows';
png.set_of_Ps = {'p1','p2','p3','p4'};
png.set_of_Ts = {'t12','t23','t34','t41','t42','t13'};

png.set_of_As = {...
    'p1','t12',1, 't12','p2',1, ... % t12
    'p2','t23',1, 't23','p3',1, ... % t23
    'p3','t34',1, 't34','p4',1, ... % t34
    'p4','t41',1, 't41','p1',1, ... % t41
    ...
    'p4','t42',1, 't42','p2',1, ... % t42
    'p1','t13',1, 't13','p3',1, ... % t12
               };
```

Listing 5.11 shows the COMMON_PRE. This COMMON_PRE is compact as we use only the time window as the condition. In addition, we may use any other additional conditions in the pre-processor if we want.

Listing 5.11 COMMON_PRE (Example 14)

```
function [fire, transition] = COMMON_PRE(transition)

global global_info
TIME_WINDOW = global_info.TIME_WINDOW;
[fire, transition] = timeWindow(transition, TIME_WINDOW, 'any');
```

The simulation result is shown in Fig. 5.10. The simulation result shows that now the cat and the mouse stay in one place for long enough to interact, as the tokens in places must stay at least for the duration of delay (TIME_WINDOW). In Fig. 5.10, the cat and the mouse stay in the same place during the following periods: In **p2** during 30–35 TU, in **p3** during 37–41 TU, and in **p4** during 43–47 TU.

5.4.4 Extending Time Windows

Multiple retention times: In the main simulation file for Example 14, we declared only one TIME_WINDOW as we assumed the holding times for all the places were the same. However, we can extend this idea to include different holding times for different places. In the main simulation file, TIME_WINDOW can be declared as an array of elements, and the length of this array is the total number of places. For example, in MSF:

Listing 5.12 Extending TIME_WINDOW in the MSF

```
% in the Main Simulation File
...
% retention time for tokens in p1, p2, p3, and p4
global_info.TIME_WINDOW = [5, 3, 2, 1];
...
```

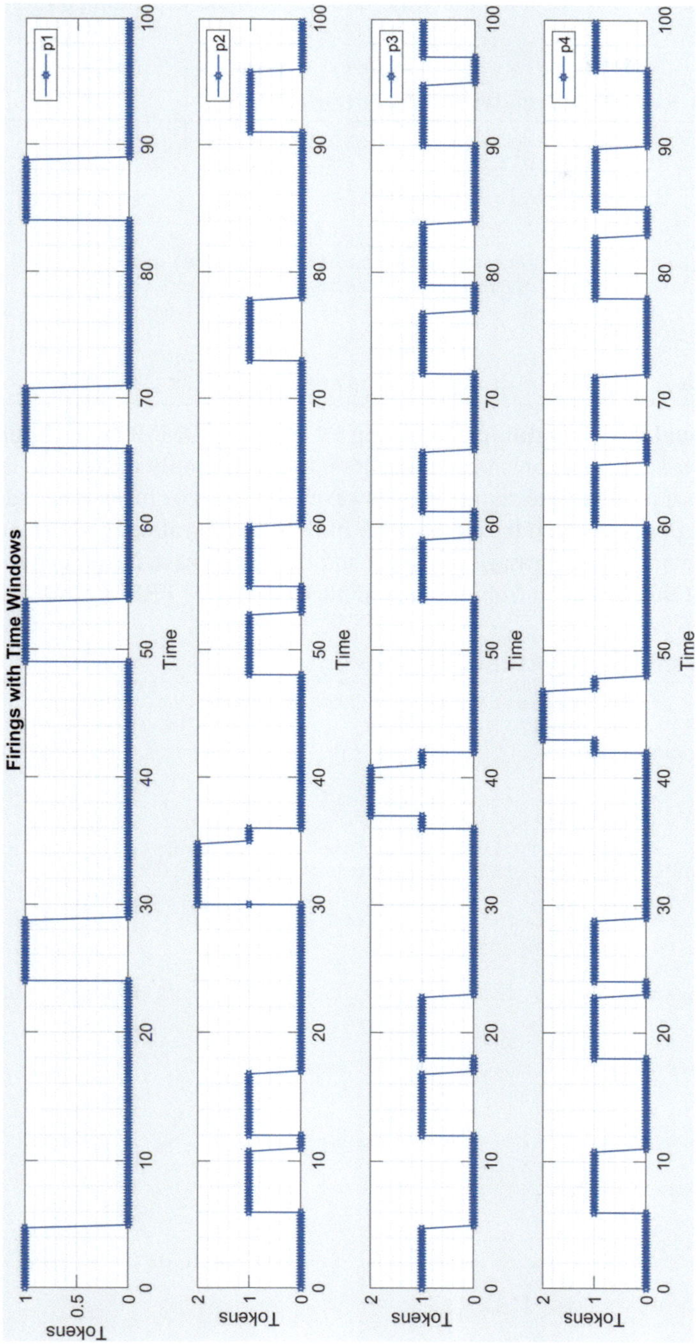

Fig. 5.10 The cat and the mouse stay in one place for long enough to interact

And, in the COMMON_PRE, different retention times are chosen depending on the input place. Also, we can modify the value if we want, depending on some other conditions.

Listing 5.13 Extending TIME_WINDOW in COMMON_PRE

```
function [fire, transition] = COMMON_PRE(transition)

global global_info

% TIME_WINDOW is declared as an array in MSF
pIDinputplace = get_inputplace(transition.name);
TIME_WINDOW = global_info.TIME_WINDOW(pIDinputplace);

% enabled transition is not allowed to fire
% until the token has stayed for at least retention time
[fire, transition] = timeWindow(transition, TIME_WINDOW, 'any');
```

Additional firing conditions: In Listing 5.11 for the COMMON_PRE for Example 14, we assumed that an enabled transition is checked **only** against the retention time before it is allowed to start firing. However, there can be many other additional conditions. For example, if the output place of the transition already has a token, then we can give a warning message as the cat and the mouse have the potential to meet and prevent this transition from firing. Sample COMMON_PRE is given below:

Listing 5.14 COMMON_PRE (Example 14-B)

```
function [fire, transition] = COMMON_PRE(transition)

global global_info

% TIME_WINDOW is declared in the main simulation file
% as an element of the global_info packet
pID = get_inputplace(transition.name);
TIME_WINDOW = global_info.TIME_WINDOW(pID);

% enabled transition is not allowed to fire
% until the token has stayed for at least
% the minimum retention time in the input place
[fire, transition] = timeWindow(transition, TIME_WINDOW, 'any');

%%%%%%%%%% Additional Conditions %%%%%%%%%%%%%%%%%%
% now, checking for the number of tokens in
% the output place

pid2 = get_outputplace(transition.name); % ID of the output ...
    place
noutP = ntokens(pid2); % number of tokens in the output place

if noutP
    disp(['The output place of ', transition.name, ' has a ...
        token']);
    disp('Therefore, not allowed to fire! ');
end

fire = and(fire, not(noutP));
```

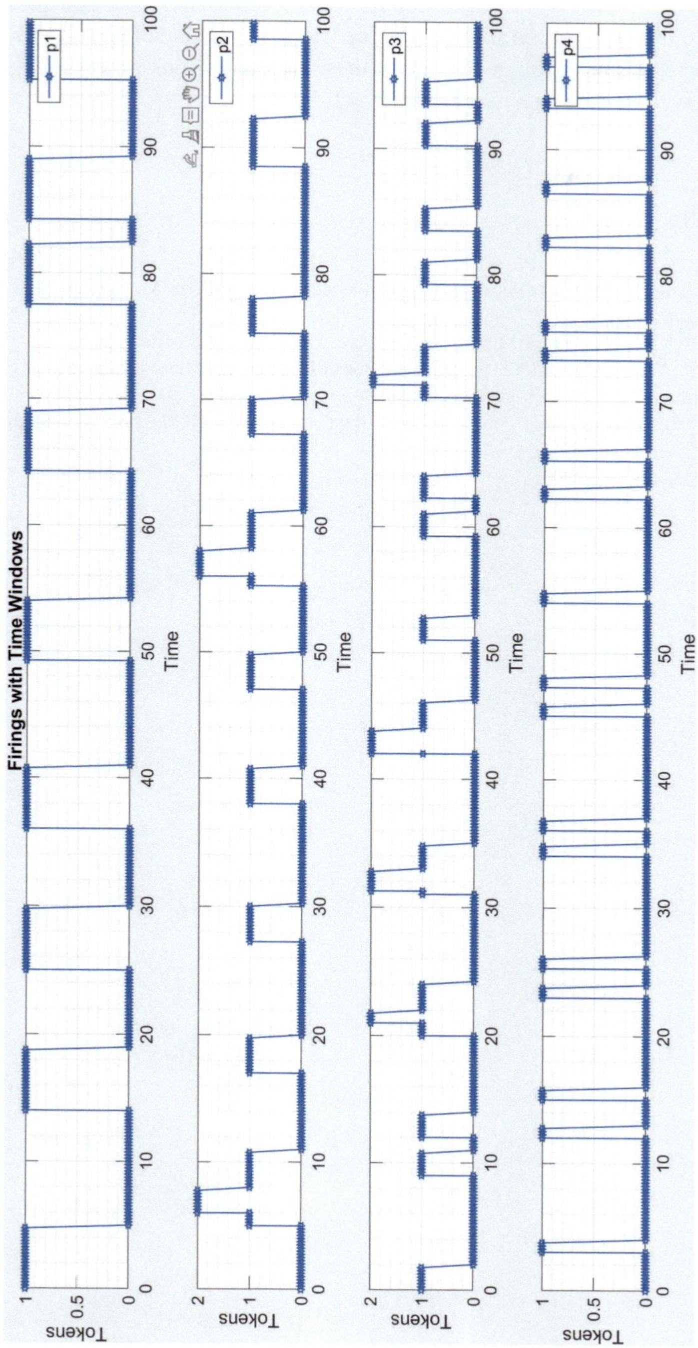

Fig. 5.11 Additional condition does not prevent the cat and the mouse lands in one place

The sample result is shown in Fig. 5.11. The result shows that the additional condition in COMMON_PRE did not prevent two tokens in **p2** and **p3**. This is because two transitions feed **p2** and **p3**. Focusing on **p2**, when **t12** and **t42** became enabled, there was no token in **p2**; hence, these two transitions were allowed to fire, and these two will deposit a token each in **p2**.

References

1. Davidrajuh R (2018) Modeling discrete-event systems with GPenSIM. Springer International Publishing, Cham
2. Davidrajuh R (2024) GPenSIM reference manual. University of Stavanger
3. Moody JO, Antsaklis PJ (2012) Supervisory control of discrete event systems using Petri nets, vol 8. Springer Science & Business Media
4. Popova-Zeugmann L (2013) Time Petri nets. Time and Petri Nets. Springer, Berlin, pp 31–137

Part II
Interfacing with External Environment

Chapter 6
Processor Files as Interfaces

This chapter focuses on the entry points GPenSIM provides in Petri net model-based software-to-software and software-to-hardware access. We will see in this chapter that the entry points in the interface are basically the set of processor files that we encountered in the previous chapters, especially in Chap. 1, "File Structure in GPenSIM."

6.1 GPenSIM Interface

Before we delve into the details, let's start with the concept of an **interface**. An Internet search on the definition of the interface provides the following three definitions.

1. The Oxford online dictionary defines an interface as "a point where two systems, subjects, organizations, etc., meet and interact".
2. The Oxford online dictionary defines an interface *in computing* as "a device or program that enables a user to communicate with a computer".
3. Wikipedia defines an interface (in computing) as "a shared boundary across which two or more separate components of a computer system exchange information".

In this chapter, we take an interface as **a meeting point** (the first definition) between **the Petri net model implemented with GPenSIM** on one side and **the external hardware and software** (anything outside the Petri net model) on the other side.

Some works use GPenSIM for Petri net model-based software-to-software and software-to-hardware control (e.g., Cameron et al. [1] and Davidrajuh [2]). Figure 6.1 shows the interface facilitating a Petri net model accessing external hardware or software.

R. Davidrajuh, *Petri Nets for Modeling Complex Discrete-Event Systems*, Asset Analytics,
https://doi.org/10.1007/978-981-96-6396-5_6

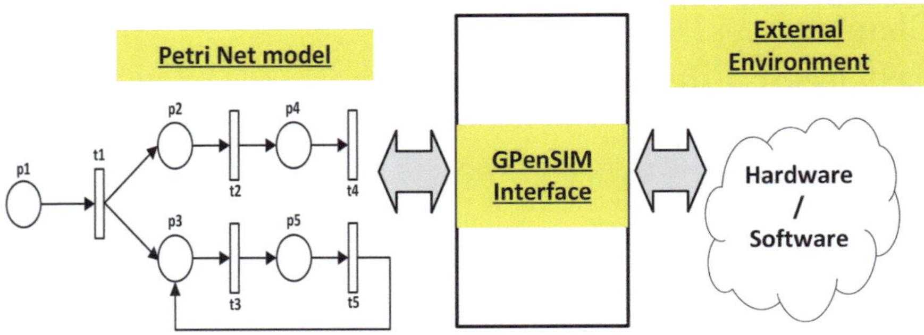

Fig. 6.1 A Petri net model accessing external hardware or software

GPenSIM treats monolithic (non-modular) Petri net models differently from Modular Petri net models, as the scopes of the transitions are different in the processor files.

6.2 Interfacing a Monolithic Petri Net

Figure 6.2 shows a small monolithic Petri net with five places and five transitions.

6.2.1 Interfacing Small Monolithic Petri Nets

Let us focus on a small monolithic Petri net. In Chap. 1, "File Structure in GPenSIM"), we learned that implementing a monolithic Petri net with GPenSIM takes some M-files [2]:

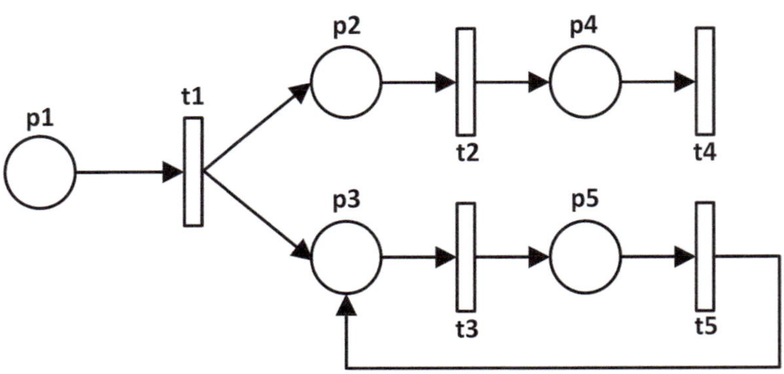

Fig. 6.2 Small monolithic Petri net

- A Petri Net Definition File (PDF), defining the static Petri net graph. **PDF will be executed only once**.
- The Main Simulation File (MSF) declares the initial dynamics and then calls the function '`gpensim`' to run the simulation. **MSF will also be executed only once**.
- (Ignoring the common preprocessor, for the time being) Specific preprocessors define the additional conditions an enabled transition needs to satisfy before firing. **Specific preprocessor file will be executed every time a transition becomes enabled**.
- (Ignoring the common postprocessor, for the time being) Specific postprocessors define the actions that need to be carried out when the transition completes firing. **Specific postprocessor file will be executed every time a transition completes firing**.

There are only five transitions in Fig. 6.2. Hence, this Petri net model will be implemented with five specific preprocessors and five specific postprocessors. We may not need some specific preprocessors as there are no additional conditions for these enabled transitions to satisfy before starting firing. Similarly, we may not need some specific postprocessors as no post-firing actions need to be performed for those transitions. Therefore, implementing this Petri net would demand a *maximum* of five specific preprocessors and a *maximum* of five specific postprocessors.

Hence, for smaller monolithic Petri net models, the interface for the Petri net model to interact with the external software and hardware is shown in Fig. 6.3.

6.2.2 Interfacing Large Monolithic Petri Nets

Suppose we are dealing with a large monolithic Petri net model, which possesses a large number of places and transitions. Implementing **a large Petri net model** will demand a large number of specific preprocessors and specific postprocessors. In addition to the large number of processor files that may clutter the folder, we may also face another issue, namely, duplication:

- Many enabled transitions may face the same conditions that are to be satisfied before they can start firing; hence, copying the same common code into multiple specific preprocessors is unnecessary.
- Similarly, the actions that are to be performed after the firing of some transitions can be the same; in this case also, copying the same common code for these actions into multiple specific postprocessors is unnecessary.

Because of these three reasons (too many processor files, duplication of conditions in specific preprocessor files, and duplication of actions in specific postprocessor files), we may choose to use only two processor files, namely, the **common processors**:

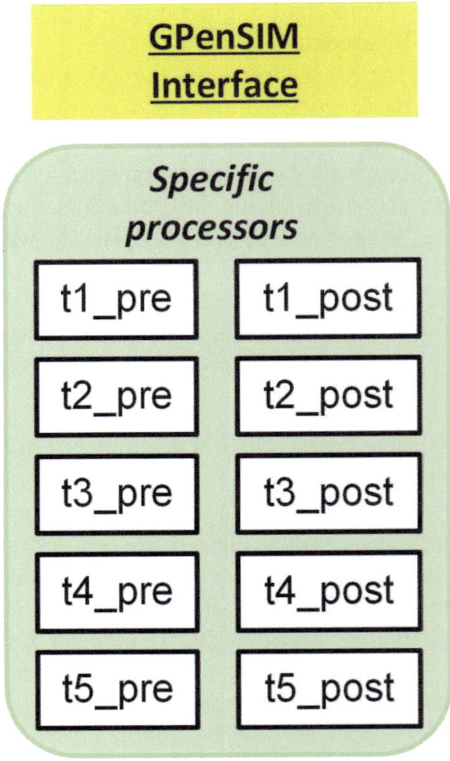

Fig. 6.3 The interface for the small monolithic Petri net shown in Fig. 6.2

- "**COMMON_PRE**" for coding the pre-conditions before starting firing.
- "**COMMON_POST**" for coding the actions after any transition completion of firing.

Figure 6.4 shows the interface for large monolithic Petri net models. COMMON_PRE and COMMON_POST (the common processors) help reduce the total number of processor files and reduce duplication of code. However, we may still need some specific processors: for example, it is not a good idea to place hardware-specific code in common processors; it is best to put them in specific pre and postprocessors of transitions that represent the hardware events.

6.3 Interfacing Modular Petri Net Models

Figure 6.5 shows a modular Petri net model consisting of two Petri Modules (Module-**Alfa** and Module-**Beta**) and two IMCs (IMC-**Driver** and IMC-**Stub**).

Figure 6.6 shows the interface of a modular Petri net. From Fig. 6.6, it may seem like the interface of a modular Petri net model becomes more detailed as it consists

Fig. 6.4 The interface for large monolithic Petri net models

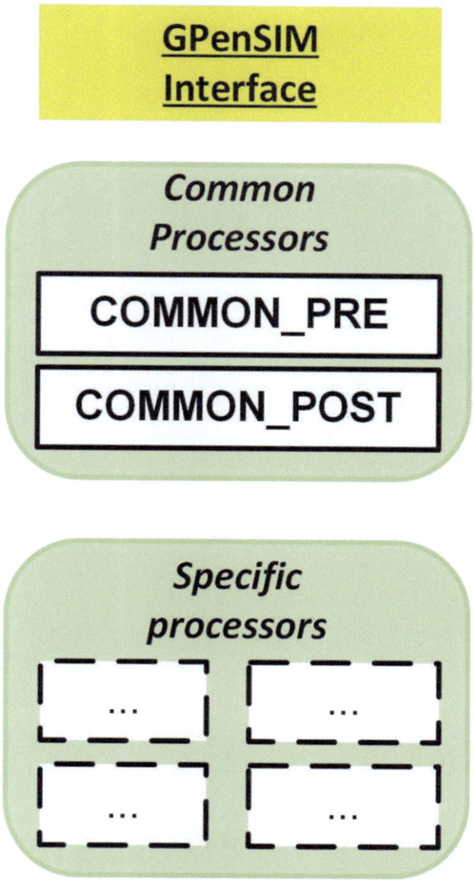

of common processors, modular processors, and some specific processors. In fact, it is not! The fundamental idea behind modular Petri net is "data hiding," which means that not all details are shared or available to everyone [3, 4]. When groups of developers develop a large modular Petri net model, each group is responsible for developing and testing their respective Petri Modules; the common processors become the "contract" between the different groups. The common processors are unique and shared (available) among the groups. Modular processors and specific processors are not shared by the groups ('data hiding').

For example, for the modular Petri net shown in Fig. 6.5, there may be up to four interfaces, one for each Petri Module and one for each IMC, as a Petri Module and an IMC can be independently run on a computer, even if it is part of a (an overall) Petri net model. An interface for a Petri Module will contain only the two Modular processes that are valid for this Petri Module (e.g., MOD_Alfa_PRE and MOD_Alfa_POST for Petri Module **Alfa**) and perhaps some other specific processors for the transitions of this module. In addition, common processors serve as the contract for how the

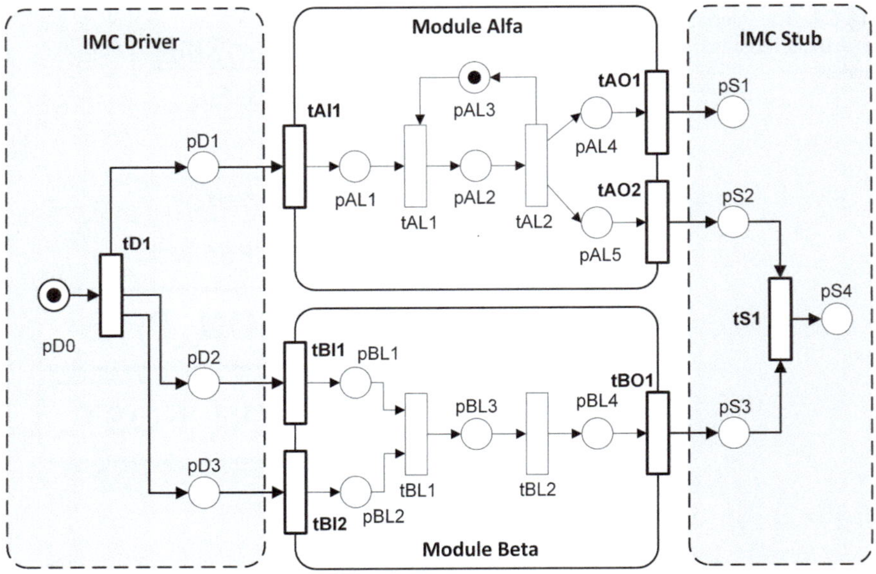

Fig. 6.5 A modular Petri net

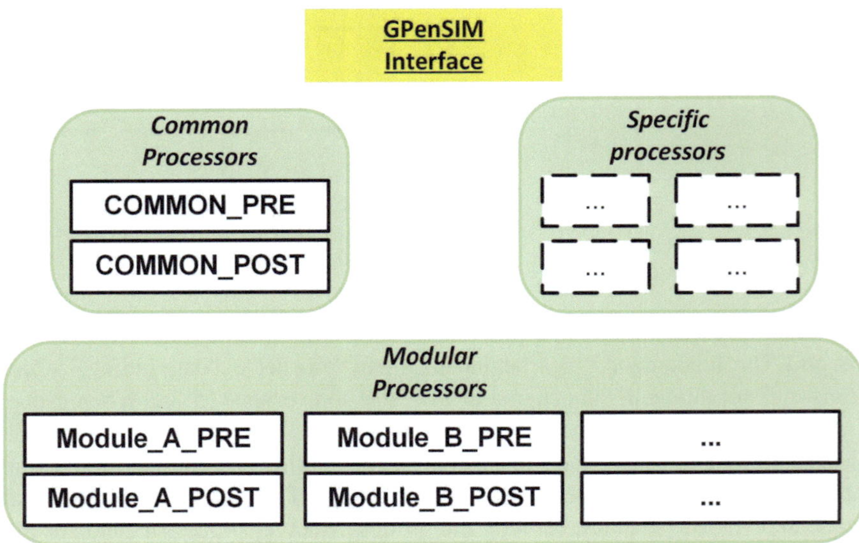

Fig. 6.6 The interface for a modular Petri net

Modules and the IMCs should communicate with each other and with the external environment. An interface consisting of common processors and all the modular processors is only possible if the developers choose to have a single interface for the whole Petri net model to interact with the external environment.

6.4 Sample Application: Interacting with External Hardware

Let us look at a simple example in which we are going to use a monolithic Petri net model to interact with external hardware. The external hardware is a LEGO robot with three buttons as the inputs ('Start', 'Yellow Light', and 'Stop') and three lights as the outputs ('Red', 'Yellow', and 'Green'). Figure 6.7 shows the robot.

The Petri net model is supposed to perform the following actions on the hardware:

- When the user presses the 'Start' button, the robot is started and the 'Green' light is switched ON; the green light will be switched on until the user presses the 'Stop' button.
- Whenever the user presses the 'Yellow Light' button, the yellow light must be switched ON for one minute.

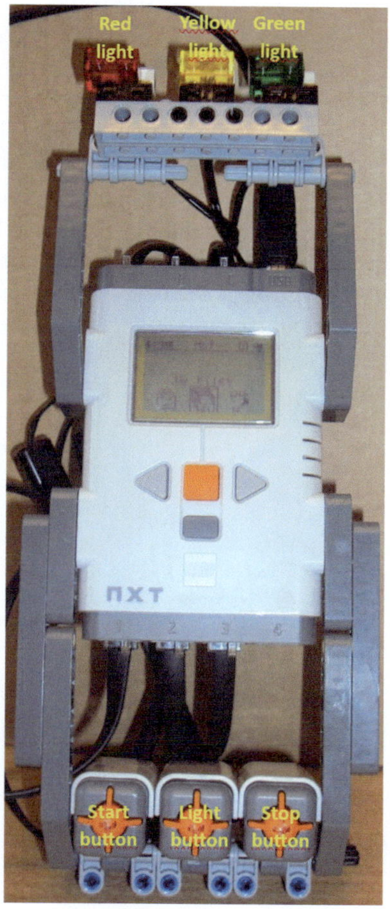

Fig. 6.7 The LEGO robot

- When the user presses the 'Stop' button, the 'Green' light must be switched OFF, and an alarm must be sounded.
- (The red light is not used in this test).

Figure 6.8 shows the Petri net model. At the start, tInit_pre (the specific preprocessor for **tInit**) initializes the hardware; after the initialization, **tInit** deposits a token into **pWait4Start**, indicating that the net is waiting for the user to press the 'Start' button.

Once the user presses the 'Start' button, it will be detected by tStart_pre (the specific preprocessor for **tStart**). tStart_pre also switches on the green light (there is no need for tStart_post). When **tStart** completes firing (firing time is immaterial), it will deposit a token into **pWait4Stop**, indicating the wait for the user to press the 'Stop' button to switch off the green light. When the user presses the 'Stop' button, it will be detected by tStop_pre and tStop_post switches off the green light and the hardware.

The Petri net also scans the 'Yellow light' button press in tWait4Yellow_pre. Once the user presses the 'Yellow light' button, tWait4Yellow_pre returns true, and the firing of **tWait4Yellow** deposits a token in **pYellowLight**. tYellowLight_pre switches on the yellow light. The firing time of **tYellowLight** is one minute. When **tYellowLight** completes firing (after one minute), tYellowLight_post will switch off the yellow light, making the yellow light switch on for one minute.

Figure 6.9 shows the interface to make the Petri net model control the LEGO Robot. Of course, since the Petri net model is small, we are using the interface shown in Fig. 6.3 (the first interface for smaller monolithic Petri net models). Also, the codes in the specific processors are hardware-specific; hence, it is a good idea to keep them away from the common processors. Should any of the hardware functions change, we need to change only the relevant specific processor, whereas common processors have some permanence.

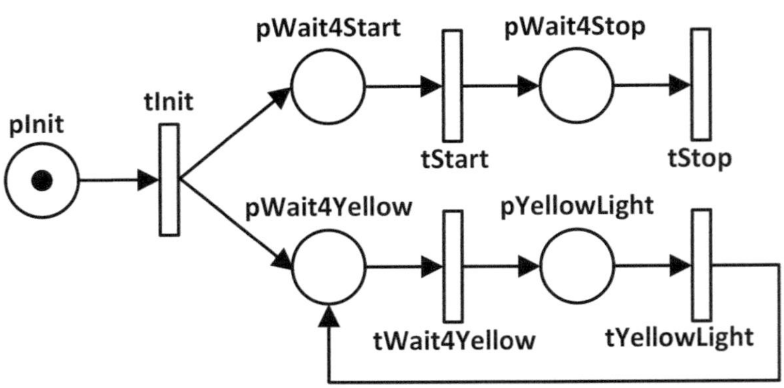

Fig. 6.8 The Petri net model for controlling the LEGO robot

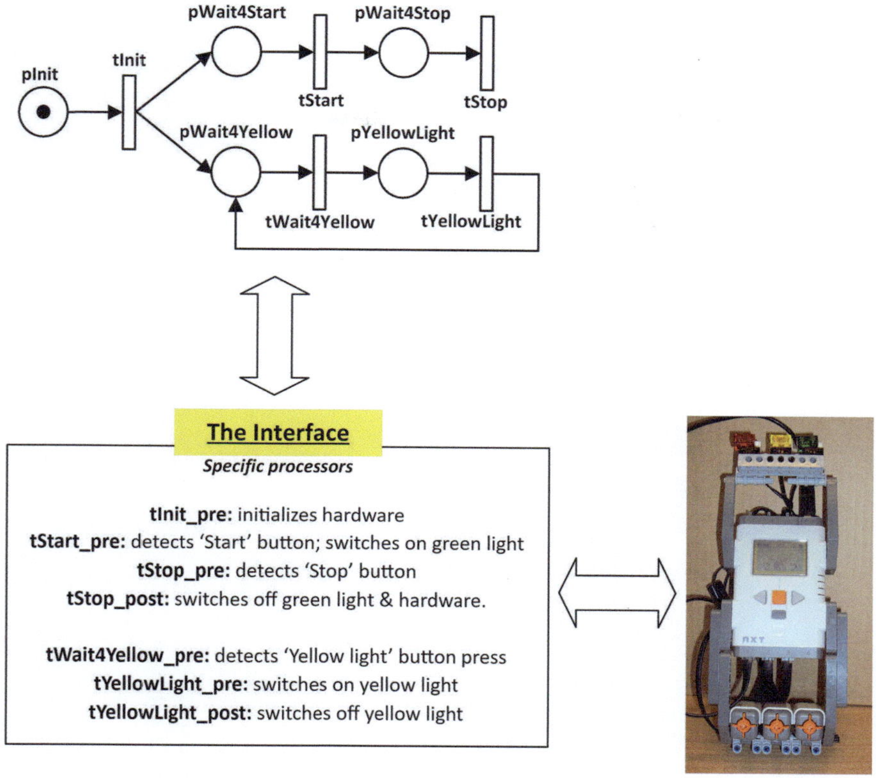

Fig. 6.9 The interface between the Petri net model and the LEGO robot

6.5 Sample Application: Interacting with External Software

Figure 6.10 shows a discrete process for dyeing (coloring or painting) tennis balls. The discrete process consists of the following steps:

1. Filling with Paint (**tPaintIn**): Paint is poured in through the pump on top of Tank-1. This pouring is a one-step event; once started, it is non-stoppable and will stop once Tank-1 is filled with the necessary volume of paint (in other words, the filling will take a fixed amount of time).
2. Tennis Balls Arrival (**tBallIn**): Once paint is poured, tennis balls are injected into Tank-1 in batches. Balls are input in **N1** batches, with **n1** balls in each batch.
3. Blender (**tBlender**): Once the tennis balls are brought in, the dyeing starts by switching on the blender. The blender will be switched on for fixed amount of time.

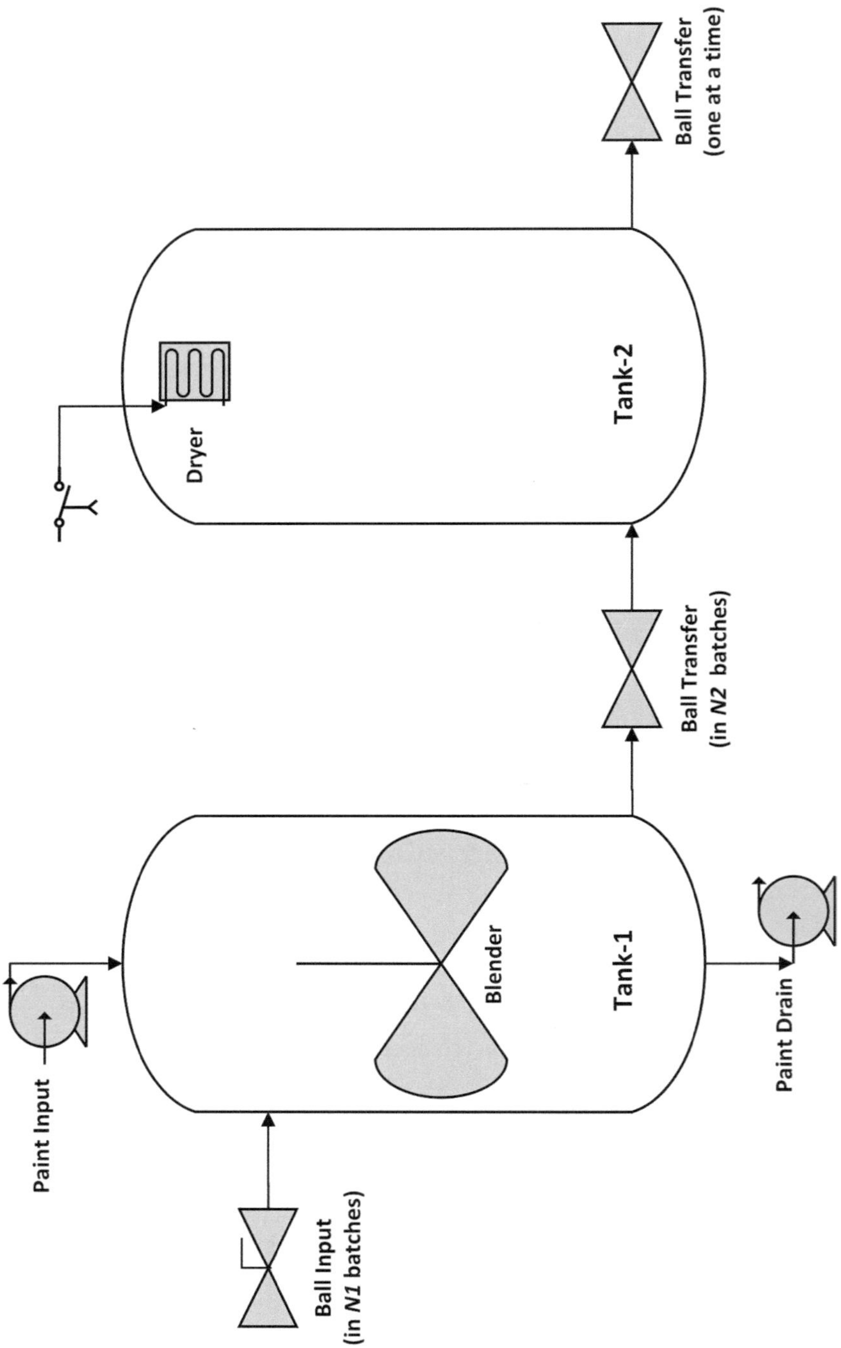

Fig. 6.10 A discrete process for dyeing tennis balls

4. Draining the paint (**tPaintOut**): Once the blender stops, the paint will be drained out of Tank-1. The suction pump for draining the paint will be switched on for a fixed amount of time.
5. Balls transfer (**tBallTransfer**) from Tank-1 to Tank-2: Once the draining of the paint is completed, balls are transferred into Tank-2 in **N2** batches. There will be **n2** balls in each batch. Note that, (**N1** × **n1**) should be equal to (**N2** × **n2**).
6. Drying (**tDrying**): Once the tennis balls are transferred into Tank-2, the drying starts by switching on the dryer, which will be on for a fixed amount of time.
7. Tennis Balls Out (**tBallOut**): Once drying is completed, tennis balls will be sucked out, one by one (for the QA by a robot).

6.5.1 A Monolithic Petri Net Model

Figure 6.11 shows a monolithic Petri net model for the discrete process of dyeing tennis balls. Once **tPaintIn** starts, all the activities will follow one after the other. In this model, the paint paths (paint, in and out of Tank-1) are shown in red, and the ball paths (balls, in and out of Tank-1 and Tank-2) are shown in violet.

We could have used a P/T Petri net for the model shown in Fig. 6.11, but some steps demand a Colored Petri net:

1. **tPaintIn** deposits one token into **pTank-1** with color 'paint'.
2. **tPaintOut** consumes one token from **pTank-1** with color 'paint'.
3. **tBallIn** fires **N1** times, each time depositing **n1** number of tokens; all these tokens must be tagged with the color 'ball'.

We can use specific preprocessors to code the coloring actions. Since we are starting with a monolithic Petri net, we could place all these actions in one file, the common preprocessor. Listing 6.1 shows the sample common preprocessor.

Listing 6.1 Sample COMMON_PRE for the monolithic model

```
function [fire, transition] = COMMON_PRE(transition)
% sample COMMON_PRE for monolithic model
% for painting tennis balls

global global_info
global_info.n2 = n2;

switch transition.name
    case 'tPaintIn'
    % color of deposited token in pTank-1 is 'paint'
        transition.new_color = 'paint';
        fire = 1;

    case 'tBallIn'
    % color of deposited tokens in pTank-1 is 'ball'
```

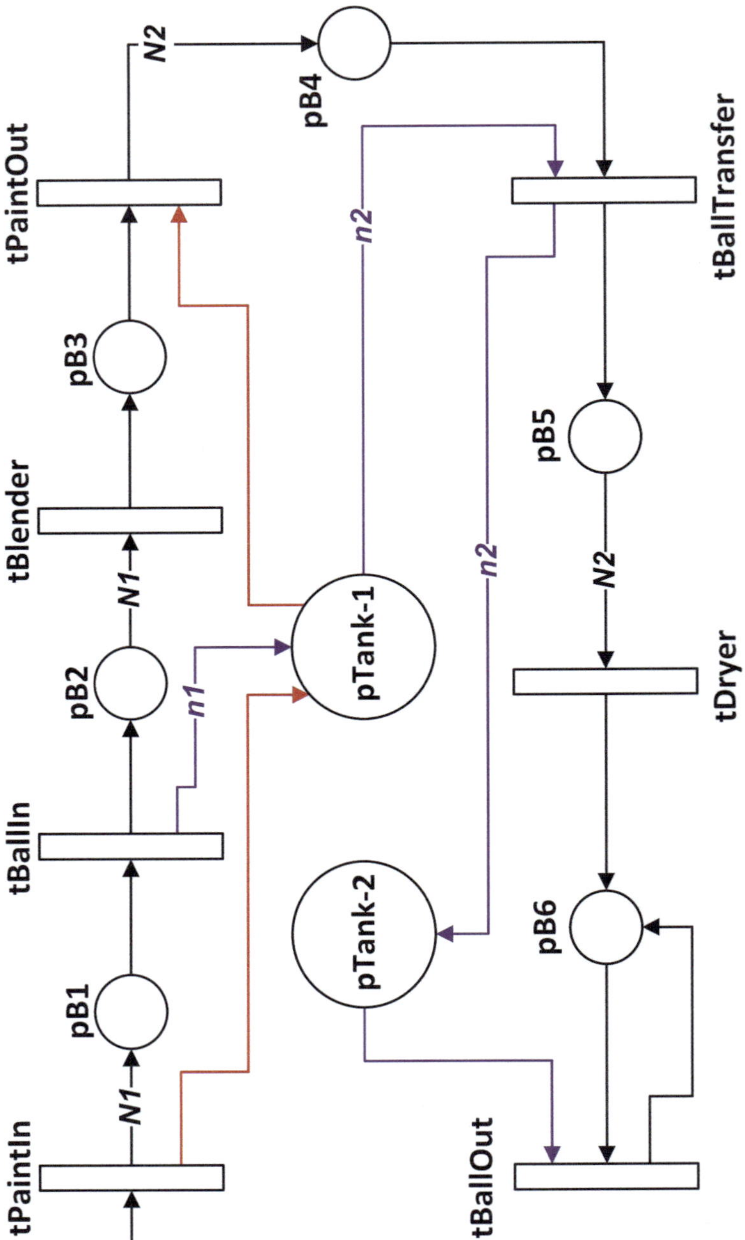

Fig. 6.11 A monolithic Petri net model

```
            transition.new_color = 'ball';
            fire = 1;

        case 'tPaintOut'
        % from pTank-1, select one token with color ...
          'paint'
            tokIDs = tokenAnyColor('pTank-1', 1, ...
                {'paint'});
            transition.selected_tokens = tokIDs;
            fire = tokIDs;

        otherwise
            fire = 1;
end
```

The files for implementation of this monolithic model: (1) Main simulation file, (2) PDF, and (3) COMMON_PRE (Listing 6.1).

6.5.2 *Interaction with External Software*

Up until now, we have assumed that the whole process of tennis ball painting is autonomous—once **tPaintIn** starts, all other activities follow after that. However, let us assume that the following activities can only be triggered by an external triggering mechanism (e.g., an external software sets some global variables):

- **Input signals from an external application**: Only external signals can start the following steps:
  - Filling in paint (**tPaintIn**, which fires only once).
  - Tennis Balls Arrival (**tBallIn**, which will fire **N1** times).
- **Output signals to the external application**: The Petri net must send signals to the external software once the following steps are completed:
  - Draining the paint (**tPaintOut**, which fires only once).
  - Tennis balls are completely emptied from Tank-2.

To realize these external interactions, let us redesign the monolithic Petri net into a modular model; the modular model is shown in Fig. 6.12.

6.5.3 *A Modular Petri Net Model*

We make four simple adjustments to the monolithic model and make it a modular model so that it can exchange data with an external application:

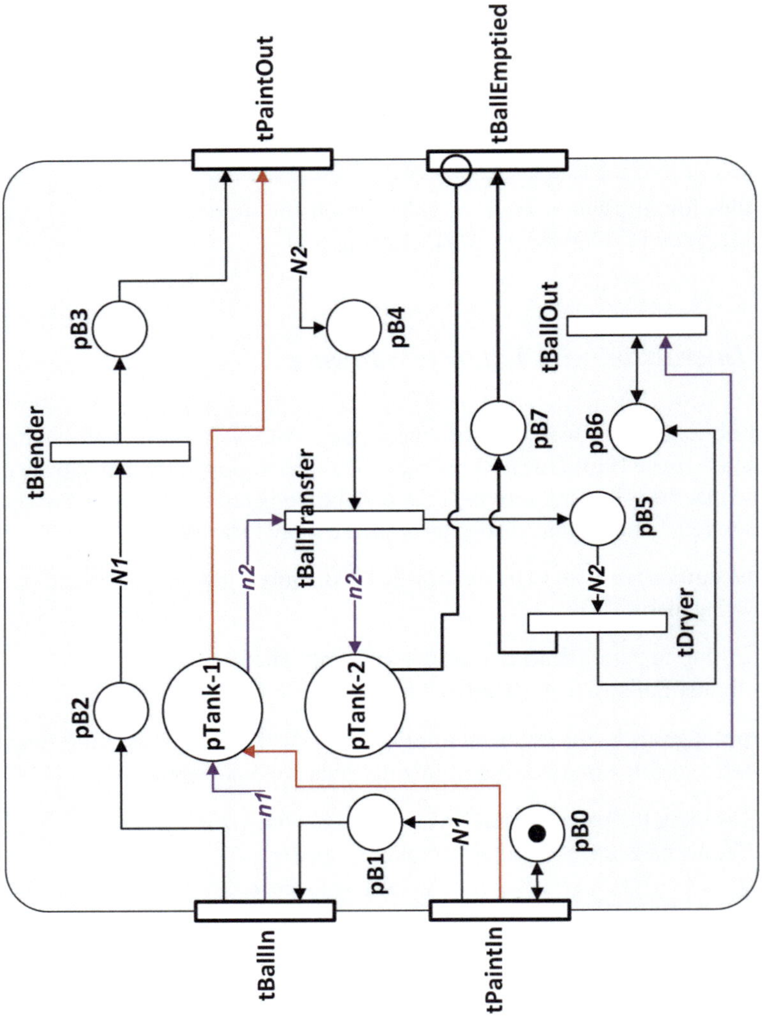

Fig. 6.12 A modular Petri net model

1. **tBallIn** and **tPaintIn** become the **Input Ports** of the module so that they can receive data directly from the external application.
2. A new place (**pB7**) and a new transition (**tBallEmptied**) are introduced. Once **tDryer** is completed, it will deposit a token into **pB7** to inform **tBallEmptied** that the ball emptying steps (by **tBallOut**) has started.
3. A new inhibiting arc is introduced from **pTank-2** to **tBallEmptied**. Once **pTank-2** is emptied and that **tDryer** is completed, **tBallEmptied** will become enabled.
4. **tBallEmptied** becomes the **Output Port** of the module so that it can send data directly to the external application.

Let us call the modular model the "PaintModule." **The files for implementation of this PaintModule**:

- Main simulation file to execute **PaintModule**.
- PDF: We will modify the PDF we used for the monolithic model by making the following changes to it:
  - Add the new elements, **pB7** and **tBallEmptied** and their arcs.
  - Add the inhibiting arc from **pTank-2** to **tBallEmptied**.
  - Declare the Input and Output Ports.

Listing 6.2 shows the sample PDF for PaintModule.

- Modular preprocessor for **PaintModule**: COMMON_PRE of the monolithic model (Listing 6.1) only deals with internal details of the process. Hence, this COMMON_PRE becomes the modular preprocessor for **PaintModule**, "MOD_PaintModule_PRE".
- COMMON_PRE: The common preprocessor should only deal with the interaction between (mainly incoming signals) the external application and the module. Listing 6.3 shows the COMMON_PRE.
- COMMON_POST: The common postprocessor also should only deal with the interaction between (mainly outgoing signals) the module and the external application. Listing 6.4 shows the COMMON_POST.

Listing 6.2 Sample PDF for "PaintModule"

```
% File: PaintModule_pdf.m (PDF of PaintModule)
function [png] = PaintModule_pdf()

png.PN_name = 'PaintModule';   % module name

% set of places (Ps), transitions (Ts), and arcs (As)
png.set_of_Ps = {'pB0','pB1','pB2','pB4','pB5',...
    'pB6','pB7','pTank-1','pTank-2'};
png.set_of_Ts = {'tBallIn','tBlender',...
    'tBallTransfer',...
    'tPaintIn','tPaintOut','tDryer',...
```

```
    'tBallOut','tBallEmptied'};
png.set_of_As = {... % all arcs are declared here
    ...
    ...
    };

% set of inhibiting arcs
png.set_of_Is = {'pTank-2','tBallEmptied',1};

% set of Input Ports and Output Ports
png.set_of_Ports = {'tBallIn', 'tPaintIn', ...
            'tPaintOut', 'tBallEmptied'};
```

COMMON_PRE of "**PaintModule**" for receiving external signals:
Every time an Input Port or an Output Port of **PaintModule** is enabled, COMMON_PRE will be executed. In the common preprocessor, we check whether the external application has already set on the relevant global variable (e.g., "start_PaintIn"). If yes, the corresponding transition can start firing (e.g., **tPaintIn**).

Listing 6.3 COMMON_PRE of "PaintModule"

```
function [fire, transition] = COMMON_PRE(transition)
% sample COMMON_PRE for external interaction

global global_info

switch transition.name
    case 'tPaintIn'
        % for tPaintIn to start, the global variable
        % "start_PaintIn" must be set ON by
        % the external application
        fire = global_info.start_PaintIn;

    case 'tBallIn'
        % for tBallIn to start, the global variable
        % "start_BallIn" must be set ON by
        % the external application
        fire = global_info.start_BallIn;

    otherwise
        % the other transitions are free to start as
        % they do not depend on external triggering
        fire = 1;
end
```

Every time an Input Port or an Output Port of **PaintModule** completes firing, COMMON_POST will be executed. In the common postprocessor, we can send (and receive signals, but not in this example) some signals to the external application. For example, when the draining of the paint is complete (**tPaintOut** has completed firing), the global variable "PaintDraining_Complete" is set to inform the external application.

Listing 6.4 COMMON_POST of "PaintModule"

```
function [] = COMMON_POST(transition)
% sample COMMON_POST for external interaction

global global_info

switch transition.name
    case 'tPaintOut'
        % inform the external application that
        % draining of paint is complete
        % by setting ON the global variable
        % "PaintDraining_Complete"
        global_info.PaintDraining_Complete = 1;

    case 'tBallEmptied'
        % inform the external application that
        % all balls have left Tank-2
        % by setting ON the global variable
        % "Balls_Emptied"
        global_info.Balls_Emptied = 1;

    otherwise
        % nothing to add
end
```

6.6 Concluding Remarks

GPenSIM provides three interfaces (Figs. 6.3, 6.4, and 6.6) that enable a developer to streamline the data exchange between Petri net models and functions in diverse MATLAB toolboxes, external software, and hardware. **All three interfaces consist only of preprocessors and postprocessors.**

Figure 6.3 shows an interface for small monolithic Petri net models, consisting of a few transitions; in this case, the interface consists of specific processors only. Figure 6.4 shows an interface for large monolithic Petri net models, composed of many transitions; in this case, the interface consists of the two common processors (in addition, some hardware-related specific processors). These two interfaces are compatible, so it is possible to switch from one to another. However, it is better to use the interface that uses common processors (Fig. 6.4) as it provides a simpler set of contact points.

Figure 6.6 shows the interface for modular Petri net models, which is not compatible with the other two interfaces due to the different visibility of transitions in modular Petri net models and monolithic Petri net models. In the case of modular Petri nets, the interface consists of two common processors and modular processors (perhaps some hardware-related specific processors in addition).

References

1. Cameron A, Stumptner M, Nandagopal N, Mayer W, Mansell T (2015) Rule-based peer-to-peer framework for decentralised real-time service oriented architectures. Sci Comput Program 97:202–234
2. Davidrajuh R (2018) Modeling discrete-event systems with GPenSIM. Springer International Publishing, Cham
3. Davidrajuh R (2021a) Literature review on modular petri nets. Petri nets for modeling of large discrete systems, pp 77–85
4. Davidrajuh R (2021b) Petri nets for modeling of large discrete systems. Springer, Berlin

Chapter 7
Introduction to Supervisory Control with GPenSIM

This chapter introduces the GPenSIM approach for supervisory control. The approach, presented in Sect. 7.4, is unique as it proposes mapping the controller into processor files for implementation. Since Petri net models of a real-life plant are usually huge, adding a controller with many control places and their arcs to the transitions of the plant will make the resulting controlled system (the plant and the controller) huge and complicated. The GPenSIM approach, while keeping the plant as it is and mapping the controller into processor files, not only reduces the overall size of the controlled system but also allows coding the processors into embedded processors for real-life hardware control.

7.1 The Basics

The chapter (and this book, too) does not present the basics of GPenSIM, as these issues are covered in the introductory book on GPenSIM, "Modeling Discrete-Event Systems with GPenSIM: An Introduction" [2]. Therefore, for a detailed study of GPenSIM, the introductory book on GPenSIM [2] is recommended.

Also, this book does not introduce the Petri Nets; the reader is expected to know some Petri Net theory beforehand. For a formal study of Petri nets, interested readers are referred to books like [1, 3, 6, 7].

Finally, for a study on supervisory control, we recommend the book by Iordache and Antsaklis [4].

R. Davidrajuh, *Petri Nets for Modeling Complex Discrete-Event Systems*, Asset Analytics,
https://doi.org/10.1007/978-981-96-6396-5_7

7.2 Linear Constraints

In supervisory control, we start with a **plant** (a Petri net model); from the simulations of this plant, we see some places of the plant get an undesirable number of tokens (e.g., a place representing a real-world buffer with limited capacity gets more tokens than the buffer can hold). Hence, we will formulate some restrictions (“**constraints**”) as a set of **linear inequalities**. For example, the total number of tokens in places **pA** and **pB** should be less than or equal to five all the time. In this section, we look into how a set of linear constraints can be coded in GPenSIM.

Consider a Petri net that possesses four places, such as **pA**, **pB**, **pX**, and **pZ**. And there are some (hypothetical) constraints, such as

- Constraint 1: Total sum of (tokens in **pA** multiplied by α) and (tokens in **pB** multiplied by β) should be less than or equal to γ.
- Constraint 2: The difference between (tokens in **pX** multiplied by δ) and (tokens in **pY** multiplied by ϵ) should be less than or equal to λ.

Where $\alpha, \beta, \delta, \epsilon, \gamma, \lambda \in N^+$ (natural numbers). Let μ_{pX} represent the number of tokens in **pX**; then, the two constraints in mathematical formulation:

$$\%Constraint\ 1\% \quad (\alpha \cdot \mu_{pA}) + (\beta \cdot \mu_{pB}) \leq \gamma$$

$$\%Constraint\ 2\% \quad (\delta \cdot \mu_{pX}) - (\epsilon \cdot \mu_{pY}) \leq \lambda$$

7.2.1 Coding the Constraints in GPenSIM

In GPenSIM, the left part of the inequality and the right part are coded separately. For example, the first constraint will be coded as follows:

Listing 7.1 Coding constraint 1 in GPenSIM

```
% linear combination (left part of the inequality)
constraints(1).L = {'pA',Alfa, 'pB',Beta};
% limiting value (right part of the inequality)
constraints(1).B = Gamma;
```

The second constraint will be coded as follows:

Listing 7.2 Coding constraint 2 in GPenSIM

```
% linear combination (left part of the inequality)
constraints(2).L = {'pX',Delta, 'pY',-Epsilon};
% limiting value (right part of the inequality)
constraints(2).B = Lambda;
```

Note that the negation operator is transferred to the constant in the code ('-Epsilon').

7.3 Basic Supervisory Control Theory

Assuming we already know the Petri net basics, let us revise the basic Supervisory Control theory, taking GPenSIM in the backseat.

7.3.1 *Incidence Matrices*

Let us focus on a Petri net with n places and m transitions. A dynamic Petri net (a Petri net with marking) can fire if the following enabling condition is met:

$$\mu \geq D^{-} \times \rho \tag{7.1}$$

where μ (dimension: $n \times 1$) is the current marking, D^{-} $(n \times m)$ is the **input incidence matrix**, and ρ $(m \times 1)$ is the vector of enabled transitions.

GPenSIM uses an extended incidence matrix A_e (dimension: $m \times 2n$), composed of D^{+} (**output incidence matrix**) and D^{-} matrices.

$$A_e = [transpose(D^{-}) \mid transpose(D^{+})]$$

If we want D^{-}, D^{+}, or D (**incidence matrix**, $D = D^{+} - D^{-}$) matrices, GPenSIM function `matrixD` will extract these from A_e:

```
[Dm, D, Dp] = matrixD(); % extract D-, D, and D+ ...
    matrices from Ae
```

When a set of transitions fire, the new marking (state), μ', is obtained by the following equation:

$$\mu' = \mu + D \times \rho \tag{7.2}$$

7.3.2 *Place Invariant*

Structural Invariants are properties that depend on the network topology (number of elements and their connections) only and are not dependent on the dynamics (e.g., firing times and marking). In other words, structural invariants are properties of static Petri nets.

A **place invariant** is a **group of places** whose **weighted token sum remains constant** for all possible firings.

Let x be a $(1 \times n)$ dimensional vector representing the set of all places, and the non-zero elements in x represent the places involved in a place invariant. In this case, for different markings μ' and μ:

$$x \times \mu' = x \times \mu \tag{7.3}$$

Since, $\mu' = \mu + D \times \rho$ (Eq. 7.2), Eq. 7.3 becomes:

$$x \times D = 0 \tag{7.4}$$

This means place invariants of a Petri net can be found by solving Eq. 7.4 for integer solutions of x.

7.3.3 *Supervisory Control: The First Step*

We can formulate some control policies as linear constraints; for example, tokens in a group of places must obey some linear constraints. For example, Sect. 8.2.2.1 presents three constraints on the number of token in places **p1** and **p2**:

$$\mu_{p1} \leq 10$$

$$\mu_{p2} \leq 5$$

$$\mu_{p1} - \mu_{p2} \leq 2$$

All these constraints can be put in a matrix form:

$$L \, \mu_P \leq B \tag{7.5}$$

where L ($n_c \times n$, where n_c is the number of constraints) is a matrix of coefficients, μ_P $(n \times 1)$ is the tokens in all places of the plant (**P**, *aka* the uncontrolled system), and B $(n_c \times 1)$ is the vector of limiting values.

To make this Eq. 7.5 an equality, we can introduce the **slack variables** (*aka* **control places**), μ_C $(n_c \times 1)$, into the equation. Hence, Eq. 7.5 becomes:

$$L \, \mu_P \; + \; \mu_C \; = \; B \tag{7.6}$$

Equation 7.6 reveals that it is about a place invariant involving some places in the plant and the control places as the weighted sum (L and I, I is the identity matrix) of tokens in these places are always a constant (B). Hence, we can extend the Eq. 7.4

to include control places too. The new equation to compute the incidence matrix of the controller, D_C, in terms of the plant (D_P) and the constraints (L):

$$x \times D = [L; I] \times [D_P, D_C] = 0 \tag{7.7}$$

In other words, Eq. 7.7 becomes:

$$L \times D_P + D_C = 0 \tag{7.8}$$

Which leads to:

$$\boxed{D_C = -L \times D_P} \tag{7.9}$$

Hence, Eq. 7.9 is the first equation for supervisory control, which computes the incidence matrix of the controller in terms of the incidence matrix of the plant.

To find the initial tokens on the control places, we go back to the Eq. 7.6; the initial tokens in all the places (plant and the controller) must satisfy Eq. 7.6. Hence:

$$L \cdot \mu_{P0} \; + \; \mu_{C0} \; = \; B \tag{7.10}$$

Which leads to:

$$\boxed{\mu_{C0} \; = \; B \; - \; L \cdot \mu_{P0}} \tag{7.11}$$

Equation 7.11 is the second equation for supervisory control, and it computes the initial tokens in the control places (μ_{C0}) in terms of the initial tokens of the plant (μ_{P0}).

7.3.4 Uncontrollable and Unobservable Transitions

In supervisory control, we use two types of transitions that are not fully available for control:

- **Uncontrollable transition**: For an uncontrollable transition, we cannot add arcs *from* control places *to* this transition. However, this transition is observable; thus, we can add arcs *from* this transition *to* the control places.
- **Unobservable transition**: since this transition is unobservable to the controller, arcs cannot be added between this transition and the control places. Hence, an unobservable transition is also uncontrollable.

For the theory behind synthesizing controllers for systems with uncontrollable and unobservable transitions, the interested reader is referred to Moody and Antsaklis [5] and Iordache and Antsaklis [4].

7.4 Supervisory Control with GPenSIM: The Approach

In the GPenSIM approach, supervisory control is done in four stages:

- **Stage A: Studying the plant and its behavior**.
- **Stage B: Synthesizing a controller** for the plant.
- **Stage C: Mapping the logic of the controller into processor files**.
- **Stage D: GPenSIM implementation**; Implementing the controlled system with the plant and the processor files.

Figure 7.1 shows the overall picture, which includes the four stages. The following subsections discuss the four stages in some detail.

7.4.1 Stage A: The Plant

We start with the plant (a Petri net) and study its behavior. Usually, we study the reachability tree and the simulation results (plots of how tokens in various places change with time). When we see that the number of tokens in some places (or a combination of these) is not acceptable, then we go to the next stage.

7.4.2 Stage B: Synthesis of a Controller

The constraints: Since the plant misbehaves (the number of tokens in some places or some combinations are not acceptable), we formulate the constraints; in Sect. 7.2, we learned how a set of constraints can be coded in GPenSIM.

Synthesis of a controller: GPenSIM functions **`supervisorSim`** and **`supervisorSyn`** will create (synthesize) a controller based on the plant and the constraints. The function `supervisorSim` works only if all the transitions are controllable and observable. If some of the transitions are uncontrollable or unobservable, we have to use the function `supervisorSyn`. Sometimes, it will not be possible to create a controller (the constraints are not realizable), and then functions `supervisorSim` and `supervisorSyn` will return an error message.

Note that functions `supervisorSim` and `supervisorSyn` create, if possible, a controller that is composed of a set of places only, known as "**control places**" or "**slack places**". A controller consists of a set of control places and arcs between these control places and the transitions of the plant. The function `supervisorSim` and `supervisorSyn` automatically label the control places as "**slack**"s. If there $\mathbf{n_c}$ number of constraints, the resulting controller would possess $\mathbf{n_c}$ number of control places, named "slack**1**" to "slack$\mathbf{n_c}$".

Verification of the controller: If we manage to create a controller for the plant based on the constraints, then we need to check whether the controlled system behaves

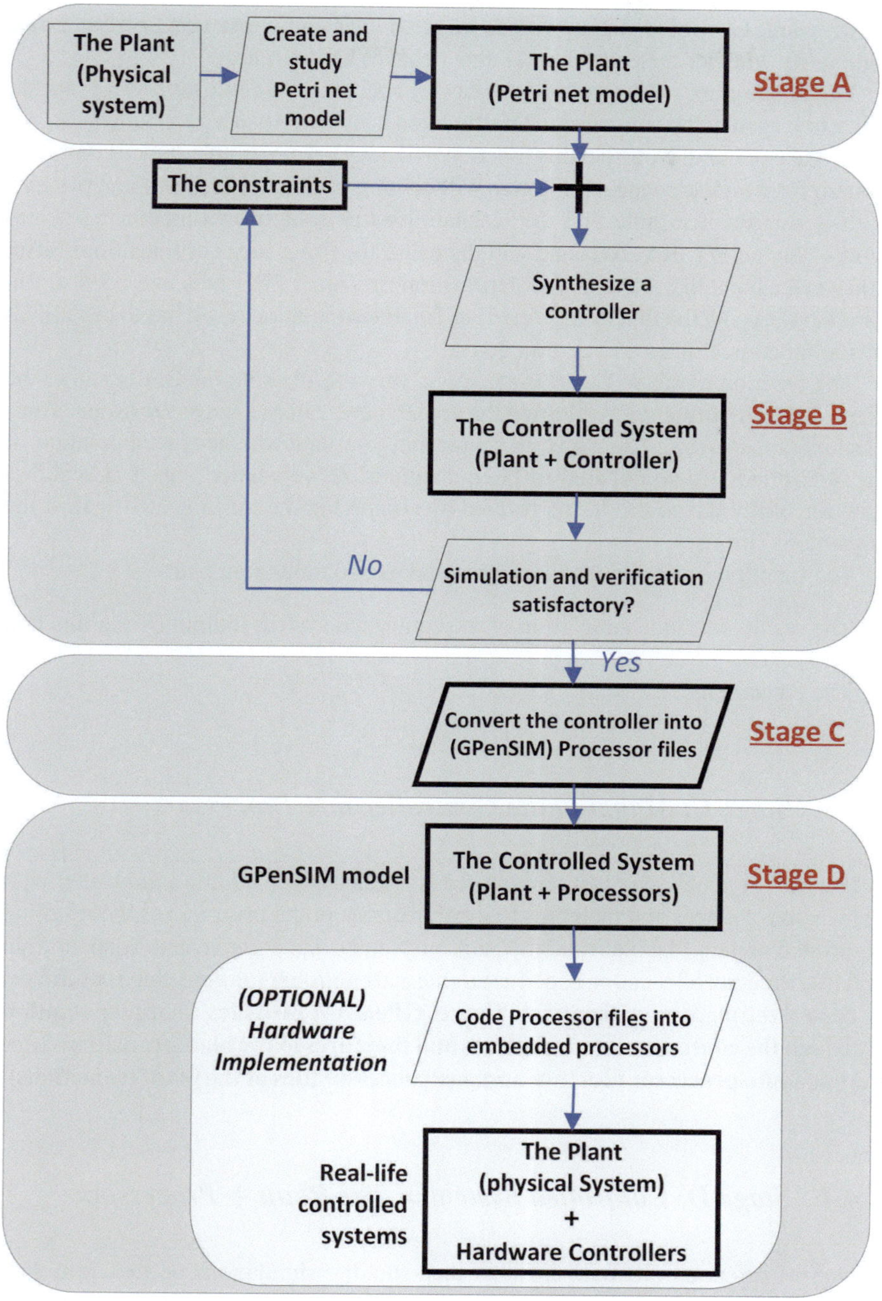

Fig. 7.1 Supervisory control with GPenSIM: an overview

as we want. GPenSIM functions **verifyCOTREE** and **controllerPerform** will verify whether the controlled system behaves appropriately.

The function `verifyCOTREE` verifies by checking the control system's reachability tree against the constraints. This function is not strictly needed, but we can run it for peace of mind. Note that this function will not work on an unbounded controlled system for which the reachability tree will contain infinite tokens for some places.

It is important to note that the reachability tree (output of function `cotree`) works only on P/T Petri Nets and will disregard the firing times of transitions (also, other extensions like colors). For verification of Timed Petri nets, we need to run simulations using the function `gpensim`, and the simulation result has to be verified by the function `controllerPerform`.

The function `controllerPerform` is very useful as it graphically shows the controller's performance by plotting the actual token values against the limits. Thus, the function `controllerPerform` not only verifies whether the simulation of the controlled system adhered to the constraints as we wanted, but it also shows how forcefully the controller performed by comparing the token values against the constraints' limits.

The function `controllerPerform` takes two input arguments:

1. The results from the simulation of the controlled system (output by the function `gpensim`).
2. The constraints.

7.4.3 Stage C: Mapping the Controller into Processors

A Petri net of a real-life plant represented is usually huge. Adding a controller with many control places and their arcs to the transitions of the plant makes the resulting controlled system (the plant and the controller) huge and complicated. Also, how, in real life, the controller can be added as an external controller (an embedded controller) to control the plant is another issue. Hence, **GPenSIM provides a simpler solution by which the controller (control places and their arcs to the plant transitions) are mapped into processor files (pre and postprocessor files of the plant transitions)**.

7.4.4 Stage D: Controlled System = The Plant + Processors

GPenSIM offers an alternative: rather than running simulations on the controlled system (plant + controller), which can be a huge and complicated Petri net, we can simulate the original Petri net (the plant) along with the processors:

- The Petri net of the resulting controlled system will be the same Petri net as the plant, as the controller (the control places along with their arcs to the transitions of the plant) will be mapped into preprocessors and postprocessors of the plant transitions.

- The preprocessors and postprocessors will be programmed into embedded controllers so that these embedded controllers can control their respective transitions (real-life machines or events).

References

1. Cassandras CG, Lafortune S (2009) Introduction to discrete event systems. Springer Science & Business Media
2. Davidrajuh R (2018) Modeling discrete-event systems with GPenSIM. Springer International Publishing, Cham
3. DiCesare F, Harhalakis G, Proth J-M, Silva M, Vernadat F (1993) Practice of Petri nets in manufacturing. Springer, Berlin
4. Iordache M, Antsaklis PJ (2007) Supervisory control of concurrent systems: a Petri net structural approach. Springer Science & Business Media
5. Moody JO, Antsaklis PJ (2012) Supervisory control of discrete event systems using Petri nets, vol 8. Springer Science & Business Media
6. Murata T (1989) Petri nets: properties, analysis and applications. Proc IEEE 77(4):541–580
7. Peterson JL (1981) Petri net theory and the modeling of systems. Prentice Hall PTR

Chapter 8
Supervisory Control with GPenSIM: Two Simple Examples

This chapter presents two simple examples of supervisory control with GPenSIM. The complete GPenSIM code for these examples can be downloaded from this book's companion website. Two sections present one example each; further, each section is divided into four subsections:

- Stage A: The first subsection deals with understanding the plant (studying its behavior).
- Stage B: The second subsection draws constraints and synthesizes a controller.
  Note: The Controlled System = The Plant + The Controller.
- Stage C: The third subsection converts the controller into processor files (pre and postprocessors).
- Stage D: Finally, in the fourth section, the plant and the processors function as the controlled system.
  Note: The Controlled System = The Plant + The Processors.

8.1 Example 15: One Constraint

This section presents a simple example (Example 15) of supervisory control with GPenSIM. This section is divided into four subsections, one for each stage. In addition, this section has two more subsections (the fifth and the sixth) that deal with uncontrollable and unobservable plant transitions.

R. Davidrajuh, *Petri Nets for Modeling Complex Discrete-Event Systems*, Asset Analytics,
https://doi.org/10.1007/978-981-96-6396-5_8

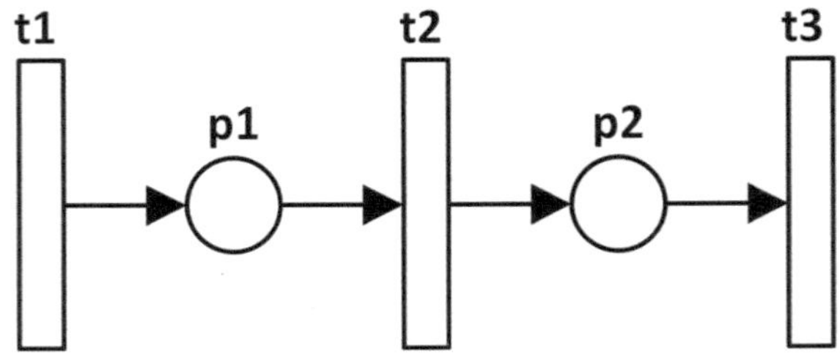

Fig. 8.1 Example 15: The plant

8.1.1 Stage A: The Plant

Figure 8.1 shows the plant—a Petri net—which involves two places, **p1** and **p2**, and three transitions, **t1**, **t2**, and **t3**.

In the plant (Fig. 8.1), transition **t1** is a "*generator*" (in GPenSIM terminology; some literature call it as a "cold start") as **t1** consumes no input tokens but generates new tokens and deposits into **p1**. Transition **t3** is a "*sink*" (in GPenSIM terminology) as **t3** consumes the input tokens but generates no new output tokens. Note that though Petri net in Fig. 8.1 lacks tokens, it is a *dynamic* Petri net as **t1** is enabled and ready to fire. Since there are no initial tokens in this Petri net, in this special case, both static and dynamic Petri nets are the same. Listing 8.1 shows the PDF.

Listing 8.1 PDF (Example 15)

```
function [png] = ex_15_pdf()
png.PN_name = 'Example 15';
png.set_of_Ps = {'p1', 'p2'};
png.set_of_Ts = {'t1', 't2', 't3'};
png.set_of_As = {'t1','p1',1, ... % t1
     'p1','t2',1, 't2','p2',1, ... % t2
     'p2','t3',1}; ... % t3
```

In the main simulation file shown below (Listing 8.2), we study the behavior of the plant.

Listing 8.2 MSF for the simulation of the plant (Example 15A)

```
clear all; clc; close all;
global global_info
global_info.STOP_AT = 30;

%%%%%%%%%%%%% the Plant %%%%%%%%%%%%%%%%%%%%%%%%%%%
pns = pnstruct('ex_15_pdf'); % static Petri net structure
dyn.m0 = {}; % no initial tokens
dyn.ft = {'t1',1, 't2',1.5, 't3',2}; % firing times
plant = initialdynamics(pns, dyn); % create the PNI
sim = gpensim(plant);
figure, plotp(sim, {'p1','p2'});
figure, cotree(plant, 1);
```

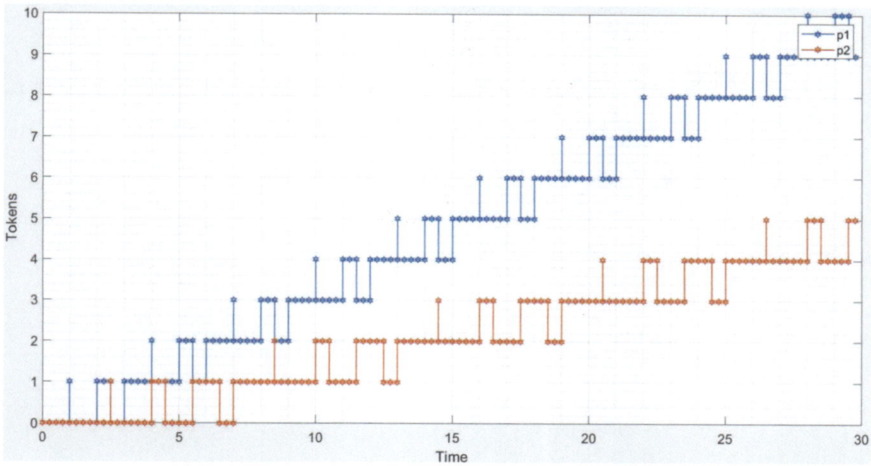

Fig. 8.2 Number of tokens in **p1** and **p2**, starting with zero initial tokens

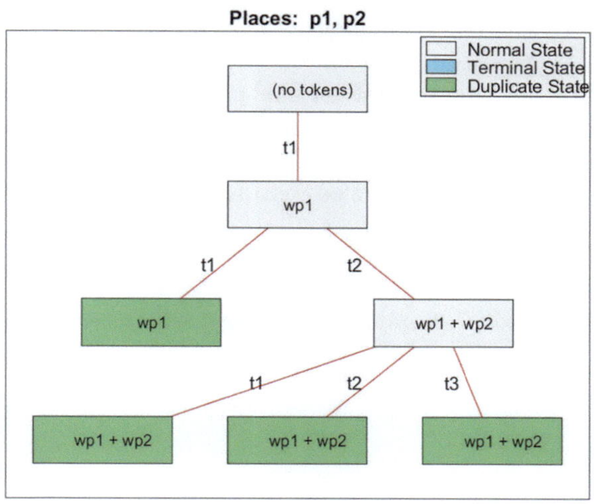

Fig. 8.3 Reachability tree, starting with zero initial tokens

Figure 8.2 shows the simulation results after a simulation time of 30 TU. Figure 8.2 indicates the number of tokens in the places **p1** and **p2**, starting with zero initial tokens and reaching 10 and 4, respectively. Figure 8.3 shows that the reachability tree is unbounded as the number of tokens in **p1** and **p2** increases toward infinity.

8.1.2 Stage B: Synthesis of a Controller

We see from Figs. 8.2 and 8.3 that the number of tokens in **p1** and **p2** increase toward infinity. If these two places represent real-world buffers, they cannot have an infinite number of tokens.

8.1.2.1 The Constraint

Suppose, due to the real-world limitations, the total number of tokens in **p1** and **p2** should not go above 2. Hence, we create a constraint such as

$$\mu_{\mathbf{p1}} + \mu_{\mathbf{p2}} \leq \mathbf{2}.$$

In GPenSIM, this constraint will be coded as follows:

Listing 8.3 Code snippet for defining the constraint

```
% linear combination
constraints(1).L = {'p1',1, 'p2',1};
% the limiting value
constraints(1).B = 2;
```

8.1.2.2 The Controller

Let us assume that all the plant transitions are controllable and observable. By imposing the constraint on the plant, the function `supervisorSim` (or `supervisorSyn`) creates the controller and the controlled system. If a controller is not possible for the stated constraints, then these two functions will return a warning message.

Listing 8.4 Code snippet for creating the controller

```
%%%%%%%%%%%%%% create the Controlled System
[controlledSys, synthesis_ok] = ...
    supervisorSyn(plant, constraints, {},{});
%%%% controller synthesis NOT possible
if not(synthesis_ok)
    disp('Controller NOT possible');
    return
end
```

8.1.2.3 The Controlled System

Listing 8.5 shows the main simulation file for the creation and simulation of the controlled system.

Listing 8.5 MSF for the simulation of the controlled system (Example 15B)

```
global global_info
global_info.STOP_AT = 30;

%%%% the Plant %%%%
pns = pnstruct('ex_15_pdf'); % static part
dyn.m0 = {}; % initial tokens
dyn.ft = {'t1',1, 't2',1.5, 't3',2};  % firing times
plant = initialdynamics(pns, dyn); % create PNI

%%%% constriant (only one constraint)  %%
constraints(1).L = {'p1',1, 'p2',1};
constraints(1).B = 2;

%%%% Controlled System %%
[controlledSys, synthesis_ok] = ...
    supervisorSyn(plant, constraints,{},{});
%%%% controller synthesis NOT possible
if not(synthesis_ok), return; end

sim_CS = gpensim(controlledSys); %%%% run simulations
prncontroller(sim_CS); % print "controller" part
```

Since a controller is possible in this example, GPenSIM function prnsys prints the following info about the controller:

```
======= Controller Composition =======

Control place: slack1
(slack1 -> t1 : 1)
t3 -> slack1 : 1)

Initial markings on the Control places:
slack1: 2
```

Note that GPenSIM automatically labels the control places as "**slack**". Since there is only one constraint, the controller would also possess only one control place named "**slack1**" (if there $\mathbf{n_c}$ constraints, the resulting controller would possess a controller with $\mathbf{n_c}$ control places, named "**slack1**" to "**slackn$_c$**").

The Petri net model of the controlled systems is shown in Fig. 8.4. Note that the control place "**slack1**" is assigned with 2 initial tokens as suggested in the controller composition.

In the plant (Fig. 8.1), as long as **t1** stands as a generator depositing tokens into **p1**, the number of tokens in **p1** (and thus in **p2**) will linearly increase. Hence, the controller forces **t1** from a generator status to a follower of **slack1** (Fig. 8.4). Since **slack1** only has two initial tokens, the maximum number of tokens in **p1** and **p2**, together, will be 2.

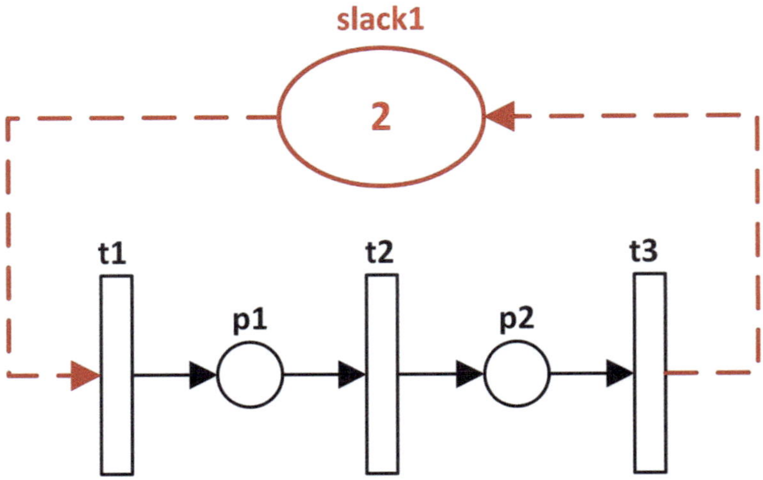

Fig. 8.4 The controlled systems

8.1.2.4 Verification of the Controlled System

In the code snippet shown below (Listing 8.6), we verify whether the controller is working properly when it is added to the plant.

Listing 8.6 MSF (continued from Listing 8.5) for verification of the controlled system (Example 15B)

```
sim_CS = gpensim(controlledSys); %%%% run simulations
prncontroller(sim_CS); % print "controller" part

%%%% print results
figure, subplot(2,1,1), plotp(sim_CS, {'p1'});
subplot(2,1,2), plotp(sim_CS, {'p2'});

%%%%% verify with COTREE %%
figure, COTREE_CS = cotree(controlledSys,1,0);
[OK, TS] = verifyCOTREE(COTREE_CS, constraints);

%%%% verify with simulation result  %%
CONT_PERFORM = controllerPerform(sim_CS, ...
   constraints);
```

The function `verifyCOTREE` compares the reachability tree (the output of the function `cotree`) of the **controlled system** against the constraint, to prove that the **controlled systems** (plant + controller) now behaves adhering to the constraint:

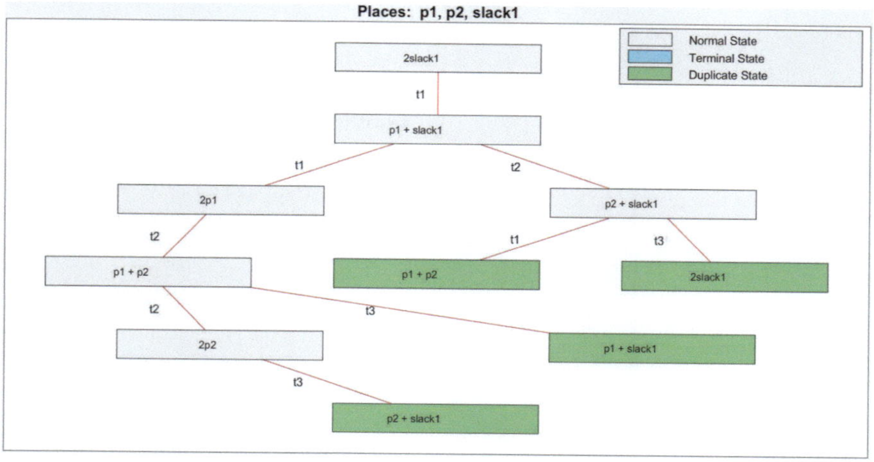

Fig. 8.5 Reachability tree showing the sum of tokens in **p1** and **p2** are always less than or equal to two

```
*******************************************
Now verifying the proposed controller action
!!!!
based on COTREE !!!!
*******************************************
All the constraints are verified !!!!
```

Also, the reachability tree (Fig. 8.5) shows that the sum of tokens in **p1** and **p2** is always less than or equal to 2.

The reachability tree (Fig. 8.5) shows that in one state, **p1** have two tokens (at the same time, tokens in **p2** will be zero), and in another state, **p2** have two tokens (at this time, **p1** will be zero). However, during simulations, these two states will not be reached; see Fig. 8.6. This is because the reachability tree does not consider the firing times of the transitions, whereas, during simulations, timing influences the outcome.

The function `controllerPerform` performs the final verification. Figure 8.7 shows the output of the function `controllerPerform`, in which the sum of tokens in **p1** and **p2** are less than or equal (the limit value) to two, except at time equals to 2.5, the token sum becomes two.

The function `controllerPerform` also returns `CONT_PERFORM` matrix, which possesses the same information presented in Fig. 8.7. See the Appendix for the details on `CONT_PERFORM` matrix.

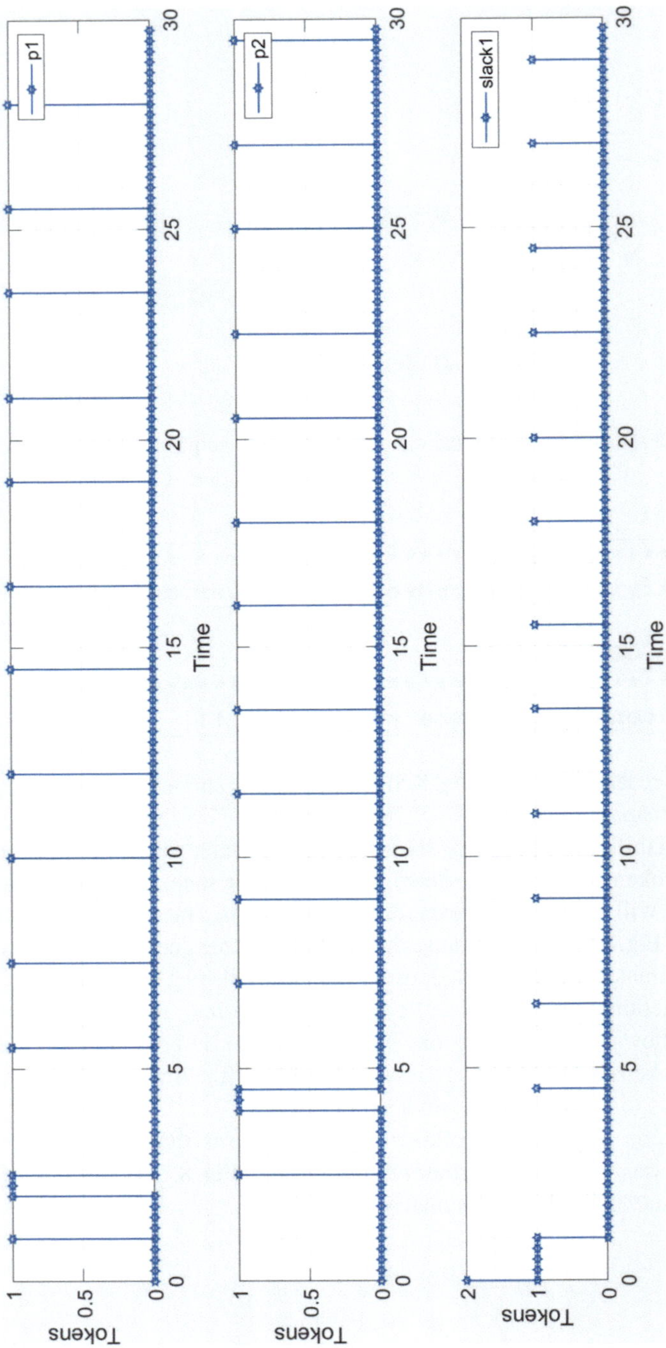

Fig. 8.6 Number of tokens in **p1** and **p2** are always less than or equal to two

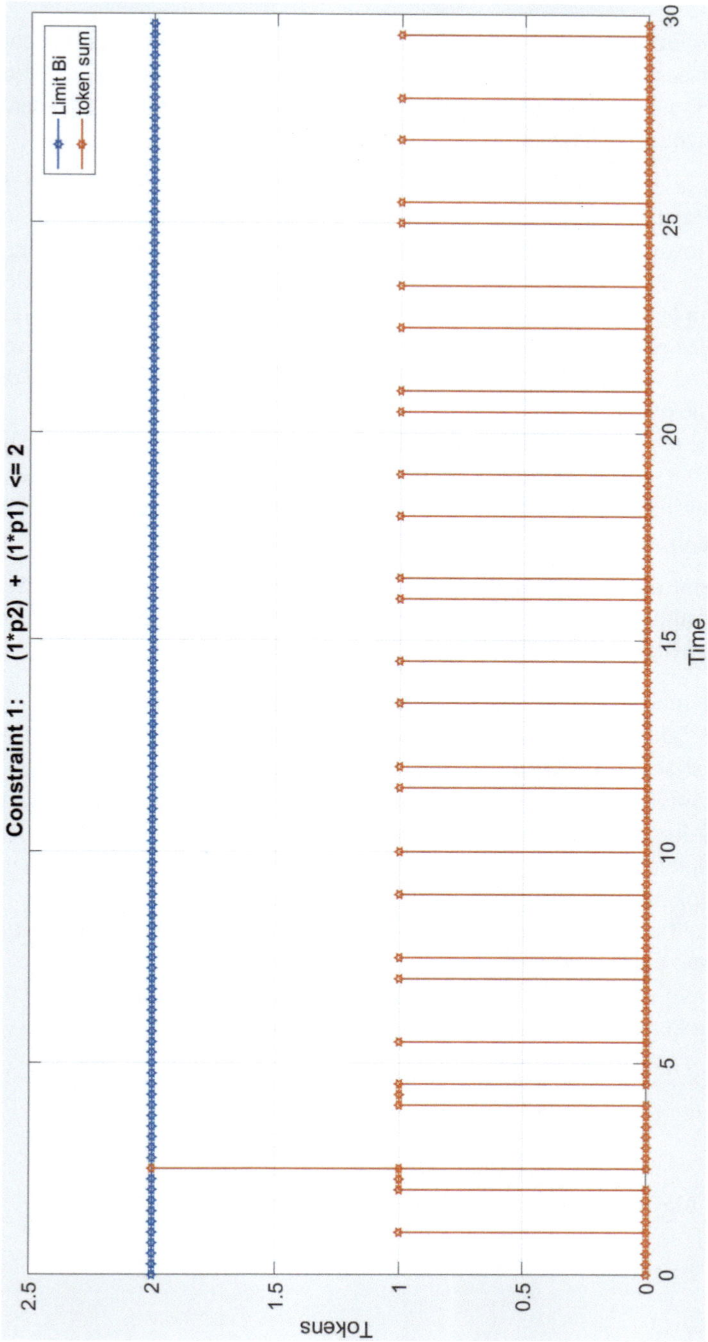

Fig. 8.7 The sum of tokens in **p1** and **p2** versus the limit value

8.1.3 Stage C: Mapping the Controller into Processors

Once the controlled system performs as expected, the next step is to map the controller (control places and their arcs to plant transitions) onto processor files. Hence, the controlled system becomes the original plant and the processor files. The idea behind this approach has two benefits:

1. Usually, a Petri net that represents the controlled system (the plant and the controller) will be more complicated than a Petri net that represents the original plant. However, in this example (Example 15), the controlled system (Fig. 8.4) is as simple as the original plant (Fig. 8.1) as Example 15 is purposely selected to be a simple one to show the GPenSIM approach.
   GPenSIM provides a convenient solution in which the Petri net in the resulting controlled system (the plant and the processor files) will be the same as the Petri net of the plant.
2. Once the controller is mapped into the processor files, the preprocessors and postprocessors will be programmed into embedded controllers so that these embedded controllers can control their respective plant transitions (real-life machines or events).

In the controller (Fig. 8.4), the control place **slack1** only feeds a token to transition **t1** and consumes a token from **t3**. GPenSIM function `control2processors` automatically codes the control logic into the specific processor files:

- First, the function `control2processors` creates one global slack variable (as a part of "global_info" packet) for each control place, and the initial value of the global variable is the corresponding number of initial tokens in the control place.
- Second, this function creates specific preprocessors for the transitions that receive tokens from the control places.
  In Example 15, only "**t1_pre**" will be created as **t1** is the only transition that will receive tokens from the control place.
- Third, the function creates specific postprocessors for the transitions that deposit tokens into control places.
  In Example 15, only "**t3_post**" will be created as **t3** is the only transition that will deposit tokens into the control place.

Listing 8.7 shows the main simulation file for the synthesis of the controller and then mapping the controller into processor files.

Listing 8.7 MSF for mapping the controller into processor files (Example 15C)

```
global global_info
global_info.STOP_AT = 30;

%%%%% the Plant %%%
pns = pnstruct('ex_15_pdf'); % static Petri net structure
dyn.m0 = {}; % initial tokens
dyn.ft = {'t1',1, 't2',1.5, 't3',2};  % firing times
```

```
plant = initialdynamics(pns, dyn); % create the PNI

%%%%% constraint (only one constraint)  %%%%%
constraints(1).L = {'p1',1, 'p2',1};
constraints(1).B = 2;

%%%%% Synthesis of Controller %%%%%
[controlledSys, synthesis_ok] = ...
    supervisorSyn(plant, constraints,{},{});
%%%% controller synthesis NOT possible
if not(synthesis_ok), return; end

%%%% update global_info and create processor files
control2processors(controlledSys);
```

Note that in the MSF shown above (Listing 8.7), after successfully synthesizing a controller, we use the function `control2processors` to code the control logic into processor files. The processor files that are automatically created by the function `control2processors` are shown below in Listings 8.8 and 8.9.

Listing 8.8 "t1_pre" (Example 15C)

```
function [fire, transition] = t1_pre(transition)
% Pre-processor for transition "t1"
%
% this file ("t1_pre.m") is automatically generated
%    by function "writePreProcessors" / "control2processors"

global global_info  % slacks are attached to global_info

fire = 1; % initial assumption
fire = and(fire, global_info.slack1);

% if the transition is allowed to fire
% then reduce the slack variables
%    (remove "tokens" from the slack (control) "places")
if fire
    global_info.slack1 = global_info.slack1 - 1;
end
```

Listing 8.9 "t3_post" (Example 15C)

```
function [fire, transition] = t1_pre(transition)
function [] = t3_post(transition)
% Post-processor for transition "t3"
%
% This file ("t3_post.m") is automatically generated
%   by function "writePostProcessors" / "control2processors"

global global_info  % slacks are attached to global_info

% after firing of the transition
% increase the slack variables
%    (add "tokens" to the slack (control) "places")
global_info.slack1 = global_info.slack1 + 1;
```

Listing 8.10 shows the file "updateGlobalInfo", which is also automatically created by the function `control2processors`.

Listing 8.10 "updateGlobalInfo" (Example 15C)

```
updateGlobalInfo()
% This function updates "global_info" packet
% with slack (control) variables
%
% this file ("updateGlobalInfo.m") is automatically generated
%    by function "writeUpdateGlobalInfo" / "control2processors"

global global_info  % slacks are attached to global_info

global_info.slack1 = 2;
```

8.1.4 *Stage D: The Controlled System = The Plant + The Processors*

In **Stage D**, the final stage, we are going to simulate **the original plant** together with **the processor files** as the controlled system. It is a good idea to create a new folder and do the following:

1. Copy the PDF to the new folder.
2. In **Stage C**, the function `control2processors` generated processors and the file "updateGlobalInfo.m"; move all these files to the new folder.
3. Create the main simulation file (for **stage D**) in this folder.

Listing 8.11 shows the main simulation file for **Stage D**. The simulated controlled system (the original plant together with the processor files) is shown in Fig. 8.8. The simulation results show that this control system behaves the same as the controlled system shown in Fig. 8.4 behaved.

Listing 8.11 MSF for simulation of the plant with processors (Stage D) (Example 15D)

```
global global_info
global_info.STOP_AT = 30;

%%%%%%% add the function "updateGlobalInfo()"
updateGlobalInfo();

%%%%% the Original Plant %%%%%%%%%%%
pns = pnstruct('ex_15_pdf'); % static Petri net structure
dyn.m0 = {}; % initial tokens
dyn.ft = {'t1',1, 't2',1.5, 't3',2};  % firing times
plant = initialdynamics(pns, dyn); % create the PNI

%%%%%% simulate the original plant with processors %%%%%
sim_plant = gpensim(plant);
plotp(sim_plant, {'p1','p2'});
```

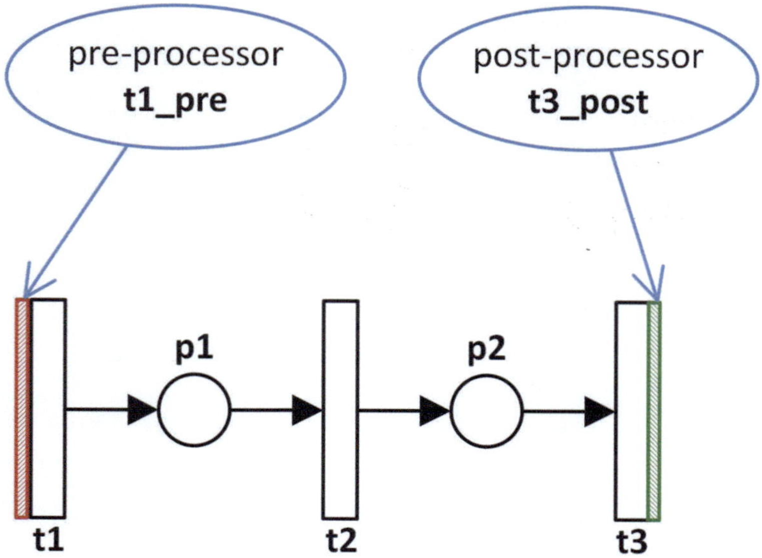

Fig. 8.8 Petri net representing the control system (the original plant + the processor files)

> **<u>CAUTION</u>: As shown in the main simulation file (Listing 8.11), we must remember to insert the function "`updateGlobalInfo()`" after declaring the global_info packet. Otherwise, the main simulation file will not work properly.**

8.1.5 Uncontrollable Transitions

The previous sections dealt with a plant in which all transitions are controllable and observable. In this subsection, we continue with Example 15 but make one transition at a time, as uncontrollable.

Let us make one of the plant transitions uncontrollable, one at a time, and see whether the synthesis of a controller is still feasible. The findings are summarized in Table 8.1 in Sect. 8.1.7.

Table 8.1 Feasibility of synthesizing a controller when a plant transition becomes uncontrollable or unobservable

	Uncontrollable	Unobservable
t1	Case-1: **Controller not feasible*	Case-4: **Controller not feasible*
t2	Case-2: **Controller_0**	Case-5: **Controller_0**
t3	Case-3: **Controller_0**	Case-6: **Controller not feasible*

8.1.5.1 Case-1: t1 is Uncontrollable

```
%%%%%%%%%%%%%% Controlled System ...
    %%%%%%%%%%%%%%%%%%%%%%%%%
[controlledSys, synthesis_ok] = ...
    supervisorSyn(plant, constraints, {'t1'}, {});
```

In this case, the function `supervisorSyn` will report that "controller not feasible". Looking at Fig. 8.4, it is obvious that if **t1** becomes uncontrollable, there is no way we can make the tokens in **p1** and **p2** under 2.

8.1.5.2 Case-2: t2 is Uncontrollable

```
%%%%%%%%%%%%%% Controlled System ...
    %%%%%%%%%%%%%%%%%%%%%%%%%
[controlledSys, synthesis_ok] = ...
    supervisorSyn(plant, constraints, {'t2'},{});
```

In this case, the function `supervisorSyn` will return a controller, the same as in Fig. 8.4 (**Controller_0**). Looking at Fig. 8.4, it is obvious that **t2** is not part of the controller; hence, its controllability does not influence the synthesis of the controller.

8.1.5.3 Case-3: t3 is Uncontrollable

```
Case-3: t3 is uncontrollable
%%%%%%%%%%%%%% Controlled System ...
    %%%%%%%%%%%%%%%%%%%%%%%%%
[controlledSys, synthesis_ok] = ...
    supervisorSyn(plant, constraints, {'t3'},{});
```

In this case, the function `supervisorSyn` will return a controller, the same as in Fig. 8.4. Looking at Fig. 8.4, it is obvious that the controller only observes **t3** (there is an arc from **t3** to **slack1**) and does not control it (there is no arc from **slack1** to **t3**). Hence, if **t3** becomes uncontrollable, the same controller, **Controller_0**, will still be synthesized.

8.1.6 *Unobservable Transitions*

Let us make one of the plant transitions unobservable, one at a time, and see whether the synthesis of a controller is still feasible. The findings are summarized in Table 8.1 in Sect. 8.1.7.

8.1.6.1 Case-4: t1 is Unobservable

```
%%%%%%%%%%%%%% Controlled System ...
    %%%%%%%%%%%%%%%%%%%%%%%%%%
[controlledSys, synthesis_ok] = ...
    supervisorSyn(plant, constraints, {}, {'t1'});
```

In this case, the function `supervisorSyn` will report that "controller not feasible".

8.1.6.2 Case-5: t2 is Unobservable

```
%%%%%%%%%%%%%% Controlled System ...
    %%%%%%%%%%%%%%%%%%%%%%%%%%
[controlledSys, synthesis_ok] = ...
    supervisorSyn(plant, constraints, {}, {'t2'});
```

In this case, the function `supervisorSyn` will return a controller, the same as in Fig. 8.4. Looking at Fig. 8.4, it is obvious that **t2** is not part of the controller; hence, its observability does not influence the synthesis of the controller.

8.1.6.3 Case-6: t3 is Unobservable

```
%%%%%%%%%%%%%% Controlled System ...
    %%%%%%%%%%%%%%%%%%%%%%%%%%
[controlledSys, synthesis_ok] = ...
    supervisorSyn(plant, constraints, {}, {'t3'});
```

In this case, the function `supervisorSyn` will also report that "controller not feasible". As the controller in Fig. 8.4 suggests, we need to observe **t3** (an arc from **t3** to **slack1**); when **t3** becomes unobservable, a controller synthesis is impossible.

8.1.7 Concluding Remarks

Table 8.1 shows that under all cases, including all transitions are controllable and observable, only one controller (**Controller_0**) exists, if it is possible at all. Hence, if we use the function `control2processors`, there will be only one set of processor files will result, the same "**t1_pre.m**" and "**t3_post.m**" presented in Sect. 8.1.3, "Stage C: Mapping the Controller into Processors".

8.2 Example 16: Three Constraints

In this example, we will impose three constraints on a plant to create a controlled system.

8.2.1 Stage A: The Plant

Figure 8.9 shows a Petri net model of a **plant**, which involves three places and four transitions. The generator **t1** is the fastest (has the least firing time), and **t3** is the slowest (has the largest firing time). Because of the firing time disparity, more and more tokens will be stuck in the interim places **p1** and **p2**, as shown in Fig. 8.10.

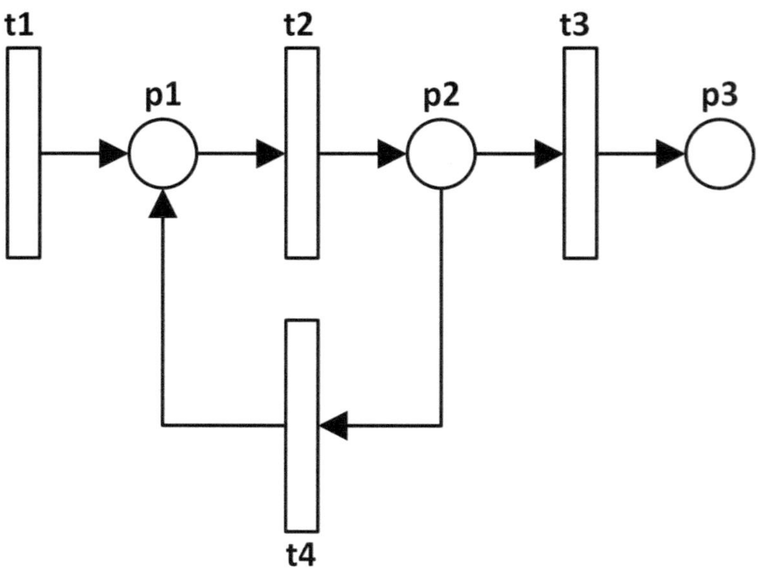

Fig. 8.9 The plant

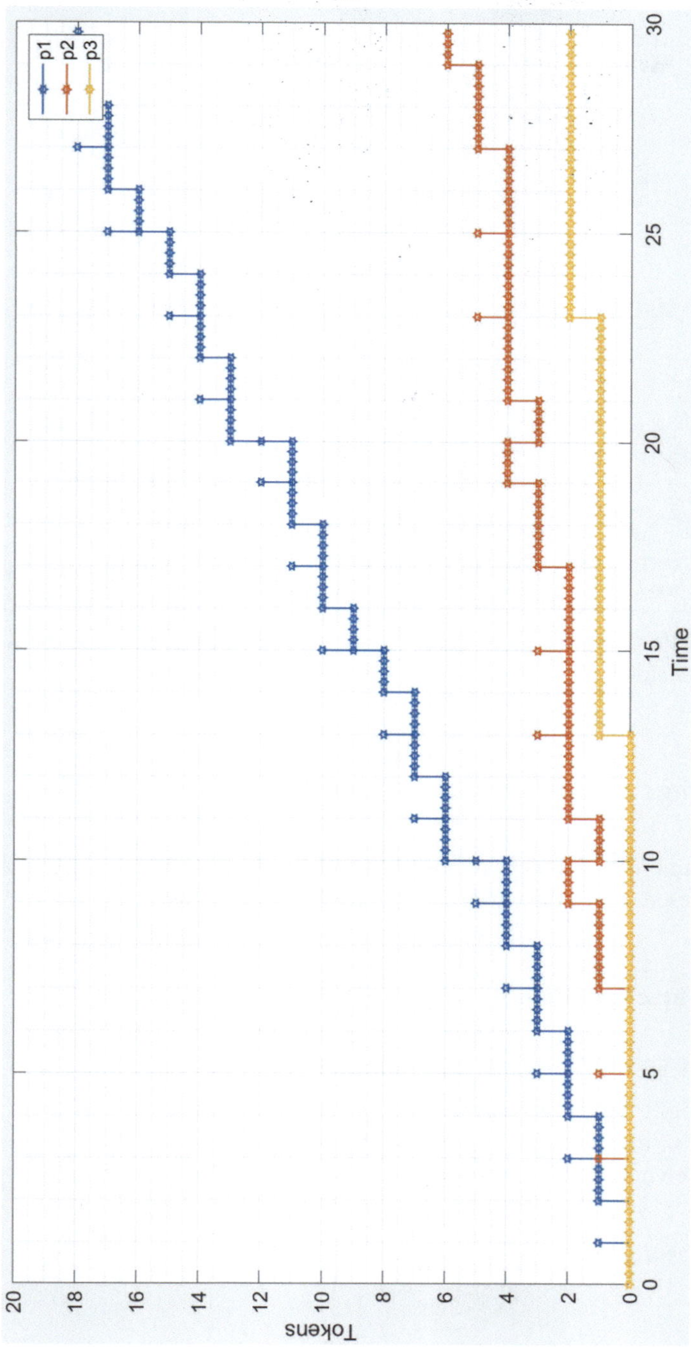

Fig. 8.10 Number of tokens in **p1**, **p2**, and **p3**

Listing 8.12 PDF (Example 16)

```
function [png] = ex_16_pdf()
png.PN_name = 'Example 16';
png.set_of_Ps = {'p1', 'p2', 'p3'};
png.set_of_Ts = {'t1', 't2', 't3','t4'};
png.set_of_As = {'t1','p1',1, ... % t1
            'p1','t2',1, 't2','p2',1, ... % t2
            'p2','t3',1, 't3','p3',1, ... % t3
            'p2','t4',1, 't4','p1',1}; % t3
```

Listing 8.13 MSF (Example 16A)

```
global global_info
global_info.STOP_AT = 30;

%%%%%%%%%%%%% plant %%%%%%%%%%%%%%%%%%%%%%%%%%%%%
pns = pnstruct('ex_16_pdf');
dyn.m0 = {}; % no initial tokens
dyn.ft = {'t1',1, 't2',2, 't3',10, 't4',5};
plant = initialdynamics(pns, dyn);
sim = gpensim(plant);
figure, plotp(sim, {'p1','p2','p3'});
```

Figure 8.10 shows the number of tokens in **p1** increases faster, whereas **p2** and **p3** increases slowly.

8.2.2 *Stage B: Synthesis of a Controller*

Let us assume that the plant represents a simple manufacturing system; thus, the places represent the buffers and, hence, have finite capacities.

8.2.2.1 Three Constraints

Let us come up with the following constraints:

1. Number of tokens in **p1** must be less than or equal to 10.
2. Number of tokens in **p2** must be less than or equal to 5.
3. The difference in the number of tokens in **p1** and **p2** must be less than or equal to 2.

In other words,

$$\mu_{\mathbf{p1}} \leq \mathbf{10}$$

$$\mu_{\mathbf{p2}} \leq \mathbf{5}$$

$$\mu_{\mathbf{p1}} - \mu_{\mathbf{p2}} \leq \mathbf{2}$$

In this simple example, in GPenSIM:

- The first constraint will be coded as follows:

```
constraints(1).L = {'p1',1};
constraints(1).B = 10;
```

- The second constraint:

```
constraints(2).L = {'p2',1};
constraints(2).B = 5;
```

- The third constraint:

```
constraints(3).L = {'p1',1, 'p2',-1};
constraints(3).B = 2;
```

We put all these three constraints together in MSF:

Listing 8.14 MSF, continued from Listing 8.13 (Example 16B)

```
constraints(1).L = {'p1',1};
constraints(1).B = 10;

constraints(2).L = {'p2',1};
constraints(2).B = 5;

constraints(3).L = {'p1',1, 'p2',-1};
constraints(3).B = 2;
```

8.2.2.2 The Controlled System

Listing 8.15 starts with the statements for synthesizing the controller and the resulting controlled system.

Listing 8.15 MSF, continued from Listing 8.14 (Example 16B)

```
%%%%%%%%%%%%%% controlled sys %%%%%%%%%%%%%%%%%%%%
[controlledSys, synthesis_ok] = ...
    supervisorSyn(plant, constraints);
%%%% controller synthesis NOT possible
if not(synthesis_ok)
    disp('Controller NOT possible'); return
end
```

```
%%%%%%%%% run simulation on the controlled sys ...
    %%%%%%%
sim2 = gpensim(controlledSys); % run simulation
figure, plotp(sim2, {'p1','p2'});
prnsys(sim2, dyn); % prnsys includes ...
    "prncontroller" part
```

GPenSIM function `prnsys` (or function `prncontroller`) prints the following info about the controller:

```
======= Controller Composition =======

Control place: slack1
(slack1 -> t1 : 1) (slack1 -> t4 : 1)
t2 -> slack1 : 1)
Control place: slack2
(slack2 -> t2 : 1)
t3 -> slack2 : 1) t4 -> slack2 : 1)
Control place: slack3
(slack3 -> t1 : 1) (slack3 -> t3 : 1) (slack3 ->
t4 : 2)
t2 -> slack3 : 2)

Initial markings on the Control places :
slack1: 10
slack2: 5
slack3: 2
```

The controller composition shows that the controller possesses three control places (as there are three constraints) named **slack1**, **slack2**, and **slack3**.

The Petri net model of the controlled systems is shown in Fig. 8.11. It is clear in the controller shown in Fig. 8.11:

- **slack1** is to ensure that the number of tokens in **p1** never exceeds 10 (constraint 1).
- **slack2** is to ensure that the number of tokens in **p2** never exceeds 5 (constraint 2).
- **slack3** is to ensure that the difference in the number of tokens in **p1** and **p2** never exceeds 2 (constraint 3).

8.2.2.3 Verification of the Controlled System

The code snippet given below (Listing 8.16) shows that the controlled system is first verified via the `COTREE` matrix (from the reachability tree). Then, the simulation result is verified by the function `controllerPerform`.

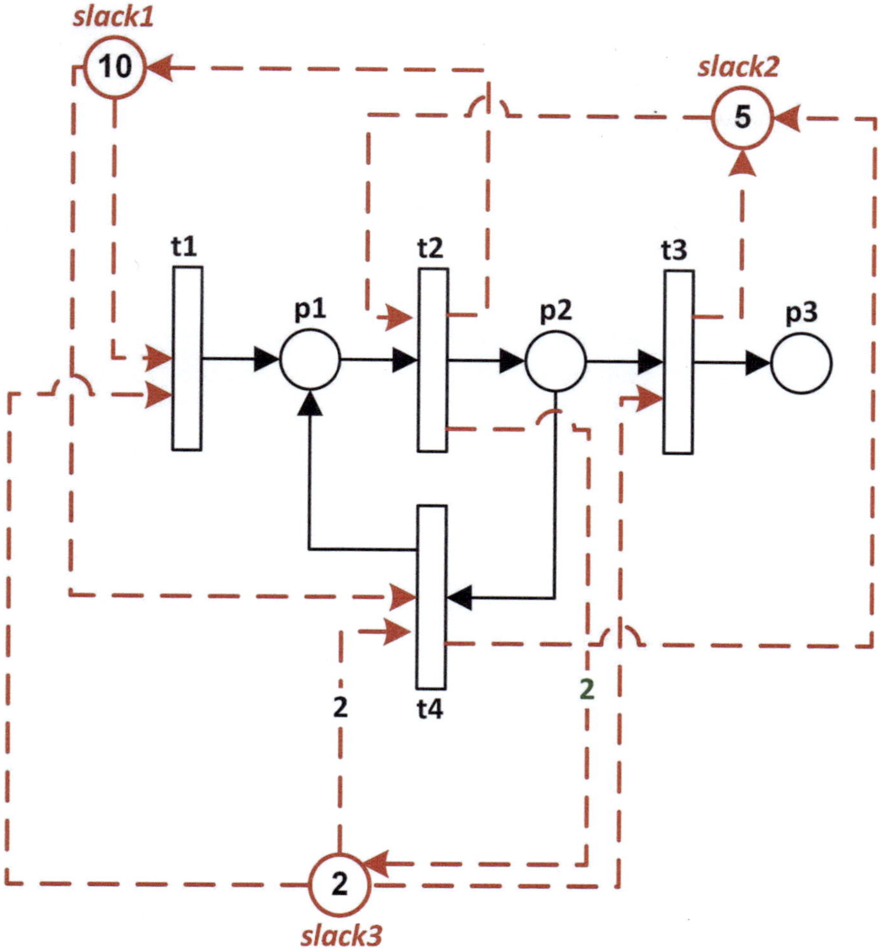

Fig. 8.11 The controlled system

Listing 8.16 MSF, continued from Listing 8.15 (Example 16B)

```
%%% sim2 = gpensim(controlledSys); % run simulation

%%%%%%%%%%%% verify with COTREE   %%%%%%%%%%%%%%
COTREE2 = cotree(controlledSys,0,0); % reachability tree
verifyCOTREE(COTREE2, constraints);

%%%%%%%% verify with simulation result  %%%%%%%%
controllerPerform(sim2, constraints);,
```

The **controlled systems** (**plant + controller**) now behaves adhering to the constraints: Fig. 8.12 shows that the number of tokens in **p1** is always less than or equal to 10, and the number of tokens in **p2** is always less than or equal to 5. Also, the difference between the number of tokens in **p1** and **p2** is always less than or equal to 2.

It is not possible to verify whether the controller behaves correctly by looking into the reachability tree (Fig. 8.13) as it will be incomprehensible. Instead, we use the function `verifyCOTREE`.

Function `verifyCOTREE` outputs the following info:

```
**********************************************
Now verifying the proposed controller action !!!!
**********************************************
Please wait ......
All the constraints are verified !!!!
```

The final checking is by the function `controllerPerform`. This function outputs three figures, Figs. 8.14, 8.15, and 8.16.

Figure 8.14 is for constraint 1; this figure shows that the number of tokens in **p1** is always less than 10. However, here we see that the controller **over-performs** (it is an "overkill"), as the number of tokens in **p1** is less than half of the allowed maximum limit.

Figure 8.15 is for constraint 2; this figure shows that the number of tokens in **p2** is always less than 5.

Figure 8.16 is for constraint 3; this figure shows that the difference in the number of tokens in **p2** and **p1** is always less than or equal to 2. This figure indicates that the token sum hits the maximum allowed value at two different times.

8.2.3 Stage C: Mapping the Controller into Processors

Once the controlled system performs as expected, we will map the controller (control places and their arcs to plant transitions) into processor files.

In the controller (Fig. 8.11):

- There are three control places, **slack1**, **slack2**, and **slack3**.
- These three control places input tokens to all four transitions.
- These three control places get tokens from **t2**, **t3**, and **t4**; all except **t1**.

Hence, GPenSIM built-in function `control2processors` automatically codes the control logic into the specific processor files:

- First, the function `control2processors` creates three global slack variables (as a part of "global_info" packet), one for each control place, and the initial value of the global variable is the corresponding number of initial tokens in the control place.

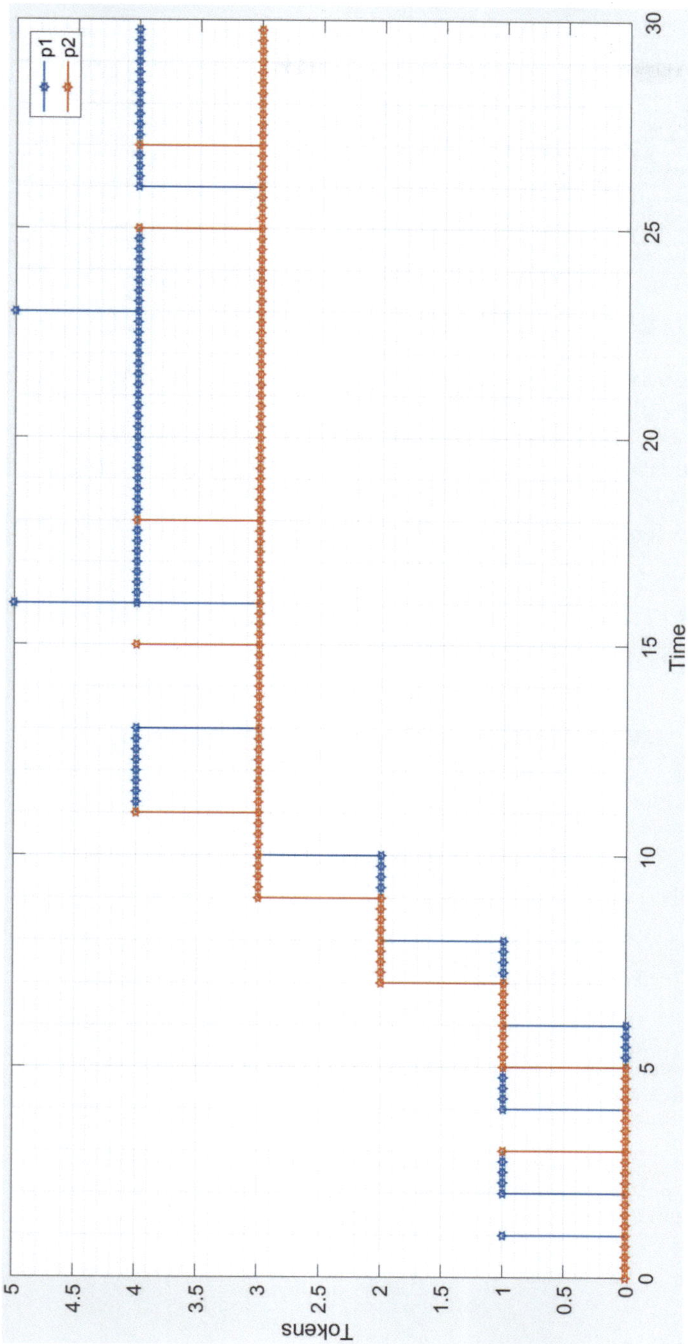

Fig. 8.12 The effect of controller on the number of tokens in **p1** and **p2**

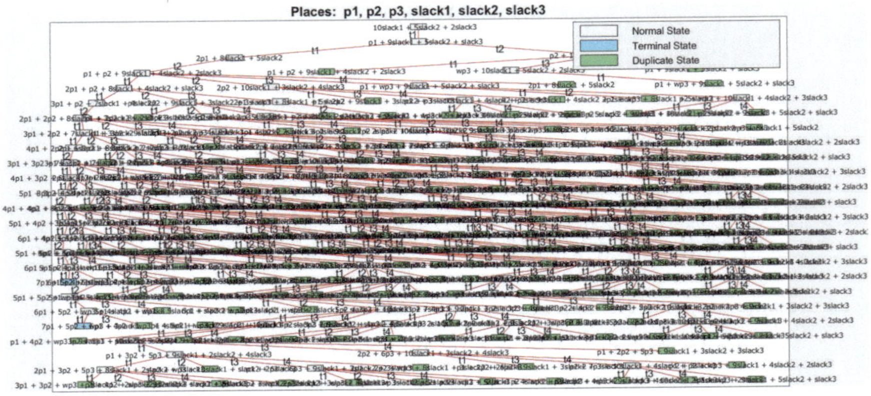

Fig. 8.13 Reachability tree showing the number of tokens in places **p2** and **p3** are always less than or equal to one

- Second, this function creates specific preprocessors for all four transitions as they receive tokens from the control places.
- Third, the function creates specific postprocessors for the transitions **t2**, **t3**, and **t4**.

Listing 8.17 shows the main simulation file for the synthesis of the controller and then mapping the controller into processor files.

Listing 8.17 MSF for mapping the controller into processor files (Example 16C)

```
clear all; clc; close all;
global global_info
global_info.STOP_AT = 100;

%%%%%%%%%%%%% plant %%%%%%%%%%%%%%%%%%%%%%%%%%%
pns = pnstruct('ex_16_pdf');
dyn.m0 = {}; % no initial tokens
dyn.ft = {'t1',1, 't2',2, 't3',10, 't4',5};
plant = initialdynamics(pns, dyn);

%%%%%%%%%%%%% constriants %%%%%%%%%%%%%%%%%%%%%%%%%%%
constraints(1).L = {'p1',1}; constraints(1).B = 10;
constraints(2).L = {'p2',1}; constraints(2).B = 5;
constraints(3).L = {'p1',1, 'p2',-1};
        constraints(3).B = 2;

%%%%%%%%%%%%% controlled sys %%%%%%%%%%%%%%%%%%%%%%%%%%%
[controlledSys, synthesis_ok] = ...
    supervisorSyn(plant, constraints);
if not(synthesis_ok), return; end

%%%%%%%%%%%%% Implement the controller %%%%%%%%%%%%%%%%
%%%% update global_info and create processor files
control2processors(controlledSys);
```

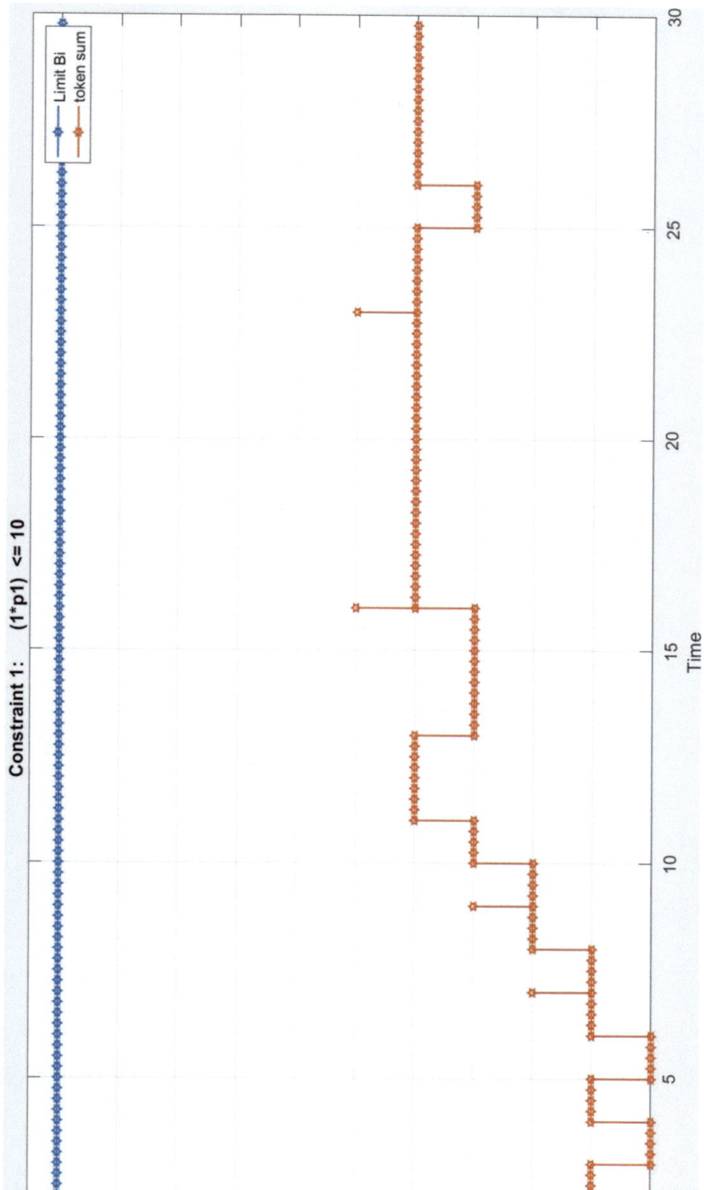

Fig. 8.14 Performance of controller against the first constraint

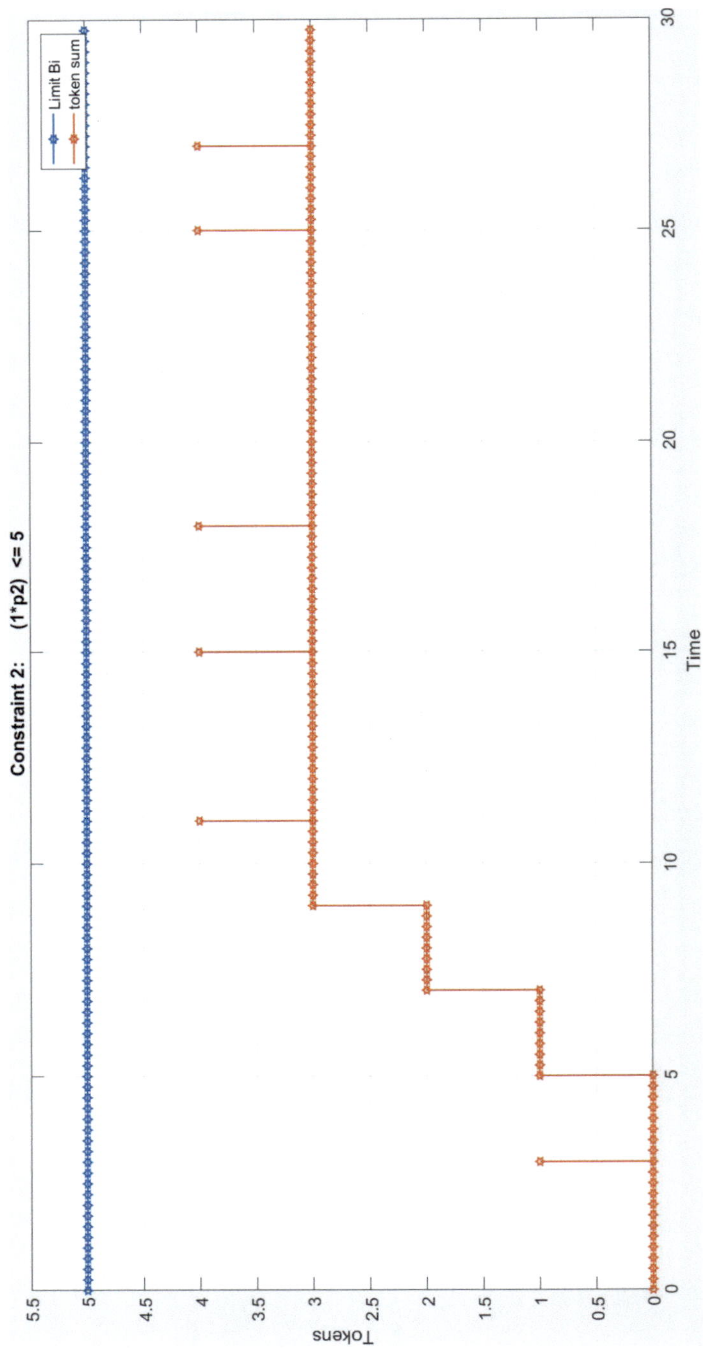

Fig. 8.15 Performance of controller against the second constraint

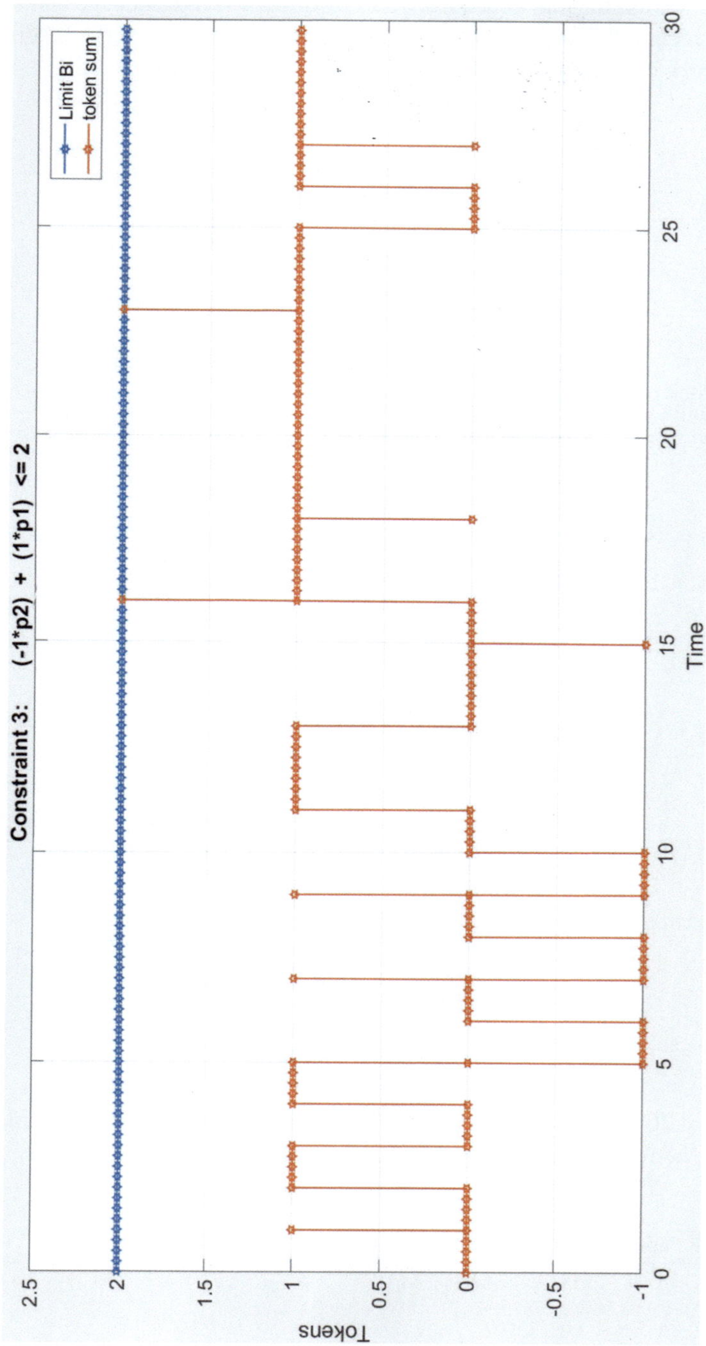

Fig. 8.16 Performance of controller against the third constraint

Note that in the MSF shown above (Listing 8.17), after successfully synthesizing a controller, we use the function `control2processors` to code the control logic into eight processor files (four preprocessors and three postprocessors). Listings 8.18 and 8.19 show one of the preprocessors and one of the postprocessors.

Listing 8.18 "t1_pre" (Example 16C)

```
function [fire, transition] = t4_pre(transition)
% Pre-processor for transition "t4"
%
% this file ("t4_pre.m") is automatically generated
%    by function "writePreProcessors" / "control2processors"

global global_info  % slacks are attached to global_info

fire = 1; % initial assumption
fire = and(fire, global_info.slack1);
fire = and(fire, ge(global_info.slack3,2));

% if the transition is allowed to fire
% then reduce the slack variables
%    (remove "tokens" from the slack (control) "places")
if fire
     global_info.slack1 = global_info.slack1 - 1;
     global_info.slack3 = global_info.slack3 - 2;
end
```

Listing 8.19 "t2_post" (Example 16C)

```
function [] = t2_post(transition)
% Post-processor for transition "t2"
%
% this file ("t2_post.m") is automatically generated
%   by function "writePostProcessors" / "control2processors"

global global_info  % slacks are attached to global_info

% after firing of the transition
% increase the slack variables
%    (add "tokens" to the slack (control) "places")
global_info.slack1 = global_info.slack1 + 1;
global_info.slack3 = global_info.slack3 + 2;
```

Listing 8.20 shows the file "updateGlobalInfo", which is also automatically created by the function `control2processors`.

Listing 8.20 "updateGlobalInfo" (Example 16C)

```
function [] = updateGlobalInfo()
% This function updates "global_info" packet
% with slack (control) variables
%
% this file ("updateGlobalInfo.m") is automatically generated
```

```
%    by function "writeUpdateGlobalInfo" / "control2processors"

global global_info  % slacks are attached to global_info

global_info.slack1 = 10;
global_info.slack2 = 5;
global_info.slack3 = 2;
```

8.2.4 *Stage D: The Controlled System = The Plant + The Processors*

For **Stage D**, let us copy and move the following files to a new folder:

1. Copy the PDF to the new folder.
2. In **Stage C**, the function `control2processors` generated processors and the file "updateGlobalInfo.m"; move all these files to the new folder.
3. Create the main simulation file (for **Stage D**, Listing 8.21) in this folder.

In the main simulation file shown below (Listing 8.21), we simulate **the original plant** together with **the processor files**. The simulated plant (together with the processor files) is shown in Fig. 8.17. The simulation of this plant with the processors behaves exactly as the controlled system shown in Fig. 8.11 behaved.

Listing 8.21 MSF for simulation of the plant with processors (Example 16D)

```
clear all; clc; close all;
global global_info
global_info.STOP_AT = 100;

%%%%%%%%%%%%% plant %%%%%%%%%%%%%%%%%%%%%%%%%%%
pns = pnstruct('ex_16_pdf');
dyn.m0 = {}; % no initial tokens
dyn.ft = {'t1',1, 't2',2, 't3',10, 't4',5};
plant = initialdynamics(pns, dyn);

% !!!!! Important !!!!!
% add the function "updateGlobalInfo()"
updateGlobalInfo();

%%%%%%%%%%%%% constriants %%%%%%%%%%%%%%%%%%%%%%%%%%%
constraints(1).L = {'p1',1}; constraints(1).B = 10;
constraints(2).L = {'p2',1}; constraints(2).B = 5;
constraints(3).L = {'p1',1, 'p2',-1};
        constraints(3).B = 2;

%%%%%%%%%%%%% run simulations %%%%%%%%%%%%%%%%%%%%%%%%%%%
sim_plant = gpensim(plant);
figure, plotp(sim_plant, {'p1','p2'});

%%%%%%%%%%%%% verfication of controller %%%%%%%%%%%%%%%%
CONT_PERFORM = controllerPerform(sim_plant, constraints);
```

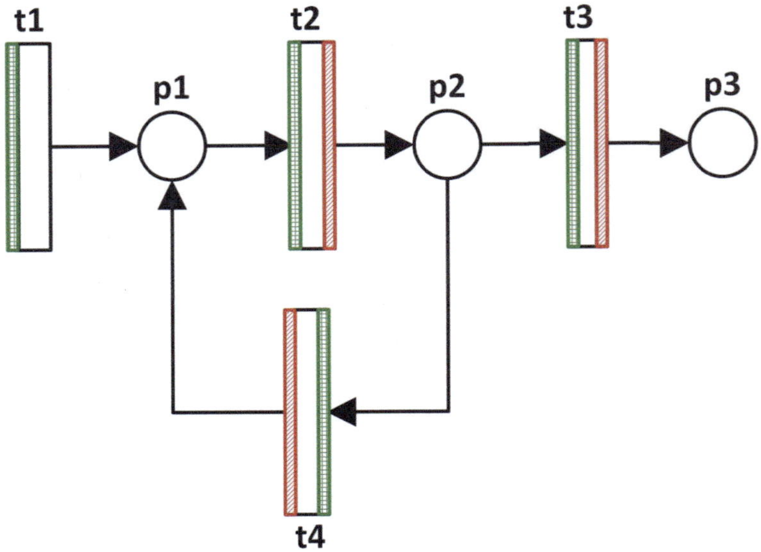

Fig. 8.17 Petri net representing the control system (the original plant + the processor files)

> **CAUTION: As shown in the main simulation file for "Stage D" (Listing 8.21), we must remember to insert the function "`updateGlobalInfo()`" after declaring the global_info packet. Otherwise, the main simulation file will not work properly.**

Chapter 9
GPenSIM Built-in Functions for Supervisory Control

This chapter lists the important GPenSIM built-in functions for supervisory control. Table 9.1 presents a summary of these functions.

9.1 Synthesis of a Controller

For supervisory control, the two most used GPenSIM built-in functions are `supervisorSim` and `supervisorSyn`; these two functions synthesize a controller.

Out of these two functions, `supervisorSyn` is the most used function as it synthesizes a controller even if the plant possesses some transitions that are uncontrollable or unobservable. However, `supervisorSyn` is not a "pure" GPenSIM built-in function as it uses a file from an external package (explained later in Sect. 9.1.2).

`supervisorSim` is a weaker function compared with `supervisorSyn` as it works only when all the transitions are controllable and observable. Hence, we don't need `supervisorSim` as `supervisorSyn` will work for all situations. However, `supervisorSim` is a "pure" GPenSIM built-in function as the complete code is developed as a part of GPenSIM version 11.

9.1.1 Function `supervisorSim`

The function `supervisorSim` can be used for the synthesis of the controller when **all transitions of the plant are controllable and observable**. Listings 9.1–9.3 show the function `supervisorSim`, piece by piece.

R. Davidrajuh, *Petri Nets for Modeling Complex Discrete-Event Systems*, Asset Analytics,
https://doi.org/10.1007/978-981-96-6396-5_9

Table 9.1 GPenSIM built-in functions for supervisory control

Function	Description
`supervisorSim`	Synthesis of a controller for a plant in which all transitions are controllable and observable
`supervisorSyn`	Synthesis of a controller for a plant in which some transitions are uncontrollable or unobservable. This function uses the function `mro_adm` in the package "spnbox" by Marian V. Iordache
`verifyCOTREE`	Checks the controlled system's reachability tree against the constraints to make sure whether the controlled systems behaved as expected
`controllerPerform`	From the simulation result, this function verifies whether the controlled system adheres to the constraints and shows how forcefully the controller performs by comparing the token values against the constraints
`control2processors`	Automatically creates the processor files that include the control logic of the controller
`prnsys`	Prints the plant and the controller in an intelligible manner
`prncontroller`	Prints the controller in an intelligible manner

The first block, Listings 9.1, shows the header. It shows that the input arguments are `pni` and constraints, where `pni` is the Petri net structure with initial dynamics, representing the plant. The output argument of the function `supervisorSim` is the `PN`, which represents the Petri net run-time structure representing the controlled system (plant + controller).

Listing 9.1 Function `supervisorSim`

```
function [PN, synthesis_ok] = supervisorSim(pni, ...
    constraints)
%     supervisor Simple
%
%    Purpose: Synthesis of a supervisor when
%             all transitions are assumed
%             controllables & observables
%
%   Input arguments:
%        1) Plant: pni - Petri net with initial ...
    dynamic
%            (output of in initialdynamics)
%        2) Constraints
%
%   Output argument:
%        1. Controlled System as PN structure
%        2. synthesis_ok: whether synthesis was ...
    successful or not
%
```

```
%        (use 'printsys' to printout the ...
   controlled system details)
%        (use gpensim to run simulations on the ...
   controlled sys)
%
%   Reggie.Davidrajuh@uis.no    (c)  08.March.2024
```

The second block (Listing 9.2) shows the extraction of **L** and **B** values by the function `extractLB` (**L**: the coefficient matrix, and **B**: the constant (or limiting) vector) from the constraints. Then, extraction of the incidence matrix (**Dp**) by the function `gpensim_2_PNCT`. Once we have the values for **L**, **B**, and **Dp**, we can synthesize the controller: compose the controller's incidence matrix (**Dc**) and the initial values for the control places (**muC0**).

Listing 9.2 Function `supervisorSim`, continued from Listing 9.1

```
global PN
PN = pni;

synthesis_ok = true;  % initial assumption

% extract L and B from constraints, and Dp
[L, B] = extractLB(constraints);
% incidence matrix of plant
[¬,¬,Dp] = gpensim_2_PNCT(PN.incidence_matrix);
mu0 = transpose(PN.X);

%%%%%%%%%% controller synthesis   %%%%%%%%%%
Dc = -1 * L * Dp;  % incidence matrix of controller
muC0 = B  - L * mu0; % initial tokens in control ...
   places

if any(muC0 < 0)
    disp('Synthesis suggests negative initial ...
       tokens ');
    disp('for some slack (control) places!! '); ...
       disp(' ');
    disp(['** Suggested initial tokens : [', ...
        int2str(transpose(muC0)), ']']);
    disp(' '); disp('Either, reduce initial ...
       tokens in plant places');
    disp('or, relax the constraints');
    synthesis_ok = false;
    return
end
```

The final block (Listing 9.3) is for combining the controller with the plant to make the controlled system. Function `imControlledSys` combines the incidence matrix of the controller together with the incidence matrix of the plant. The function addSlacks2GP adds the control places to the global places and assigns the initial marking (muC0) to the control places.

Listing 9.3 Function supervisorSim, continued from Listing 9.2

```
%%%%%%%%%%%% Update Controlled Sys %%%%%%%%%%%%
% update incidence matrix for the controlled system
imControlledSys(Dc, size(L,1));

% add slack variables to the list of global_places
addSlacks2GP(muC0);
```

9.1.2 *Function* supervisorSyn

In the previous subsection, we assumed all transitions are observable and controllable. This subsection will take **some of the transitions as uncontrollable and unobservable**. In this case, the function supervisorSim cannot be used; only supervisorSyn can help.

The function supervisorSyn on the core uses function mro_adm, which is a function in the package "**spnbox**" and written by **Marian V. Iordache**. The package "spnbox" accompanies the book by Iordache and Antsaklis [1].

Listings 9.4–9.7 show the function supervisorSyn.

The first block (Listing 9.4) is the header. The input arguments are pni (the Petri Net with initial dynamics) representing the plant, the constraints, the set of uncontrollable transitions, and the set of unobservable transitions. The output arguments are PN representing the Petri Net dynamic structure for the controlled system, and "synthesis_ok" is a Boolean variable stating whether the synthesis was successful or not.

Listing 9.4 Function supervisorSyn

```
function [PN, synthesis_ok] = supervisorSyn(pni, ...
                  constraints, uncontrollables, ...
                      unobservables)
% function [PN, synthesis_ok] = ...
    supervisorSyn(pni, ...
%                   constraints, uncontrollables, ...
    unobservables)
%       supervisor synthesizer
%
%     Purpose: Synthesis of a supervisor when
%              some transitions are
%              uncontrollables and/or unobservables
%
```

```
%   Input arguments:
%        1) Plant: pni - Petri net with initial ...
    dynamic
%             (output of in initialdynamics)
%        2) Constraints: set of linear inequalities
%        3) uncontrollables: set of uncontrollable ...
    trans
%        4) unobservables: set of unobservable trans
%
%
%   Output argument:
%        Controlled System as PN
%   (use 'printsys' to printout the controlled sys)
%   (use 'gpensim' to run simulations on the ...
    controlled sys)
%
%   Functions used:  mro_adm
%                    extractLB, gpensim_2_PNCT,
%                    imControlledSys, addSlacks2GP,
%                    get_transitions
%
%   NOTE: This functions uses "mro_adm", which is
%         function in the package "spnbox" and ...
    written by
%         Marian V. Iordache.
%         Package "spnbox" accompany the book:
%         Iordache and Antsaklis (2007) n
%
%   Reggie.Davidrajuh@uis.no   (c)  08.March.2024
```

The second block (Listing 9.5) extracts **L**, **B**, the incidence matrix of the plant (**Dp**), and the initial marking on the plant so that the controller can be synthesized in the next block (Listing 9.6).

Listing 9.5 Function `supervisorSyn`, continued from Lisiting 9.4

```
global PN
PN = pni;

% extract L and B from constraints
[L, B] = extractLB(constraints);

% incidence matrix and mu0 of plant
[¬,¬,Dp] = gpensim_2_PNCT(PN.incidence_matrix);
mu0 = transpose(PN.initial_marking);
```

In the third block (Listing 9.6), we use the function '**`mro_adm`**' from the spnbox toolbox written by Marian V. Iordache. The function `mro_adm` is for realizing **L1** and **B1**, in case there are uncontrollable or unobservable transitions.

Listing 9.6 Function supervisorSyn, continued from Lisiting 9.5

```
%%%%%%%%%%%%%%%%%%%%%%%%%%%%%%%%%%%%%%%%%%%%%%%%%%%%%
% Some transitions are uncontrollable/unobservable
%%%%%%%%%%%%%%%%%%%%%%%%%%%%%%%%%%%%%%%%%%%%%%%%%%%%%
nuc = 0; uc_ts = []; % initial assumption on ...
    uncontrollables
nuo = 0; uo_ts = []; % initial assumption on ...
    unobservables

if ge(nargin, 3)  % get the set of uncontrollable ...
    transitions
     [nuc, uc_ts] = get_transitions(PN, ...
         uncontrollables);
end
if ge(nargin, 4)  % get the set of unobservable ...
    transitions
     [nuo, uo_ts] = get_transitions(PN, ...
         unobservables);
end

if or(nuc, nuo) % there are ...
    uncontrollable/unobservable trans
     [L1, B1, R1, R2, how, dhow] = mro_adm(L, B, ...
         Dp, uc_ts, uo_ts, mu0, 0);
else
     % simple supervisor, with all trans ...
         observable & controllable
     L1 = L; B1 = B; how = 'ok';
end

synthesis_ok = strcmp(how, 'ok');
if not(synthesis_ok)
     disp('Controller not feasible ...');
     return
end
```

In the fourth and final block (Listing 9.7), with **L1** and **B1** obtained in the previous block, we synthesize the controller, computing **Dc** (the incidence matrix of the controller) and **muC0** (the initial marking on the control places). After that, we combine the plant and the controller to make the controlled system; this is done by the function `imControlledSys`, which combines **Dc** and **Dp**, and the function `addSlacks2GP`, which expands the global places with the control places and assigns the initial tokens (**muC0**) to the control places.

Listing 9.7 Function supervisorSyn, continued from Lisiting 9.6

```
%%%%%%%%%%%%%%%%%%%%%%%%%%%%%%%%%%%%%%%%%%%%%%%%%%%
% controller
Dc = -1 * L1 * Dp;
muC0 = B1  - L1 * mu0;
%%%%%%%%%%%%%%%%%%%%%%%%%%%%%%%%%%%%%%%%%%%%%%%%%
```

```
%%%%%%%%%%%% Update Controlled Sys ...
    %%%%%%%%%%%%%%%%%%%%%%%%%
% update incidence matrix for the controlled system
imControlledSys(Dc, size(L,1));
% add slack variables to the list of global_places
addSlacks2GP(muC0);
```

9.2 Verifying Controller Performance

There are two GPenSIM built-in functions for the verification of controller performance; these functions are `verifyCOTREE` and `controllerPerform`.

9.2.1 Function verifyCOTREE

Listings 9.8–9.10 show the function `verifyCOTREE`.

The first block (Listing 9.8) is the header of the function. The input arguments are `COTREE` is the matrix output by the function `cotree` and the constraints. The output arguments:

1. TokenSUM: A matrix in which the number of rows equals the number of rows of the `COTREE` matrix, and the number of columns equals the number of constraints. Each column represents the token sum (linear combination of tokens on the left side of the inequality) of each constraint.
2. 'all_ok': a Boolean value informing whether the verification was successful or not.

Listing 9.8 Function verifyCOTREE

```
function [all_ok, TokenSUM] = ...
    verifyCOTREE(COTREE, constraints)
%      Verify supervisor's action with COTREE
%
%     Purpose: To verify whether the controlled systems
%              behaves as demanded by the constraints
%
%   NOTE: *** this function will NOT work for ...
    reachability tree with
%                infinite (omega) tokens *** ...
    (unbounded net)
%
%   Input arguments:
%       1) COTREE: reachability tree (output of ...
    'cotree'
```

```
%                       on controlled system
%           2) Constraints: linear inequalities in ...
    GPenSIM formulation.
%
%   Output argument:
%           1) all_Ok : (Boolean value) verification ...
    is successful?
%           2) TokenSUM: sum of tokens in places ...
    satisfying constraints
%
%   Functions used:  (none)
```

The second block (Listing 9.9) extracts the **L** and **B** values, the number of constraints, and the number of rows (states) in COTREE; all these values are for the main loop in the final block (Listing 9.10).

Listing 9.9 Function `verifyCOTREE`, continued from Listing 9.8

```
disp(' ');
disp('****************************************************');
disp('Now verifying the proposed controller action !!!!');
disp('****************************************************');
disp('');

Ps = simResults.No_of_places;

% extract L and B
[L, B] = extractLB(constraints);

% number of constraints
lenConstr = length(constraints);

% number of states in COTREE
rows_of_CT = size(COTREE, 1);
```

The third and final block (Listing 9.10) possesses the main loop for verification. The outer loop runs for each constraint and the inner loop for each state (row) in COTREE. If any state violates a constraint, an error message is printed out and the program exits.

Listing 9.10 Function `verifyCOTREE`, continued from Listing 9.9

```
all_ok = true; % optimistic assumption, at start
% the main loop
for ci = 1:lenConstr  % for each constraint
    Li = L(ci, :);
    bi = B(ci, :);

    % check each state in COTREE
    for rowj = 1:rows_of_CT
        tokens = COTREE(rowj, 1:Ps);
        toksum = tokens * Li';
        if gt(toksum, bi)
```

```
                disp(['invalid control action in ...
                    row-',...
                            int2str(rowj)]);
                disp('wrong here');
                all_ok = false;
                return
            end
        end
end
disp([simResults.name, ' with controller:']);
disp('All the constraints are verified !!!!');
```

NOTE: The function verifyCOTREE **will NOT work for reachability trees with infinite (ω) tokens**. For unbounded systems, the function cotree outputs reachability trees (COTREE matrix) with infinite (ω) tokens. In this case, the function verifyCOTREE will only display a warning about its inability to verify the reachability tree against the constraints. For unbounded systems, the function controllerPerform (discussed in the next subsection) can be used for verification.

9.2.2 *Function* controllerPerform

The first block (Listing 9.11) is the header of the function. The input arguments are "simResults," the simulation result output by the function gpensim, and the constraints. The output argument, 'CONT_PERFORM,' is a matrix.

- Rows of CONT_PERFORM: The number of rows in CONT_PERFORM is equal to the number of rows in simResults, which is the number of states.
- Columns of CONT_PERFORM: The number of columns in CONT_PERFORM is equal to the number of constraints plus one:
  - The first column of CONT_PERFORM is the time series, which is the last column of simResults.
  - The other columns (second column to the last column): each column represents the token sum (linear combination of tokens on the left side of the inequality) of each constraint.

Listing 9.11 Function controllerPerform

```
function [CONT_PERFORM] = ...
    controllerPerform(simResults, constraints)
% function [CONT_PERFORM] = ...
    controllerPerform(simResults, constraints)
%       Quantify conttoller's performance
%
%    Purpose: To quantify how well the controller ...
    performs
```

```
%              by checking token sums against ...
    constraint limits
%
%   Input arguments:
%        1) simResults: output of gpensim on ...
    controlled sys
%        2) Constraints: linear inequalities
%
%   Output argument:
%        1) CONT_PERFORM: sum of tokens in places ...
    satisfying constraints
%
%   Functions used:  (none)
%
%   Reggie.Davidrajuh@uis.no    (c)  10.March.2024
```

In the second block (Listing 9.12), we extract **L**, **B**, and the number of constraints to prepare for the main loop for filling the CONT_PERFORM in the third block (Listing 9.12).

Listing 9.12 Function `controllerPerform`, continued from Listing 9.11

```
Ps = simResults.No_of_places; % number of places
LOG = simResults.LOG;  % LOG: simulation results

% extract L and B
[L, B] = extractLB(constraints);

% number of constraints
lenConstr = length(constraints);

% number of states in LOG
rows_of_LOG = size(LOG, 1);

% prepare the output file
CONT_PERFORM = zeros(rows_of_LOG, lenConstr);
```

In the third block (Listing 9.13), we fill the CONT_PERFORM matrix.

Listing 9.13 Function `controllerPerform`, continued from Listing 9.12

```
    Li = L(ci, :);  bi = B(ci, :);

    % check each state in LOG
    for rowj = 1:rows_of_LOG
        tokens = LOG(rowj, 1:Ps);   % a marking
        toksum = tokens * Li';      % combination ...
            of marking
        CONT_PERFORM(rowj, ci) = toksum;
        if gt(toksum, bi)  % check whether the ...
            state is valid
```

```
                disp(['invalid control action in ...
                    row-',...
                           int2str(rowj)]);
                error('verification went wrong here ...
                    ...');
                load gong.mat; sound(y);
                return
           end
      end
end
time_series = LOG(:, Ps+6);
CONT_PERFORM = [time_series CONT_PERFORM];
```

The fourth and final block (Listing 9.14) is for displaying the figures for each constraint, showing the performance of the controller.

Listing 9.14 Function `controllerPerform`, continued from Listing 9.13

```
% plot the findings
for ci = 1:lenConstr
     tokens = CONT_PERFORM(:, 1+ci); % extract ...
         relevant token sum
     bi = B(ci, :);
     Bs = bi * ones(size(tokens));
     figure, plot(time_series', [Bs tokens], ...
          '-h', 'linewidth', 1, 'MarkerSize', 5);
     ylim([-inf, bi+0.5]), ...
     xlabel('Time'); ylabel('Number of tokens');
     % The title of the plot
     current_constraint = constraints(ci);
     lenCurrConstr = length(current_constraint.L);
     label = '';
     for j = lenCurrConstr:-2:2
          label = [label, ' + (', ...
               int2str(current_constraint.L{j}), ...
               '*', current_constraint.L{j-1}, ')'];
     end
     title(['Constraint ', int2str(ci), ':     ',...
          label(4:end), ' ≤ ', int2str(bi)]);
     legend({'Limit Bi', 'token sum'}); grid on;
end
```

9.3 Creating Processors from Controller

Once a supervisor controller is created by the functions `supervisorSim` or `supervisorSyn`, the controller can be mapped into processor files by the function `control2processors`. The function `control2processors` is basically a shell that uses three subfunctions, such as `writeUpdateGlobalinfo`, `writePreProcessors`, and `writePostProcessors`. All these four functions are described in the following subsections.

9.3.1 Function `control2processors`

This function (shortened for "control logic to processor files"), as we have seen in the example in Sect. 8.1.3, "Stage C: Mapping the Controller into Processors," maps the control logic of the controller into processor files. The automatic creation of specific preprocessors and postprocessors (in addition to the file "updateGlobalInfo") is done in three steps:

1. Creates the file "updateGlobalInfo" using the function `writeUpdateGlobalInfo`.
2. Creates preprocessor files using the function `writePreProcessors`.
3. Creates postprocessor files using the function `writePostProcessors`.

The sole input argument to this function is the controlled system, which is output by the function `supervisorSyn` (alternatively, `supervisorSim`).

9.4 Print Functions

This section presents two functions for printing the details: the plant, the controller, and the controlled system.

9.4.1 Function `prnsys`

The function `prnsys` (shortened for "print the controlled system info") takes two input arguments: (1) the simulation results of the controlled system. (2) the initial dynamics.

This function prints the following information:

- **The plant** and the initial tokens on the places of the plant.
- **The controller** (the control places ("slack" places)).
- **The controlled system**:
  - The connections between the control places and the transitions in the plant.
  - The initial tokens on the slack places.

Note: this function uses the function `prncontroller` (given in the next subsection) for printing the controller part.

9.4.2 *Function* `prncontroller`

The function `prncontroller` (shortened for "print the controller part") prints the details of the controller on screen in an intelligible manner, with control (slack) places and their arcs to the plant transitions. This function takes only one input argument, namely the simulation results on the controlled system, which is output by the function `gpensim`.

Reference

1. Iordache M, Antsaklis PJ (2007) Supervisory control of concurrent systems: a Petri net structural approach. Springer Science & Business Media

Chapter 10
Case Study on Supervisory Control with GPenSIM

In Chap. 8, "Supervisory Control with GPenSIM," we studied the four stages of implementing supervisory control-based controllers for Petri nets. This chapter presents a case study in which we will put the first three stages (**Stages A–C**) together to develop controllers and map them into processors. The final stage (**Stage D**) is for implementing the controllers as processors and verifying them.

10.1 Case Study: Car Wash

This case study is on **car washing bays**. This case study presents a car washing system where up to two cars can be washed at a time (Fig. 10.1). This case study is adapted from [3].

In this car washing system (Fig. 10.1):

1. Arrival of cars: Cars arrive at a faster rate and queue up outside the main entrance.
2. Wait Area inside the system: If the two wash bays are in use, up to four more cars can stay in the waiting area in front of the wash bays.
3. The wash bay: At most, one car can occupy a wash bay. When a wash bay is free and a car starts rolling towards it, the bay entrance will automatically open and let the car inside.
4. Car wash: Washing starts immediately when you enter the bay.
5. Bay exit: The bay exit door will always open when a car rolls towards it (usually after the completion of washing).
6. Leaving the system: Cars leave the system through the main exit; the door will always open for an approaching car.

R. Davidrajuh, *Petri Nets for Modeling Complex Discrete-Event Systems*, Asset Analytics,
https://doi.org/10.1007/978-981-96-6396-5_10

Fig. 10.1 Car washing Bays

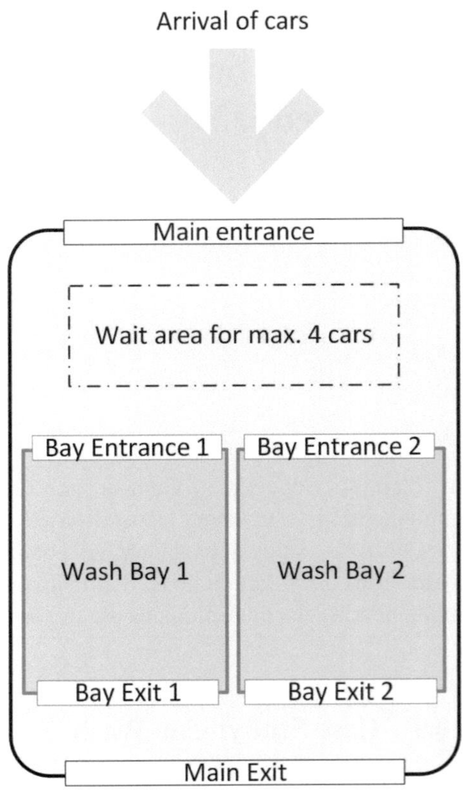

10.2 Stages A–C: From Plant to Processors

Figure 10.2 shows the Petri net model. Table 10.1 explains the elements of the model.

Let us assume the following timing: cars arrive every 1 TU (firing time of **tArrival** is 1), at a faster rate than the washing, which takes 5 TU (firing times of **tWash1** and **tWash2** are 5). Finally, all door openings and closings take 0.1 TU. Listing 10.1 shows the main simulation file, which consists of **Stages A–C**.

Listing 10.1 **MSF**, Example 17-A-C: Wash Bay

```
global global_info
global_info.STOP_AT = 30;

%%%%%%%%%%%%%%%%%%%%%%%%%%%%%%%%%%%%%%%%%%%%
% Stage A: Study behavior of the plant
%%%%%%%%%%%%%%%%%%%%%%%%%%%%%%%%%%%%%%%%%%%%
pns = pnstruct('wash_bay_pdf');
dyn.m0 = {}; % no initial tokens
dyn.ft = {'tArrival',1, 'tWash1',5, 'tWash2',5,...
```

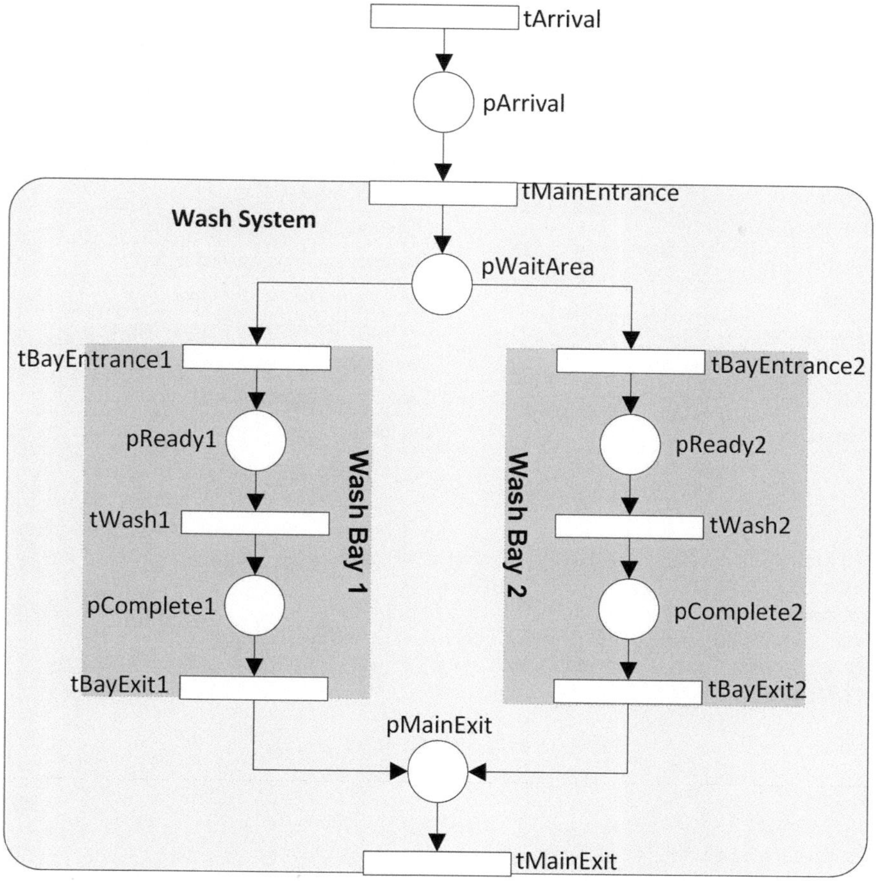

Fig. 10.2 Petri net model

```
    'allothers',0.1};
plant = initialdynamics(pns, dyn);
sim = gpensim(plant);
subplot(5,1,1), plotp(sim, {'pArrival'});
title('Behavior of the Plant');
subplot(5,1,2), plotp(sim, {'pWaitArea'});
subplot(5,1,3),plotp(sim,{'pReady1','pComplete1'});
subplot(5,1,4),plotp(sim,{'pReady2','pComplete2'});
subplot(5,1,5), plotp(sim, {'pMainExit'});

%%%%%%%%%%%%%%%%%%%%%%%%%%%%%%%%%%%%%%%%%%%%
% Stage B: Synthesis of a controller
%%%%%%%%%%%%%%%%%%%%%%%%%%%%%%%%%%%%%%%%%%%%
%%%%% B1: Constraints
WaitArea.L = {'pWaitArea',1};
WaitArea.B = 4; % wait area
```

Table 10.1 Interpretation of places and transitions

Element	Purpose
tArrival	Arrival of cars to the wash system
pArrival	Cars arrived before the main entrance
tMainEntrance	The main entrance
pWaitArea	Wait area inside the system
tBayEntrance*i*	The entrance of wash bay *i*
pReady*i*	Car readying to be washed in bay *i*
tWash*i*	The washing of a car in bay *i*
pComplete*i*	Car washed and ready to leave bay *i*
tBayExit*i*	The exit door of bay *i*
pMainExit	Car about to leave the wash system
tMainExit	Car leaving the system

```
WashBay1.L  = {'pReady1',1, 'pComplete1',1};
WashBay1.B  = 1; % wash bay 1
WashBay2.L  = {'pReady2',1, 'pComplete2',1};
WashBay2.B  = 1; % wash bay 2
MainExit.L  = {'pMainExit',1};
MainExit.B  = 1; % main exit

constraints = [WaitArea, WashBay1, ...
               WashBay2, MainExit];

%%%%% B2: Synthesis of Controlled System
[controlledSys, synthesis_ok] = ...
    supervisorSyn(plant, constraints, {}, {});
if not(synthesis_ok), return; end

%%%%% B3: run simulations on controlled system
sim_CS = gpensim(controlledSys);
prnsys(sim_CS, dyn);
figure, subplot(5,1,1), plotp(sim_CS, {'pArrival'});
title('Behavior of the Controlled System');
subplot(5,1,2), plotp(sim_CS, {'pWaitArea'});
subplot(5,1,3),plotp(sim_CS, ...
    {'pReady1','pComplete1'});
subplot(5,1,4),plotp(sim_CS, ...
    {'pReady2','pComplete2'});
subplot(5,1,5), plotp(sim_CS, {'pMainExit'});

%%%%% B4: Verify performance of controller
COTREE_CP = cotree(sim_CS, 0, 0);
verifyCOTREE(COTREE_CP, constraints);
controllerPerform(sim_CS, constraints);

%%%%%%%%%%%%%%%%%%%%%%%%%%%%%%%%%%%%%%%%%%%%%
```

```
% Stage C: Mapping controller into Processors
%%%%%%%%%%%%%%%%%%%%%%%%%%%%%%%%%%%%%%%%%%%%%
control2processors(controlledSys);
```

In Stage A, we study the behavior of the plant; the simulation result (Fig. 10.3) reveals that many cars are inside the wash bays, as places **pReady1** and **pReady2** hold more than one token, which is not acceptable.

In Stage B, we synthesize a controller.

- **Step B1**: We formulate the constraints.
- **Step B2**: Synthesize a controller.
- **Step B3**: We simulate the controlled system (The plant and the controller
- **Step B4**: We verify whether the controlled system performs as we wanted.

In **Step B2**, the function `prnsys` also prints the following info about the controller.

```
======= Controller Composition =======

Control place: slack1
(slack1 -> tMainEntrance : 1)
tBayEntrance1 -> slack1 : 1)
tBayEntrance2 -> slack1 : 1)
Control place: slack2
(slack2 -> tBayEntrance1 : 1)
BayExit1 -> slack2 : 1)
Control place: slack3
(slack3 -> tBayEntrance2 : 1)
tBayExit2 -> slack3 : 1)
Control place: slack4
(slack4 -> tBayExit1 : 1) (slack4 ->
tBayExit2 : 1)
tMainExit -> slack4 : 1)

Initial markings on the Control places:
slack1: 4
slack2: 1
slack3: 1
slack4: 1
```

Figure 10.4 shows the Petri net model of the controlled system in which the controller is superimposed on the plant. In the controlled system, control places:

- **slack1** is to ensure the number of tokens in **pWaitArea** never exceeds 4.
- **slack2** and **slack3** ensure that there is a maximum of one token each in Wash Bay 1 and Wash Bay 2, respectively.
- **slack4** ensures that there is at most one token in **pMainExit**.

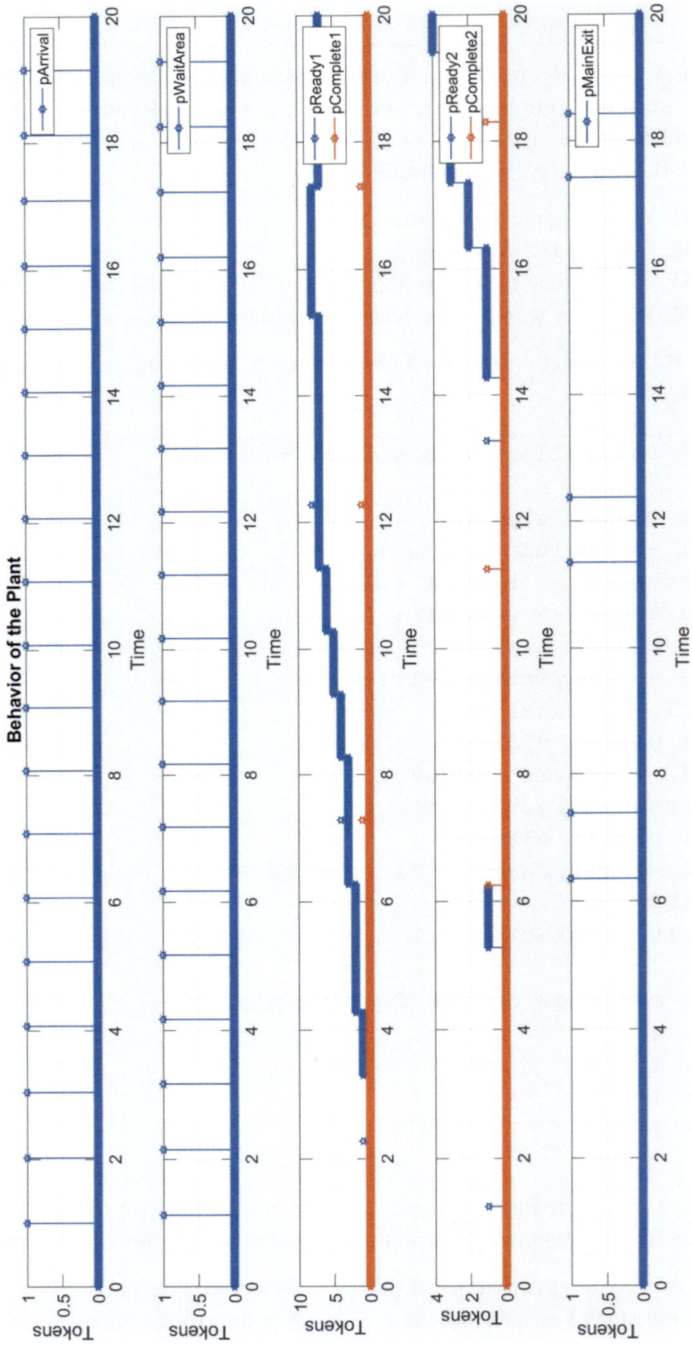

Fig. 10.3 Simulation when all transitions are controllable and observable

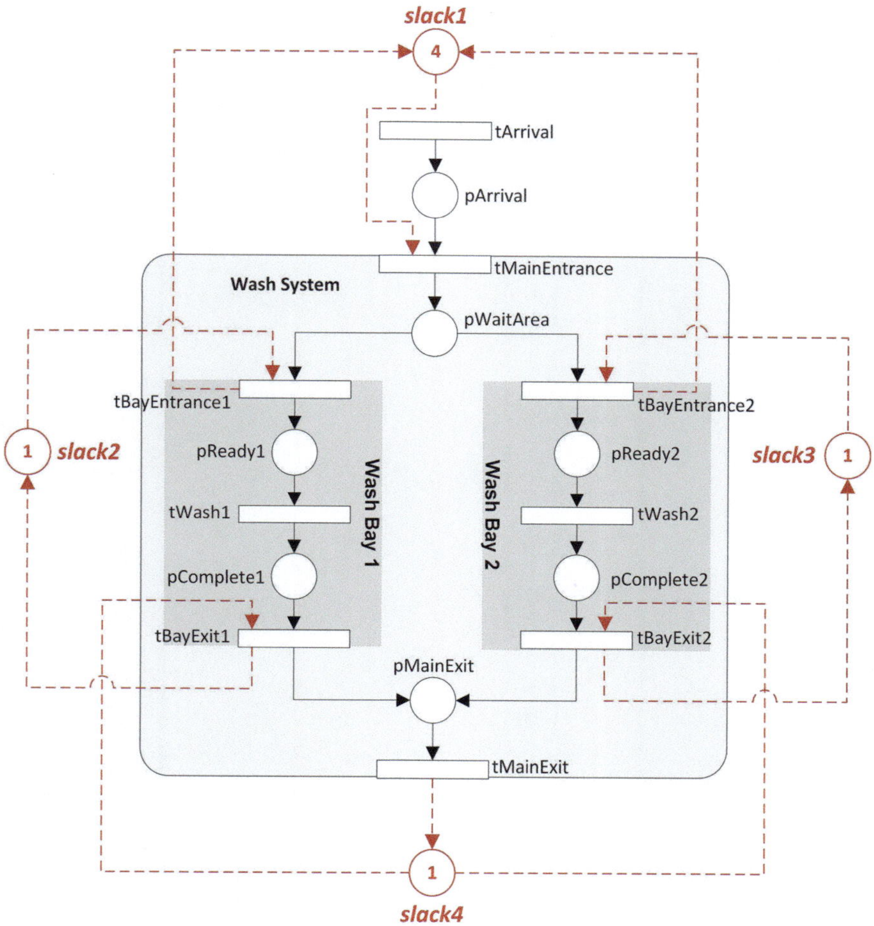

Fig. 10.4 Petri net model of the controlled system

In **Step B3**, the simulation of the controlled system is performed. Figure 10.5 shows that the queue of cars is now shifted outside the facility (**pArrival**) and that there are only a maximum of four cars in the waiting area inside the facility (**pWaitArea**). Also, there is at most one car inside each bay (**pReady1** + **pComplete1**) and (**pReady2** + **pComplete2**).

In **Step B4**, we verify the performance of the controller. Figure 10.6 shows that the number of cars in the waiting area is always under the limit (the first constraint). The number of cars in the waiting area starts at zero initially and then starts climbing up until it reaches the limit of four cars. Due to brevity, the figures from the verification of the other three constraints are not shown.

In Stage C: (After completing Stages A–B) We map the controller into processors with the help of the function `control2processors`.

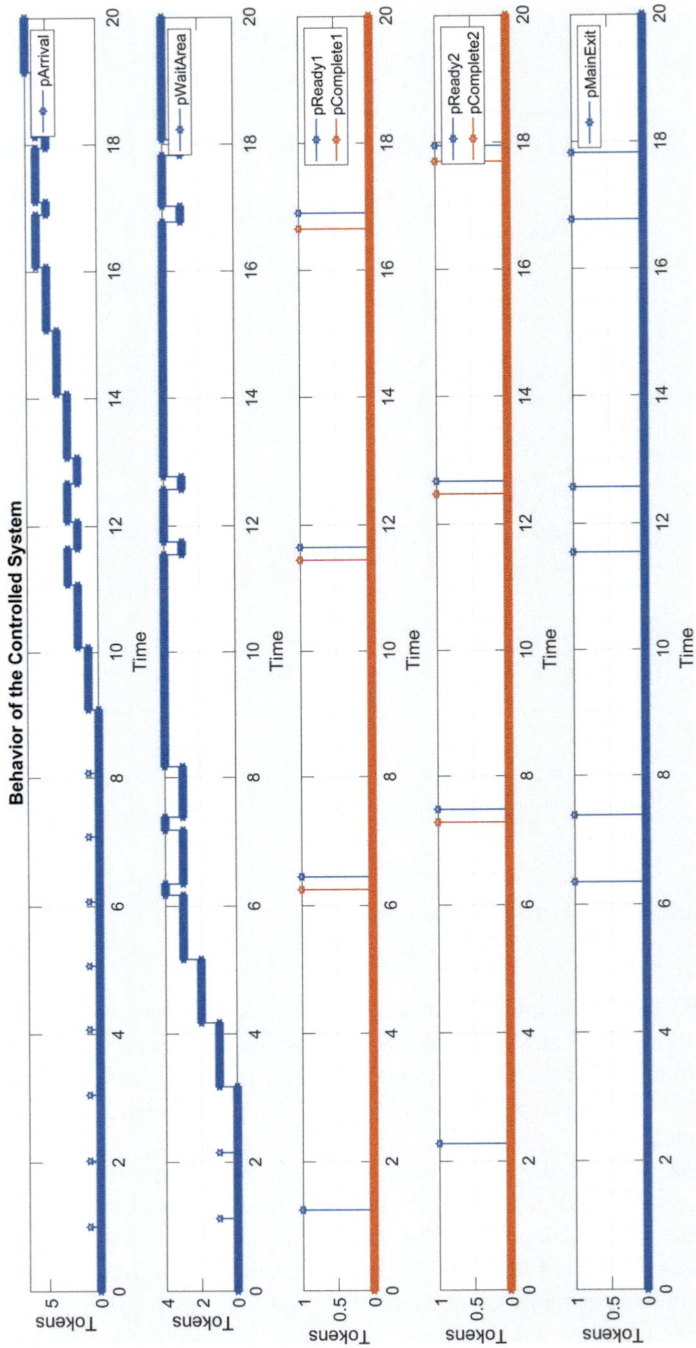

Fig. 10.5 Simulation of the controlled system (The plant and the controller)

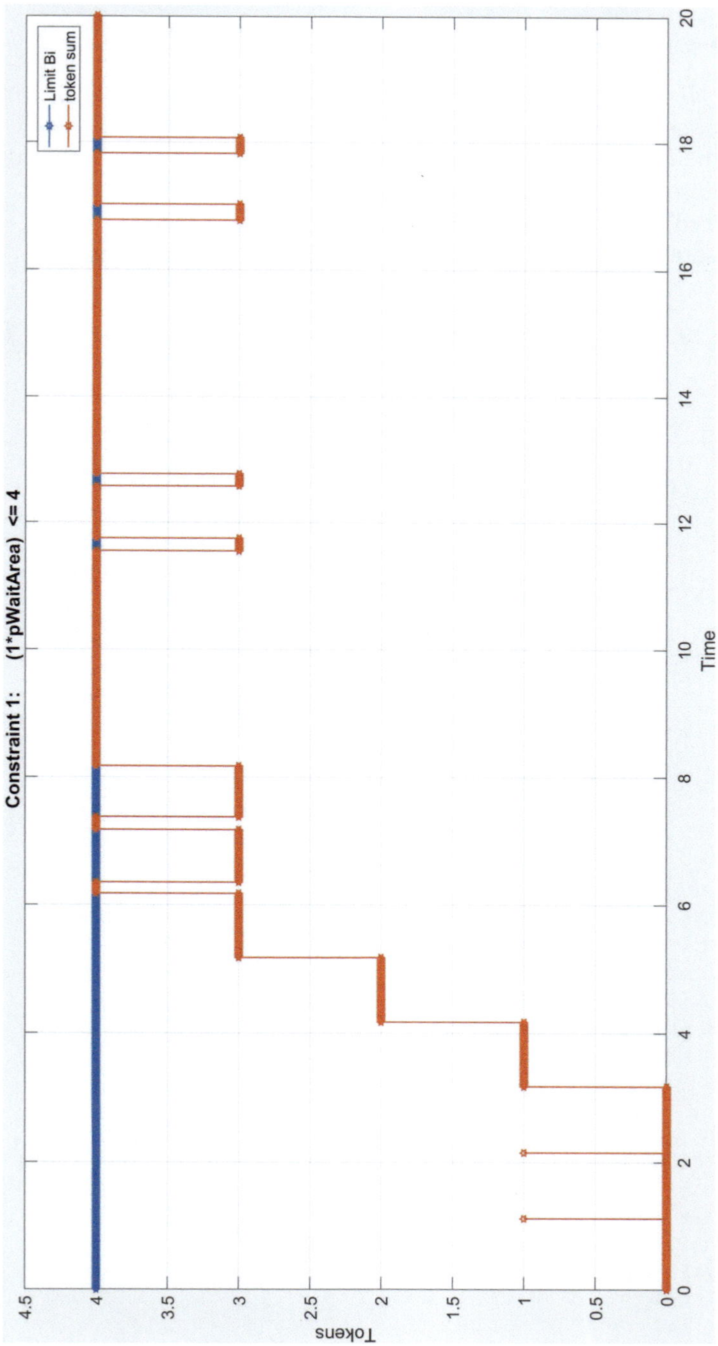

Fig. 10.6 Controller performance on the number of cars in the wait area

10.3 Stage D: Implementing the Controller with Processors

Before we start **Stage D**, we have to do the following:

1. Copy all the **processor files** (generated by the function `control2processors`) to a new folder; let us call the folder **"Stage-D-Folder"**.
2. Copy the file "updateGlobalInfo" (also generated by the function `control2processors`) to the new folder "Stage-D-Folder".
3. Copy the PDF "ex_17_wash_bay_pdf.m" also to this folder.
4. Make sure the main simulation file "ex_17D_wash_bay.m" also exists in this folder.

Listing 10.2 shows the main simulation file for **Stage D**, "ex_17D_wash_bay.m"

Listing 10.2 MSF, Example 17D: Wash Bay (Stage D)

```
global global_info
global_info.STOP_AT = 30;

%%%%%%%%%%%%%%%%%%%%%%%%%%%%%%%%%%%%%%%%%%%%%%%
% Step D: Study behavior of plant with Processors
%%%%%%%%%%%%%%%%%%%%%%%%%%%%%%%%%%%%%%%%%%%%%%%

% remember to add all the processor files and PDF
%    to this folder

updateGlobalInfo();

pns = pnstruct('ex_17_wash_bay_pdf');
dyn.m0 = {};  % no initial tokens
dyn.ft = {'tArrival',1, 'tWash1',5, 'tWash2',5,...
    'allothers',0.1};
plant = initialdynamics(pns, dyn);
sim = gpensim(plant);
subplot(5,1,1), plotp(sim, {'pArrival'});
title('Behavior of the Plant (with Processors!)');
subplot(5,1,2), plotp(sim, {'pWaitArea'});
subplot(5,1,3),plotp(sim,{'pReady1','pComplete1'});
subplot(5,1,4),plotp(sim,{'pReady2','pComplete2'});
subplot(5,1,5), plotp(sim, {'pMainExit'});

%%%%%%% verify controller (the Plant and the ...
   processors) performance
%%%%% Constraints
WaitArea.L = {'pWaitArea',1};
WaitArea.B = 4; % wait area
WashBay1.L = {'pReady1',1, 'pComplete1',1};
WashBay1.B = 1; % wash bay 1
WashBay2.L = {'pReady2',1, 'pComplete2',1};
WashBay2.B = 1; % wash bay 2
MainExit.L = {'pMainExit',1};
```

```
MainExit.B = 1; % main exit
constraints = [WaitArea, WashBay1, ...
               WashBay2, MainExit];
%%%%% verification via simulation result
controllerPerform(sim, constraints);
```

In Stage D, the main simulation file ("ex_17D_wash_bay.m", shown in Listing 10.2) will generate many figures that will show that the plant with the processor files satisfies all the constraints.

10.4 Uncontrollables in Wash Bay

In the previous subsections, we assumed all the plant transitions were controllable and observable. In this case, the resulting controller (with four control places, **slack1** to **slack4**) is shown in Fig. 10.4. Let us call this controller "**Controller_0**" (when all the plant transitions are controllable and observable).

In this subsection, we shall run some experiments with uncontrollable transitions. The experiment with uncontrollable transitions involves eight cases:

- Case 1: **tArrival** is uncontrollable.
- Case 2: **tMainEntrance** is uncontrollable.
- Case 3: **tMainEntrance** and **tArrival** are uncontrollable.
- Case 4: **tBayEntrance** is uncontrollable.
- Case 5: **tBayEntrance1** and **tBayEntrance2** are both uncontrollable.
- Case 6: **tBayExit1** is uncontrollable.
- Case 7: **tBayExit1** and **tBayExit2** are both uncontrollable.
- Case 8: **tMainExit** is uncontrollable.

Table 10.2 shown below summarizes the resulting controllers when some transitions become uncontrollable.

10.5 Unobservables in Wash Bay

Table 10.3 shown below summarizes the resulting controllers when some transitions become unobservable.

10.6 GPenSIM Style Supervisory Control

Figure 10.4 shows "Controller_0" as the controller when all transitions are controllable and observable. Tables 10.2 and 10.3 present up to eight different controllers when one or more plant transitions become uncontrollable or unobservable. Though the other controllers are not shown, it is clear that in all the controllers:

Table 10.2 Controllers when plant transitions become uncontrollable

Case	Uncontrollables	Controller
1	tArrival	**Controller_0** (no change)
2	tMainEntrance	**Controller_1** (new controller with the same optimal performance as **Controller_0**)
3	tArrival & tMainEntrance	*(Controller not feasible)*
4	tBayEntrance1	**Controller_2** (new controller with **sub-optimal** performance)
5	tBayEntrance1 & tBayEntrance2	*(Controller not feasible)*
6	tBayExit1	**Controller_3** (new controller with the same optimal performance as **Controller_0**)
7	tBayExit1 & tBayExit2	*(Controller not feasible)*
8	tMainExit	**Controller_0** (no change)

Table 10.3 Controllers when plant transitions become unobservable

Case	Unobservables	Controller
9	tArrival	**Controller_0** (no change)
10	tMainEntrance	**Controller_4** (new controller with the same optimal performance as **Controller_0**)
11	tArrival & tMainEntrance	*(Controller not feasible)*
12	tBayEntrance1	**Controller_5** (new controller with **sub-optimal** performance)
13	tBayEntrance1 & tBayEntrance2	*(Controller not feasible)*
14	tBayExit1	**Controller_6** (new controller with the same optimal performance as **Controller_0**)
15	tBayExit1 & tBayExit2	*(Controller not feasible)*
16	tMainExit	***Controller_7**: Controller is feasible?* The controller will allow ONLY one token through **tMainExit**; after that, the system will freeze, resulting in a token each stuck in **pComplete1** and **pComplete2**, and four tokens in **pWaitArea**. All other tokens will pile up at **pArrival**

- Before firing: Control places control plant transitions by limiting the input tokens.
- After firing: Plant transitions deposit tokens back into the control places.

GPenSIM proposes mapping control places and their arcs to plant transitions as:

- Control places are mapped into global variables known as "slack" variables as a part of the "global_info" packet.
- Preprocessors: The act of control places feeding tokens into a plant transition, which is mapped as reducing the value of slack variables in the preprocessor.
- Postprocessors: The act of a plant transition depositing tokens back into control places, which is mapped as increasing the value of slack variables in the postprocessor.

The advantage of using processor files (preprocessors and postprocessors) is that the resulting controlled system is slim (Petri nets representing the controlled system and the plant are the same), and **modelers can add any other logical conditions to the processor files**. Also, the processors can be programmed into embedded controllers for real-world control.

10.7 Extending the Model with Additional Conditions

The model obtained after **Stage C** (and the one that is used **in Stage D**) is the plant and the processor files:

- The static Petri net model is represented by the same PDF (PDF doesn't change for different stages).
- The main simulation file (ex_17D_wash_bay.m, shown in Listing 10.2) is for assigning the initial tokens and firing times and simulating the plant and the processors.
- Processors: there will be many preprocessors and postprocessors generated by the function `control2processors`.
- updateGlobalInfo: the file for updating the global_info packet with slack variables.

For simplicity, let us assume again that all the plant transitions are controllable and observable. Let us make the following improvements to the model (Fig. 10.2):

- Improvement 1 (cars waiting outside the main entrance):
  Since cars arrive at a faster rate, they tend to queue up outside the main entrance in large numbers, which is not realistic. Let us limit the number of cars waiting outside the main entrance to 5.
- Improvement 2 (First Come First Served):
  Up to four cars are waiting in the waiting area. When a wash bay becomes available, the car that arrived first must be allowed to enter the wash bay. The current model shown in Fig. 10.2 does not realize this issue.

Improvement 1 (limiting the cars waiting outside the main entrance):
It is easy to realize this improvement by adding another control place with five initial tokens; this control place only inputs a token to **tArrival** and **tMainEntrance** deposits the token back into the control place. However, this needs a change in Petri net (Fig. 10.2). Instead (without adjusting the Petri net), we can make this improvement by utilizing the preprocessor of **tArrival**, as shown below (Listing 10.3).

Listing 10.3 tArrival_pre

```
function [fire, transition] = ...
    tArrival_pre(transition)
% Pre-processor for transition "tArrival"
%
global global_info  % slacks are attached to ...
    global_info

% number of tokens in "pArrival" ( == number of cars
%       waiting outside the main entrance)
npArr = ntokens('pArrival');

% fire, only if number of cars less than or equal ...
    to 5
fire = le(npArr, 5):
```

Improvement 2 (First Come First Served):
When up to four cars wait in the waiting area, if a wash bay becomes available, the car that came first must be served. This logic cannot be realized in P/T Petri nets. However, GPenSIM offers a rich set of built-in functions [2]. To realize the second improvement, we can use GPenSIM built-in function `tokenArrivedEarly`, which is part of the Colored Petri net functions [1]. Listing 10.4 shows the preprocessor of **tBayEntrance1**; the preprocessor of **tBayEntrance2** looks similar.

Listing 10.4 tBayEntrance1_pre

```
function [fire, transition] = ...
    tBayEntrance1_pre(transition)
% Pre-processor for transition "tBayEntrance1"

global global_info  % slacks are attached to ...
    global_info

%%%%%%%%%%%%%%%%%%%%%%%%%%%%%%%%%%%%%%%%%%%%%%%%%%
%%%%%%%%%%%%%%%% the control part %%%%%%%%%%%%%%
fire = 1; % initial assumption
fire = and(fire, global_info.slack2);

% if the transition is allowed to fire
% then reduce the slack variables
%    (remove "tokens" from the slack "places")
```

```
if fire
     global_info.slack2 = global_info.slack2 - 1;
end

%%%%%%%%%%%%%%%%%%%%%%%%%%%%%%%%%%%%%%%%%%%%%%%%%%
%%%%%%%%%% select the earliest car %%%%%%%%%%%%%%
tokID = tokenArrivedEarly('pArrival',1);
transition.selected_tokens = tokID;
```

References

1. Davidrajuh R (2023) Colored Petri nets for modeling of discrete systems: a practical approach with GPenSIM. Springer Nature
2. Davidrajuh R (2024) GPenSIM reference manual. University of Stavanger
3. Davidrajuh R, Skolud B, Krenczyk D (2018) Gpensim for performance evaluation of event graphs, Advances in manufacturing, number 201519 in Lecture notes in mechanical engineering. Springer International Publishing, Cham, pp 289–299

Appendix A
Reference Manual for Functions for Supervisory Control

This appendix lists GPenSIM's built-in functions for supervisory control.

Table A.1 presents a summary of these functions. The implementation details of these functions are given in **Chap.** 9, **"GPenSIM Built-in Functions for Supervisory Control"**.

A.1 Function `supervisorSim`

Function name: `supervisorSim`
Full name: Simple synthesizer of supervisory control.
Purpose: For supervisory control, `supervisorSim` is a simple function that synthesizes a controller **only when all the transitions are controllable and observable**.
Input Parameters:
(1) `pni` (Petri net structure with initial dynamics);
(2) constraints: a set of linear constraints GPenSIM formulation.
Output Parameter:
(1) Controlled System as `PN` structure.
(2) synthesis_ok: whether synthesis was successful or not.
This function uses:
`extractLB`: to extract **L** and **B** values.
`gpensim_2_PNCT`: to convert GPenSIM's extended incidence matrix to **D** matrix.
`imControlledSys`: to update incidence matrix for controlled system.
`addSlacks2GP`: add slack variables to the list of global_places.
Further info: Sects. 9.1 and 9.1.1 of this book.
Sample use:

```
...
[controlledSys, synthesis_ok] = ...
    supervisorSim(pni, constraints);
```


R. Davidrajuh, *Petri Nets for Modeling Complex Discrete-Event Systems*, Asset Analytics,
https://doi.org/10.1007/978-981-96-6396-5

Table A.1 GPenSIM built-in functions for supervisory control

Function	Description
`supervisorSim`	Synthesis of a controller for a plant in which all transitions are controllable and observable
`supervisorSyn`	Synthesis of a controller for a plant in which some transitions are uncontrollable or unobservable. This function uses the function `mro_adm` in the package "spnbox" by Marian V. Iordache
`verifyCOTREE`	Checks the controlled system's reachability tree against the constraints to make sure whether the controlled systems behaved as expected
`controllerPerform`	From the simulation result, this function verifies whether the controlled system adheres to the constraints and shows how forcefully the controller performs by comparing the token values against the constraints
`control2processors`	Automatically creates the processor files that include the control logic of the controller
`prnsys`	Prints the plant and the controller in an intelligible manner
`prncontroller`	Prints the controller in an intelligible manner

```
%%%% controller synthesis NOT possible
if not(synthesis_ok), return; end

sim_CS = gpensim(controlledSys); %%%% run simulations
...
```

Related function: `supervisorSyn`

A.2 Function `supervisorSyn`

Function name: `supervisorSyn`
Full name: Synthesizer of supervisory control.
Purpose: For supervisory control, `supervisorSyn` synthesizes a controller **even if some of the transitions are uncontrollable or unobservable**.
Input Parameters:
(1) `pni` (Petri net structure with initial dynamics);
(2) constraints: a set of linear constraints GPenSIM formulation.
(3) set of uncontrollable transitions.
(4) set of unobservable transitions.

Output Parameter:
(1) Controlled System as PN structure.
(2) synthesis_ok: whether synthesis was successful or not.
This function uses:
mro_adm: to synthesize the controller.
extractLB: to extract **L** and **B** values.
gpensim_2_PNCT: to convert GPenSIM's extended incidence matrix to **D** matrix.
imControlledSys: to update incidence matrix for controlled system.
addSlacks2GP: add slack variables to the list of global_places.
NOTE: The function supervisorSyn on the core uses function mro_adm, which is a function in the package "**spnbox**" and written by **Marian V. Iordache**. The package "spnbox" accompanies the book by Iordache and Antsaklis Iordache and Antsaklis (2007).
Further info: Sects. 9.1 and 9.1.2 of this book.
Sample use:

```
...
[controlledSys, synthesis_ok] = ...
    supervisorSyn(pni, constraints, ...
        uncontrollables_set, unobservables_set);
%%%% controller synthesis NOT possible
if not(synthesis_ok), return; end

sim_CS = gpensim(controlledSys); %%%% run simulations
...
```

Related function: supervisorSim

A.3 Function verifyCOTREE

Function name: verifyCOTREE
Full name: Verify supervisor's action with COTREE.
Purpose: To verify whether the controlled system behaves as demanded by the constraints.
NOTE: **The function verifyCOTREE will NOT work for reachability trees with infinite (ω) tokens**. For unbounded systems, the function cotree provides reachability trees (COTREE matrix) with infinite (ω) tokens. In this case, the function verifyCOTREE will only display a warning about its inability to verify the reachability tree against the constraints. For unbounded systems, the function controllerPerform (discussed in the next subsection) can be used for verification.
Input Parameters:
(1) COTREE: reachability tree (output of function "cotree" on controlled system.
(2) Constraints: a set of linear inequalities in GPenSIM formulation.

Output Parameter:
(1) all_Ok : (Boolean value) verification is successful?
(2) TokenSUM matrix: sum of tokens in places satisfying constraints; see Section A.5 for details.
Output to screen: Text printout informing whether the verification was successful or not.
This function uses: (none)
Further info: Sects. 9.2 and 9.2.1 of this book.
Sample use:

```
...
[controlledSys, synthesis_ok] = ...
    supervisorSyn(plant, constraints,{},{});
%%%% controller synthesis NOT possible
if not(synthesis_ok), return; end

figure, COTREE_CS = cotree(controlledSys,1,0);
[OK, TS] = verifyCOTREE(COTREE_CS, constraints);
```

Related function: controllerPerform

A.4 Function controllerPerform

Function name: controllerPerform
Full name: Quantify controller's performance.
Purpose: From the simulation result, this function verifies whether the controlled system adheres to the constraints and shows how forcefully the controller performs by comparing the token values against the constraints.
Input Parameters:
(1) simulation_Results: output of the function gpensim from the simulation of the controlled system.
(2) Constraints: a set of linear inequalities in GPenSIM formulation.
Output Parameter:
CONT_PERFORM matrix: sum of tokens in places satisfying constraints; see Section A.6 for details.
Output to screen: Plots showing how the controlled system performs against each constraint.
This function uses: (none)
Further info: **Further info**: Sects. 9.2 and 9.2.2 of this book.
Sample use:

```
...
[controlledSys, synthesis_ok] = ...
    supervisorSyn(plant, constraints,{},{});
%%%% controller synthesis NOT possible
```

```
if not(synthesis_ok), return; end

sim_CS = gpensim(controlledSys); %%%% run simulations
%%%%%%%%%%%%%% verify with simulation result  %%
CONT_PERFORM = controllerPerform(sim_CS, ...
    constraints);
```

Related function: `verifyCOTREE`

A.5 TokenSUM Matrix

`TokenSUM` is a matrix output by the function `verifyCOTREE`. The composition of `TokenSUM` is ("`COTREE`" is the matrix, output of the function `cotree`):

- Rows of `TokenSUM`: The number of rows in `TokenSUM` is equal to the number of rows in "`COTREE`, which is the number of states.
- Columns of `TokenSUM`: The number of columns in `TokenSUM` is equal to the number of constraints. Each column represents the token sum (linear combination of tokens on the left side of the inequality) of each constraint.

A.6 CONT_PERFORM Matrix

`CONT_PERFORM` is a matrix output by the function `controllerPerform`. The composition of `CONT_PERFORM` is ("simulation_results" is the output of the function `gpensim`):

- Rows of `CONT_PERFORM`: The number of rows in `CONT_PERFORM` is equal to the number of rows in simulation_results, which is the number of states.
- Columns of `CONT_PERFORM`: The number of columns in `CONT_PERFORM` is equal to the number of constraints plus one. The first column of `CONT_PERFORM` is the time series, which is the last column of simulation_results. The other columns (second column to the last column): each column represents the token sum (linear combination of tokens on the left side of the inequality) of each constraint.

A.7 Function control2processors

Function name: `control2processors`
Full name: Control logic to processor files.
Purpose: Maps the control logic of the controller (control places and their arcs to plant transitions) into processor files. The automatic creation of specific pre-processors and post-processors (in addition to the file "updateGlobalInfo") is done in three steps:

1. Creates the file "updatGlobalInfo" using the function `writeUpdateGlobalInfo`.
2. Creates pre-processor files using the function `writePreProcessors`.
3. Creates post-processor files using the function `writePostProcessors`.

Input Parameters: `PN`, the Petri net structure representing the controlled system, which is output by the function `supervisorSyn` (alternatively, `supervisorSim`).
Output Parameter: (none).
Output Files: Processor files and `updatGlobalInfo`.
This function uses:
`writeUpdateGlobalInfo`, `writePreProcessors`, `writePostProcessors`.
Further info: Sects. 9.3 and 9.3.1 of this book.
Sample use:

```
...
[controlledSys, synthesis_ok] = ...
    supervisorSyn(plant, constraints,{},{});
%%%% controller synthesis NOT possible
if not(synthesis_ok), return; end

%%%% update global_info and create processors files
control2processors(controlledSys);
```

Related function: `writePreProcessors`, `writePostProcessors`, `writeUpdateGlobalInfo`

A.8 Function `writeUpdateGlobalInfo`

Function name: `writeUpdateGlobalInfo`
Full name: write the file "updateGlobalInfo.m"
Purpose: creates the file "updateGlobalInfo.m", so that the function "updateGlobalInfo()" can be added to the main simulation file in Stage D of supervisory control with GPenSIM.
File "updateGlobalInfo.m" contains code to add slack variables (representing the control places and their arcs) to global_info data packet.
Input Parameters: `PN`, the Petri net structure representing the controlled system, which is output by the function `supervisorSyn` (alternatively, `supervisorSim`).
Output Parameter: (none).
Output File: File "updatGlobalInfo.m".
This function uses: (none).
This function is used by: `control2processors`.

Further info: Sects. 9.3 and 9.3.1 of this book.
Related function: `control2processors`, `writePreProcessors`, `writePrePostcessors`.

A.9 Function `writePreProcessors`

Function name: `writePreProcessors`
Full name: write pre-processor files.
Purpose: to write (create) pre-processor files, mapping the input arcs from control places to plant transitions.
Control places are mapped as "slack" variables as part of global_info.
Input arcs from control places to plant transitions are mapped as the reduction (–1) of slack variables.
Input Parameters: `PN`, the Petri net structure representing the controlled system, which is output by the function `supervisorSyn` (alternatively, `supervisorSim`).
Output Parameter: (none).
Output Files: Pre-processor files.
This function uses: (none).
This function is used by: `control2processors`.
Further info: Sects. 9.3 and 9.3.1 of this book.
Related function: `control2processors`, `writePostProcessors`, `writeUpdateGlobalInfo`.

A.10 Function `writePostProcessors`

Function name: `writePostProcessors`
Full name: write post-processor files.
Purpose: to write (create) post-processor files, mapping the output arcs from plant transitions to control places.
Control places are mapped as "slack" variables as part of global_info.
Output arcs from plant transitions to control places are mapped as the increment (+1) of slack variables.
Input Parameters: `PN`, the Petri net structure representing the controlled system, which is output by the function `supervisorSyn` (alternatively, `supervisorSim`).
Output Parameter: (none).
Output Files: Post-processor files.
This function uses: (none).
This function is used by: `control2processors`.
Further info: Sects. 9.3 and 9.3.1 of this book.

Related function: `control2processors`, `writePreProcessors`, `writeUpdateGlobalInfo`.

A.11 Function prnsys

Function name: `prnsys`
Full name: Print the system info.
Purpose: This function prints the following information:

- **The plant** and the initial tokens on the places of the plant.
- **The controller** (the control places ("slack" places)).
- **The controlled system**:
  - The arcs between control places and plant transitions.
  - The initial tokens on the slack places.

Input Parameters: (1) the simulation results of the controlled system. (2) the initial dynamics.
Output Parameter: (none).
Output on screen: Prints two sections on screen:

1. The composition of the plant (process) with places, transitions, arcs, and initial tokens.
2. The composition of the controller with control (slack) places and initial tokens on the control places.

This function uses:
`prncontroller` for printing the controller part.
`prnsys_connection`, `get_initial_marking`, `marking_string`.
Further info: Sect. 9.4.1 of this book.
Sample use:

```
...
%%%%%%%%%%%%%% Controlled System ...
   %%%%%%%%%%%%%%%%%%%%%%%%%%%
[controlledSys, synthesis_ok] = ...
    supervisorSyn(plant, constraints,{},{});
%%%% controller synthesis NOT possible
if not(synthesis_ok), return; end

sim_CS = gpensim(controlledSys); %%%% run simulations

%%%% print the system info (incl. the controller)
prnsys(sim_CS, dyn);
```

Related function: `prncontroller`

A.12 Function `prncontroller`

Function name: `prncontroller`
Full name: Print the controller part.
Purpose: Prints the details of the controller on screen in an intelligible manner, with control (slack) places and their arcs to plant transitions.
Input Parameters: The simulation results of the controlled system.
Output Parameter: (none).
Output on screen: Prints only the composition of the controller with control (slack) places and initial tokens on control places.
This function uses: (none).
This function is used by: `prnsys`; [also, in the main simulation file].
Further info: Sect. 9.4.1 of this book.
Sample use:

```
...
%%%%%%%%%%%%%% Controlled System ...
    %%%%%%%%%%%%%%%%%%%%%%%%%%%%
[controlledSys, synthesis_ok] = ...
    supervisorSyn(plant, constraints,{},{});
%%%% controller synthesis NOT possible
if not(synthesis_ok), return; end

sim_CS = gpensim(controlledSys); %%%% run simulations

%%%% print the controller info
prncontroller(sim_CS); % print "controller" part
```

Related function: `prnsys`

Bibliography

1. Iordache M, Antsaklis PJ (2007) Supervisory control of concurrent systems: a Petri net structural approach. Springer Science & Business Media

Appendix B
GPenSIM Webpage

GPenSIM website: http://www.davidrajuh.net/gpensim/.

This website presents some material on GPenSIM; for example, GPenSIM systems files (version 11) can be freely downloaded from this website. Also, this website functions as a companion website for all the books published on GPenSIM. The code for examples presented in the books on GPenSIM can be downloaded from the GPenSIM website.

GPenSIM Books

- Figure B.1 shows the basic book on GPenSIM, titled "**Modeling Discrete-Event Systems with GPenSIM**", Davidrajuh (2018), which can be considered as a simple user manual.
- Figure B.2 shows the "**GPenSIM Reference Manual**", Davidrajuh (2024), which describes about 150 built-in functions. This book is an "Open-Access" book.
- Figure B.3 shows the third book on GPenSIM, titled "**Petri Nets for Modeling Large Discrete Systems**", Davidrajuh (2021). This book discusses modular model building with a new modular Petri Net theory, focusing on modeling large discrete systems.
- Figure B.4 shows the fourth book on GPenSIM, titled "**Colored Petri Nets for Modeling of Discrete Systems**", Davidrajuh (2023). This book is for modeling real-world discrete systems for which Colored Petri Nets are needed. This book focuses on coloring of tokens, resources, and cost calculation.

R. Davidrajuh, *Petri Nets for Modeling Complex Discrete-Event Systems*, Asset Analytics,
https://doi.org/10.1007/978-981-96-6396-5

Fig. B.1 A simple introduction to GPenSIM

Fig. B.2 GPenSIM reference manual (**Open-Access**)

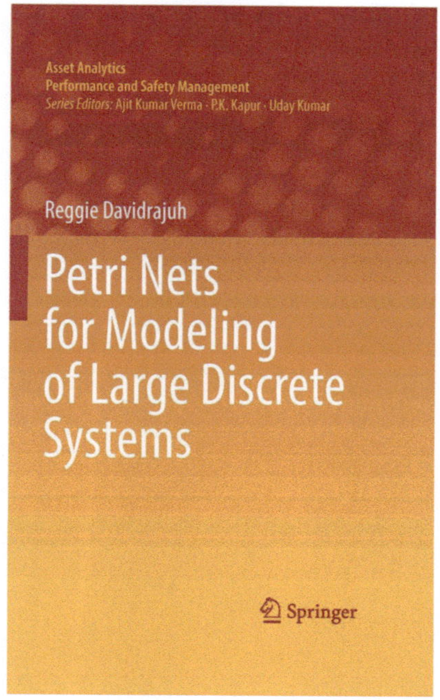

Fig. B.3 Petri nets for modeling large discrete systems

Fig. B.4 Colored Petri nets with GPenSIM

Bibliography

1. Davidrajuh R (2018) Modeling discrete-event systems with GPenSIM. Springer International Publishing, Cham
2. Davidrajuh R (2021) Petri nets for modeling of large discrete systems. Springer
3. Davidrajuh R (2023) Colored Petri nets for modeling of discrete systems: a practical approach With GPenSIM. Springer Nature
4. Davidrajuh R (2024) GPenSIM reference manual. University of Stavanger

Index

R. Davidrajuh, *Petri Nets for Modeling Complex Discrete-Event Systems*, Asset Analytics,
https://doi.org/10.1007/978-981-96-6396-5

Index

R. Davidrajuh, *Petri Nets for Modeling Complex Discrete-Event Systems*, Asset Analytics,
https://doi.org/10.1007/978-981-96-6396-5

MIX
Papier aus verantwortungsvollen Quellen
Paper from responsible sources
FSC® C105338

If you have any concerns about our products,
you can contact us on
ProductSafety@springernature.com

In case Publisher is established outside the EU,
the EU authorized representative is:
Springer Nature Customer Service Center GmbH
Europaplatz 3, 69115 Heidelberg, Germany

Printed by Libri Plureos GmbH
in Hamburg, Germany